300 best Homemade Candy recipes

Brittles, caramels, chocolates, fudge, truffles & so much more

Jane Sharrock

Robert **ROSE**

For complete cataloguing information, see page 279.

Disclaimer
The recipes in this book have been carefully tested by our kitchen and our tasters. To the best of our knowledge, they are safe and nutritious for ordinary use and users. For those people with food or other allergies, or who have special food requirements or health issues, please read the suggested contents of each recipe carefully and determine whether or not they may create a problem for you. All recipes are used at the risk of the consumer.

We cannot be responsible for any hazards, loss or damage that may occur as a result of any recipe use.

For those with special needs, allergies, requirements or health problems, in the event of any doubt, please contact your medical adviser prior to the use of any recipe.

Design and production: Daniella Zanchetta/PageWave Graphics Inc.
Editor: Carol Sherman
Recipe editor: Jennifer MacKenzie
Proofreader: Karen Campbell-Sheviak
Techniques photographer: Ricky Rhodes
Techniques food stylist: Melissa McClelland
Techniques hand model: Kaitlin Rhodes
Recipe photographer: Colin Erricson
Recipe associate photographer: Matt Johannsson
Recipe food stylist: Kathryn Robertson
Recipe prop stylist: Charlene Erricson

Cover image: *From top down and left to right:* Bullet Fudge (page 119), Lemon-White Chocolate Fudge, variation (page 166), White Cherry Fudge (page 164), Out-of-This-World Maple Fudge (page 155), Microwave Rocky Road Fudge (page 131) and Pumpkin Fudge (page 162).

The publisher gratefully acknowledges the financial support of our publishing program by the Government of Canada through the Canada Book Fund.

Published by Robert Rose Inc.
120 Eglinton Avenue East, Suite 800, Toronto, Ontario, Canada M4P 1E2
Tel: (416) 322-6552 Fax: (416) 322-6936
www.robertrose.ca

Printed and bound in USA

1 2 3 4 5 6 7 8 9 CKV 22 21 20 19 18 17 16 15 14

Contents

The Day I Became a Candy Maker (and Why I Wrote This Book)

One Christmas when I was in my mid-thirties, my mother was visiting and she walked into my kitchen carrying a sack in her hands. She smiled coyly and said, "I have something for you." She hesitated a minute and then said, "I am giving this to you because I think you will be the next candy maker in the family." She reached into the sack and pulled out her late-1940s heavy aluminum pressure cooker as I clapped my hands and squealed with delight.

"Really?" I said excitedly! "I get the candy pot?"

"Yes," she said, enjoying my childlike enthusiasm. "I think you will use it the most."

As I took the old pressure cooker from her hands, I felt the torch pass from one generation to the next. I was still marveling that I had been chosen as the keeper of family tradition when she smiled again and said, "I have something else for you." She was clutching it tightly to her chest so I could not see what it was. She raised an eyebrow and said, "Before I give this to you, you have to promise to hold onto it and take care of it because I have never seen another one like it." I promised, though I had no idea what I was promising. She looked at me for reassurance so I promised again.

Then, in a ceremonious fashion, Mom handed me her only candy cookbook. It was a tattered, 16-page pamphlet that she had cherished and protected for over 40 years. She explained that she knew the author, they were former colleagues, and this pamphlet was the only printed source of candy-making advice Mom had ever seen. I was delighted by my newfound wealth.

Over the next few years I discovered Mom was right — candy cookbooks are hard to find, and very few explain the basics of candy making. Most of what I knew came from watching my mother or calling her to ask for advice. I began collecting recipes and trying new candies, and when I discovered that Mom had a stash of recipes I had never seen, the temptation was just too great — I had to combine her lessons with our recipe collection and share this treasure with others.

My mother died before *300 Best Homemade Candy Recipes* was published, but she knew the impact she had on the generations that would follow her. Several times when she was with me on candy-related adventures, she received standing ovations from those who knew our story. You see, without that mother-daughter exchange in my kitchen all those years ago, we would have had no inspiration for this book, no sage advice or recipes to share, and no love for heirloom candy pots.

· ·

In Memory of Martha Sharrock
(1917 – 2012)

· ·

Acknowledgments

Thank you to all who contributed to this book, but especially:

Tom and Sherry Muchmore of the *Ponca City News* for allowing me to include lovely, old recipes printed in my hometown newspaper long ago.

Jim and Nancy Sharrock, and Lynda Mayo, for your daily support and encouragement.

Joann White, for listening to my stories.

My agent, Coleen O'Shea; my publisher, Robert Dees; and my editor, Carol Sherman, for your vision and wisdom.

Daniella Zanchetta and PageWave Graphics, for creating such a beautiful book.

The many friends, neighbors and family members, who shared special recipes, tasted my creations and supported this effort in every way imaginable.

The candy makers and candy cookbook authors who came before me, including Eula Morris and my mother's former colleagues on the Oklahoma A & M (now Oklahoma State University) School of Home Economics teaching staff, and the authors at Kansas State University School of Home Economics who wrote *Practical Cookery and the Etiquette and Service of the Table*, published in 1945. Your lessons serve a new generation.

Our fourth-generation candy makers — Lindsay and Hilary — and our fifth-generation candy makers — Mallory, Hadley and Shelby — for allowing Mima's tradition to live through you.

Preface

300 Best Homemade Candy Recipes is a cherished collection of homemade candy recipes, many of which date back 60 years or more. Both novice and experienced candy makers will find an incredible selection of recipes to explore, along with detailed instructions, step-by-step photographs, tips, and an explanation of the science behind candy making.

Compiled from my personal recipe collection and the collections of family and friends, *300 Best Homemade Candy Recipes* is also a tribute to generations past. Many of our mothers, grandmothers and great-grandmothers were experts in the art of candy making, having learned their craft at the knee of the generation before them. Armed with a glob of butter the size of an egg or a pinch of soda the size of a bean, they could turn out a batch of homemade goodies that would rival even the most expensive of confections that we now purchase.

Few of us bother to make our own candies today, perhaps because we do not have time or perhaps because we do not know how. Regardless of the reasons, the art of candy making is quickly vanishing from the North American home. *300 Best Homemade Candy Recipes* is an effort to preserve the recipes of another generation, as well as the bit of Americana they represent, before they are lost to us forever.

Basic Things to Know

Many of us are intimidated at the thought of making our own candies, but only because we have not mastered a few basic principles every candy maker should know. By following just a few simple steps, even the novice candy maker can produce delicious homemade goodies that everyone will enjoy.

Choosing the Right Candy Kettle

The ideal cooking pan is a saucepan or kettle made of heavy aluminum or cast iron. Nonstick coatings are not required and make little difference in cooking or cleanup. The pan should have a sturdy handle to grip during stirring, beating and pouring. Lids are required in some recipes but not all. Lightweight stainless-steel pans are not recommended for most candies because ingredients such as milk, cream and butter can easily scorch.

Saucepans with bowed sides are beautiful but are often not practical for candy making. The bowed sides often do not distribute the heat evenly throughout the pan, meaning that candy ingredients may not cook properly. Pans should have straight sides or rounded sides with an opening larger than the base. Place the saucepan or kettle on a burner that is as wide or wider than the sides of the pan so that the sides of the pan remain heated during cooking.

My official candy kettle is a deep 4.5-quart banged-up beauty that began life as a heavy cast aluminum pressure cooker over 60 years ago. This coveted family heirloom has probably produced a few thousand batches of candy, yet it still cooks candy as well today as it did when my mother first christened it "The Candy Pot" in the late 1940s. Similar pans are often available at garage sales or estate sales for only a few dollars. For smaller recipes, I use nonstick heavy aluminum saucepans from one of two sets of everyday cookware.

As I was putting the finishing touches on this book, one of my younger family members entertained me with tales about her first solo batch of fudge. Her story reminded me that old candy makers sometimes forget to tell new candy makers a thing or two, like candy ingredients that barely cover the bottom of a huge kettle when cold may boil over when hot. A boiling candy mixture has a tendency to take on a life of its own, with some increasing in volume by as much as 500 percent, especially if the recipe includes buttermilk and baking soda. To avoid a major cleanup effort use a pan larger than you think you need.

Guide to Selecting Candy Pans

One of the nice things about being in charge of the kitchen is that we can decide how we want our candies to look. Much of this is determined by the pan size we choose to mold the candy. I grew up believing that all fudge had to be about ¾ inch (2 cm) thick because that is how my mother's fudge looked. When I took command of my own kitchen I realized that if I poured the same amount of candy into a slightly smaller pan my candy would be taller and prettier, at least to my eye.

I prefer using smaller pans to create taller candies, but that is a personal preference and some may choose another size pan for the same recipe. Pan size will not affect taste, only appearance, so you may want to experiment to find what appeals to you.

The pan sizes recommended in each recipe are just a guideline based on my preference for the thickness of that candy. Once you've made a few batches you can decide your own preference. To judge what pan size you'd like to use, look at the weight yield of the candy you plan to make and compare the pan sizes with other candies you've made, then use a larger pan (or pans) if you prefer a thinner candy or a smaller pan (or pans) if you prefer a taller candy. For small batches (1 to 1½ lbs/500 to 750 g), most candies can also be poured onto a buttered dinner-size plate, or onto a baking sheet, lined with buttered parchment paper, instead of a pan. Remember that if you do not have the perfect pan, you can improvise and create your own by lining a box with buttered parchment paper.

Cooking with Candy Thermometers

I strongly recommend investing in a good, sturdy candy thermometer. I rarely make candy without mine. Why toy with disaster when a little gadget will tell us all we need to know?

Candy thermometers should have very specific markings showing temperatures in 2-degree increments. Those encased in about a 12-inch (30 cm) strip of metal are often sturdier, easier to use and less likely to break than those made only of glass. This type of thermometer is available at stores that sell kitchen supplies or candy-making equipment. Two brand names are Taylor and Comark, though other brands may work equally well. More expensive digital thermometers are also available in specialty stores. Glass thermometers are available in some grocery stores for only a few dollars, but the least expensive models can be difficult to read.

Clip the thermometer to the side of the pan so that the tip is covered by the candy mixture. Do not let the thermometer rest on the bottom of the pan, where it can give a false reading. Most metal-encased thermometers have a bottom lip to prevent the glass portion from touching the pan. Depending on the size and shape of the pan, thermometers may also be placed in the middle of the pan, with the thermometer resting on the pan's outer edge. During cooking, it is important to move the thermometer occasionally and stir underneath it. Do not place the thermometer

in the pan until after the sugar dissolves and the mixture comes to a boil.

To clean a thermometer, soak it in hot, soapy water until the sugar mixture dissolves and then rinse it and pat it dry. Scrubbing a thermometer may erase the markings, making it difficult to read. Thermometers can be damaged if not carefully stored away from knives and other heavy cooking utensils.

If a candy thermometer is not available, refer to the Candy-Cooking Guide (page 11).

Final Cooking Temperatures

The purpose of cooking candy is to change the texture of ingredients by reducing or "cooking out" excess moisture. The temperature rises as the moisture evaporates, with sugar changing forms as it cooks. Cooked sugar gradually progresses through a series of stages known as the soft ball, medium ball, firm ball, hard ball, soft crack and hard crack stages. Each of these stages defines a candy's moisture content and affects texture, which is why it is necessary to monitor cooking temperatures so closely.

Cooking temperatures can be adjusted for personal preferences as long as they fall within a range of temperatures appropriate for that type of candy. For example, one person may prefer a specific fudge recipe when cooked to 236°F (113°C), while another prefers that same recipe cooked to 234°F (112°C) for a slightly softer fudge or to 238°F (114°C) for a slightly firmer fudge. For this reason, many of the temperatures cited in this book are recommendations rather than edicts. If the recipe offers a recommended temperature, I advise cooking to that temperature the first time you try the recipe.

If a candy is too dry for your taste, cook it 1 to 2 degrees lower next time, thus letting it retain more moisture. If it is too soft, sticky or tacky, cook it 1 to 2 degrees higher next time, thus decreasing the moisture. Record temperatures as you cook so that you can duplicate your best candies again.

Cooking Candies in Humid Conditions

Most candy experts recommend cooking candies on a clear day if possible and increasing the temperature by 1 to 2 degrees on particularly damp or humid days. While bad weather is broadly thought to adversely affect candies, I have not found it to be a major factor in the success or failure of any particular recipe. I tend to pay more attention to seasons rather than cloud cover, sometimes cooking soft candies like fudge a little longer in the summer to fortify them against Oklahoma's notorious summer heat.

Cooking Candies at High Altitudes

Those who live in high altitudes must adjust cooking temperatures for their specific altitude. To make these adjustments, insert a candy thermometer into a pan of cool water and place over medium heat. Bring the water to a boil, noting the precise temperature on the candy thermometer as the water reaches the boiling point. Subtract that temperature reading from 212°F (100°C) (the boiling point of water at sea level) and then reduce the cooking temperature by the difference.

For example, if the water boils at 202°F (94°C), subtract 202°F (94°C) from 212°F (100°C). The result is 10°F (6°C), meaning that candy cooked at that altitude will reach the desired consistency sooner than when cooked at sea level. Therefore, reduce the recommended cooking temperature of your candies by 10°F (6°C).

Temperatures for Cooking Candies

Unless directed otherwise, candies should be cooked slowly over low or medium to medium-high heat, but never on high heat. The objective is to keep a consistent boil without rushing the candy along, as cooking too quickly can cause candies to scorch or become grainy.

Stirring Candy

In candy making, the phrase "stir constantly" means to keep the mixture moving so it does not scorch on the bottom or the sides of the pan. This usually means a slow, gentle stir rather than fast, vigorous stirring. I stir in a slow, rhythmic figure-eight pattern through the center of the pan, occasionally lifting the thermometer to stir underneath and behind it. Too much stirring may cause candy to be grainy, so do not stir more than necessary.

Many old-time candy makers believe that candy should only be stirred or beaten with wooden spoons, often warning that anything but a wooden spoon will ruin the candy. While I usually use a wooden spoon, I have cooked with metal spoons without noticing any significant difference. In one recipe, Aunt Bill's Brown Candy (page 28), I often choose a metal spoon because it gives me a better feel for what is happening on the bottom of the kettle. If the metal spoon drags across the pan, I know the caramelized sugar has not yet fully dissolved.

Preventing Sugar Crystals

Some recipes call for removing sugar crystals that form on the sides of the pan as a result of undissolved sugar. This can be a crucial step, as even one crystal can prompt a chain of crystals to form and make a candy grainy.

The two most common methods for removing crystals are (1) to place the lid on the pan for a few minutes so that crystals will dissolve in the trapped moisture or (2) to wash the crystals (or wipe them) from the sides of the pan with a damp pastry brush or cloth-wrapped fork while cooking. I prefer the lid method, but brushing the sides of the pan with a pastry brush that has been dipped in water can be equally effective. If in doubt about sugar crystals, cover the pan for 2 to 3 minutes just after it begins to boil. This requires very little effort and can only improve the candy, not harm it. Be aware that covered candy can boil over the sides of the pan very easily, so lift the lid occasionally to make sure you are not headed for disaster.

Some recipes may specify not to stir, move or shake a mixture while it is cooking or to pour without scraping the sides or bottom of the pan. For example, Grace's Walnut Butter Fudge (page 115) calls for pouring the cooked mixture into a clean, dry container without scraping the pan. This is because moving, shaking and scraping can prompt a chain of sugar crystals to form, making a candy grainy.

candies made from a mixture of sugar and corn syrup, such as Glass Candy (page 54), Horehound Candy (page 56) or Hardtack Candy (page 55). These types of candies should always be cooled at room temperature.

As a general rule, if a finished candy can be stored in the refrigerator or freezer, it can be cooled in the refrigerator or freezer. Cool others at room temperature.

Beating Candy

Unless directed otherwise, candies that require beating should be beaten by hand until they cool, lose their gloss and begin to stiffen. These are signs that the chemical changes that affect texture are complete. Electric mixers are a poor substitute for hand beating and will not necessarily yield the same results. Additionally, many old-fashioned candies are too thick and heavy to beat with most electric mixers without causing motor damage. Unless a recipe specifies to use an electric mixer, consider it a risk. The one exception may be fudges containing marshmallow creme. A few short minutes of beating with an electric mixer does not seem to hurt these candies and can often help them.

In most recipes, it is important to use a clean spoon for beating. For example, in Grace's Walnut Butter Fudge (page 115), the only time a spoon is used to stir the mixture is at the very beginning of the cooking process. If we later pick up that same spoon to beat the cooked candy, the undissolved sugar left on the spoon will be mixed into the candy and may cause a chain of sugar crystals to form.

Cooling Candy

Many candies may be cooled on the countertop or in the refrigerator or freezer. Some candies, especially fudges, often cut more neatly if slightly chilled first. Occasionally, a candy cooled in the refrigerator or freezer develops a sticky coating. This is especially true of hard

Storing Candy

Store candy in airtight containers to prevent drying. Refrigeration is often a matter of personal choice, though many candies will keep longer if properly covered and chilled.

Hard candies like toffees or brittles may absorb moisture and become sticky if stored with soft candies like fudge, so it is best to store them in separate containers.

Because most candies that come through my kitchen are ingested within a matter of days, it is difficult to say exactly how long candies might keep in a home graced with willpower. Cooked candies such as fudge should retain their freshness at least 1 month if properly covered and stored in the refrigerator. Aunt Bill's Brown Candy (page 28) is rumored to keep indefinitely, though indefinitely has never visited my home. Some pralines seem to lose their eye appeal after only a few days yet are still tasty at least 2 weeks after cooking, especially when individually sealed in plastic wrap. Some truffles and ball-type candies may begin to show their age after a week or so, though the majority of these same candies can be frozen for later use. Certainly any candy containing uncooked eggs should be stored in the refrigerator and eaten within 2 to 3 days, if not sooner. (See Cook's Note, page 176, concerning eating uncooked eggs.) This rule does not apply to divinity, as the hot syrup that is poured over the beaten egg whites should heat the whites sufficiently to consider them cooked.

Packaging Candy for Gifts

Some craft stores and candy-making supply stores offer specially coated, direct-pour candy boxes in 1/2-lb or 1-lb (250 to 500 g) sizes that are perfect for gift giving. Simply pour the warm candy into these boxes, allow the candy to cool and then seal the box in plastic wrap. Place the lid on the box, tie it with a decorative bow and the candy is ready to hand to a friend or ship across the country.

Any clean, sturdy, decorative box can be made into a direct-pour candy box with a set of kitchen shears, a little parchment paper and some butter. Cut a piece of parchment paper to exactly fit the bottom of the box and then generously butter both the parchment paper and the sides of the box. Place the buttered parchment paper into the bottom of the box. Once the candy is finished as directed, simply pour the warm candy on top of the parchment paper. After the candy cools, seal the box in plastic wrap and then add the lid and a decorative bow. Both types of boxes work very well for candies such as fudge, and the final presentation is worth the effort.

Cellophane bags are an impressive yet inexpensive way to present favorite toffees, brittles, barks and hard candies to family, friends and coworkers, especially when tied with a festive bow. These bags can also be used to package candies like fudges, pralines or caramels, especially if each piece of candy is individually wrapped in plastic wrap. Large craft store chains often sell packages of these bags near candy-making supplies. Shop early because cellophane bags seem to disappear from the shelves just as the holiday season approaches.

Most craft stores and some grocery stores carry small, fluted paper candy cups designed to hold bonbons, truffles and other chocolate-dipped candies. When small candies are placed into these cups and then into a decorative box, they can be just as beautiful as professionally packaged candies. Coordinating the color of the candy cup with the candy's flavor, such as using red or pink candy cups for Luscious Raspberry-Fudge Truffles (page 220), is a nice way to let friends distinguish one chocolate-coated candy from another.

The Candy Maker's Personality: Getting the Right Frame of Mind

I spent years wondering why my mother was more successful with some candy recipes than I was, and I finally uncovered the secret while writing this book. My mother had the ideal personality to be a candy maker. She never hurried her candy along, she never put much effort into stirring and she was more than happy to let some candies simmer quietly on the stove while tending to another task. Above all, she never worried, became frustrated or took shortcuts.

I, on the other hand, spent years turning the heat to the highest possible setting, often pushing it to the extreme. My spoon never stopped moving, as I was certain constant clatter and activity in my kitchen would somehow make candy cook faster. I chained myself to the stove, watching every bubble, every degree and every tick of the clock. If patience is a virtue, my mother got my share.

Eventually I discovered that the more patient I became, the better my candies tasted. My date and pecan rolls were smoother, my fudges creamier and my Aunt Bill's Brown Candy (page 28) began to rival my mother's. That may be my finest achievement yet.

As a result of this "research," my single best piece of advice for anyone wanting to become a candy maker is to be slightly lazy about it. Pull up a chair, sit near the stove, turn down the heat and daydream while you stir. Candy will cook at its own pace if you let it.

Safety First

Candy mixtures can be dangerously hot, especially for little ones standing underfoot. Use great caution when cooking, stirring, carrying or pouring hot candy to prevent burns and spills on children, pets and yourself. Nothing is more satisfying than introducing a child to candy making, but place safety above all else. Provide full-time adult supervision, and never leave a child alone with hot candies.

Candy-Cooking Guide

Cold Water Testing Procedure

I strongly recommend using a candy thermometer in most recipes, but if preferred you can determine where a candy is in the cooking process by dropping a small amount of the hot candy mixture into cold water. The water cools the candy enough that you can touch it and feel how soft, firm or brittle it might be. Then it is up to you to use your judgment to determine if it has reached the right consistency for that kind of recipe. This method often produces inconsistent results but generations of candy makers relied on it exclusively. My mother always used a candy thermometer yet I saw her drop candy into cold water many times, often as a way to entertain herself or to check the accuracy of her thermometer. If you are new to candy making you may want to experiment with this method a few times even when using a candy thermometer just so you can learn about the changes in texture that occur as candy escalates in temperature.

First remove the kettle or saucepan from the heat so the temperature does not rise during testing. Drop about $\frac{1}{2}$ tsp (2 mL) of the boiling hot syrup or candy mixture into a glass or small bowl filled with cold water. Test the firmness of the mixture by shaping it with your fingers. Use fresh cold water for each test.

Sugar Stages

For step-by-step photographs, see color page L.

Soft Ball Stage	234°F to 240°F (112°C to 116°C) *For fondants, fudges and penuches* Soft ball may be formed under cold water but flattens some when picked up.
Medium Ball Stage	241°F to 244°F (116.5 to 118°C) (Not indicated on candy thermometers) *For old-fashioned fudge-like candies* Medium ball firmer than soft ball.
Firm Ball Stage	244°F to 248°F (118°C to 120°C) *For caramels* Firm ball may be formed and holds its shape unless pressed.
Hard Ball Stage	250°F to 265°F (121°C to 129°C) *For divinities, marshmallows, nougats, popcorn balls and taffies* Hard ball may be formed and retains its shape. The ball is hard enough to be rolled on a buttered surface.
Soft Crack Stage	270°F to 290°F (132°C to 143°C) *For butterscotches* Hard threads form as the hot syrup strikes the cold water. They will be chewy and stick to the teeth.
Hard Crack Stage	300°F to 310°F (149°C to 154°C) *For brittles and toffees* Hard, brittle threads form as the hot syrup strikes the cold water.

Skill Levels: What Do They Mean?

Many candy makers often want guidance in choosing recipes appropriate for their level of expertise. The recipes in this book can be classified into one of five categories, ranging from those candies that anyone can make to those best reserved for experienced candy makers. Keep in mind that most of these groupings are based upon the amount of skill required to make the recipe rather than the amount of time required. (See also Jane's Top 40, page 17, and Recipes by Skill Level, page 277.)

Novice, Super Simple

For the most part, Super Simple recipes require opening a few packages, measuring a few ingredients and stirring a few things together. Even those who claim they cannot boil water should have no trouble with these recipes since no cooking is involved.

Novice, Easy

Easy recipes do not require exceptional culinary skill, though some may be time-consuming. For example, most chocolate-coated candies are stirred together, formed into balls and dipped into melted chocolate. Recipes of this nature are not difficult, though shaping and dipping individual candies takes time. Most truffle recipes are also grouped into this category since they involve heating, mixing and shaping ingredients.

Average

Most candies in the Average category must be cooked to a specific temperature but do not require significant hand beating. Examples are marshmallow fudges, toffees, brittles, caramel popcorn and most old-fashioned hard candies. Those who have a basic understanding of cooking procedures should make these candies successfully.

Advanced

Candies in the Advanced category involve some level of precision cooking. The candy must cook to a specific temperature and be beaten by hand, usually until it loses its gloss and begins to hold its shape. Often deciding when a candy is properly beaten is more of a judgment call than an exact science. Advanced recipes are not as difficult as they appear so if you are comfortable with recipes categorized as Average then you should be prepared to tackle Advanced. Most traditional cooked candies and old-fashioned fudge recipes fall within this category, as do the divinity recipes.

Expert

These candies involve extra time or multiple steps and should be attempted by those who are experienced candy makers or those who have excellent cooking skills. For example, Aunt Bill's Brown Candy (page 28) not only requires precision cooking, but it also requires cooking and stirring two mixtures simultaneously. Though it is a wonderful old recipe to be enjoyed by many, it is not the place for novices to begin. If you want to try the Expert recipes then consider asking a more experienced friend to help you.

The Science of Candy Making

Candy making is based upon sugar chemistry, with different ingredients and different methods producing different candies. Some fundamental knowledge of how the different ingredients interact with the sugar is very useful if we want to improve a candy's texture or compare one recipe to another.

Most traditional candies fall into one of two categories, crystalline or non-crystalline. Crystalline candies include old-fashioned fudges, penuches, divinities, nougats, pecan rolls, date rolls and cooked fondants. All of these candies ideally contain very fine sugar crystals that form due to the combination of ingredients, the cooking temperature and the beating process. If small crystals form slowly, the candy will be smooth and creamy. If large crystals form rapidly, the candy may become sugary or grainy. As candy makers, our job is to help the sugar crystals form slowly so that our candies will be extra delicious.

The purpose of cooking candies slowly and beating by hand is to encourage small crystals to form. Some crystalline candy recipes also recommend a cooling period between cooking and beating, often cooling the candy until it is lukewarm (110°F/43°C) or until you can comfortably hold your hand on the bottom of the pan. This cooling period is just one more step candy makers add to promote the formation of small crystals. Cooling is also a bonus for the cook because cooled candies usually require less beating than hot candies.

Ingredients also affect the crystallization process, with certain ingredients aiding crystallization and others hindering it. Some candy makers prefer recipes that include corn syrup, which is known for producing ultra-smooth candies. Butter and cream also reduce the size of sugar crystals and give our candies that silky texture that we love. Non-crystalline candies, such as brittles, toffees, butterscotches, caramels and taffies,

ideally do not contain any sugar crystals and, therefore, often call for large amounts of these ingredients. Acidic ingredients, such as vinegar, lemon juice and cream of tartar, also work to prevent crystallization. Some of the creamiest candies in this collection often contain at least one, if not two, forms of acid, along with corn syrup, butter and cream.

Modifying Recipes

This example shows how to put this knowledge to practical use. I had the following recipe for pineapple fudge.

3 cups	granulated sugar	750 mL
1 tbsp	light (white) corn syrup	15 mL
½ cup	heavy or whipping (35%) cream	125 mL
1	can (8 oz/227 mL) crushed pineapple, drained	1
2 tbsp	butter	30 mL
½ tsp	vanilla extract	2 mL
1 cup	coarsely chopped walnuts or black walnuts (optional)	250 mL

At first glance, I expected the candy to be creamy, but instead it was grainy and best used as a brick. The small amount of heavy cream did not give it the moisture it needed so the candy cooked too quickly, even when placed over low heat. I modified the recipe, adding slightly more corn syrup to prevent crystallization; plus I added ½ cup (125 mL) light (5%) cream to give it moisture. My second version was better, but it still was not what I wanted.

On the third try, I added lemon juice, cream of tartar and a little more corn syrup. Because half-and-half (10%) cream has more moisture than heavy cream, I chose to use all half-and-half rather than a mixture of the two creams. Though I could have adjusted my cooking temperature down 1 or 2 degrees to correct the dryness, I added a little more butter after the candy was cooked. This is the modified list of ingredients.

3 cups	granulated sugar	750 mL
3 tbsp	light (white) corn syrup	45 mL
1 cup	half-and-half (10%) cream	250 mL
1	can (8 oz/227 mL) crushed pineapple, drained	1
2 tsp	lemon juice	10 mL
1/4 tsp	cream of tartar	1 mL
1/4 cup	butter	60 mL
1/4 tsp	pure lemon extract	1 mL
1 cup	coarsely chopped walnuts (optional)	250 mL

In the end, I had an ultra-smooth, light-colored, pineapple-speckled fudge, which is exactly what I wanted when I started. My last-minute decision to use lemon extract versus vanilla extract was nothing more than an adventure, but it gave the flavor an extra boost and branded the recipe as my own.

Comparison of Three Recipes for Pralines

As you can see, the science of making candy is not nearly as complicated as it first appears to be. Just a little knowledge helps us customize a recipe to our tastes. Understanding how ingredients interact with one another also helps us choose which recipes might have the texture we like.

For example, Perfect Pralines (page 63) tend to be somewhat creamier than most traditional pralines. This is due to the buttermilk used in the recipe, as buttermilk contains acid and acid helps prevent crystallization.

Ingredients for Perfect Pralines

1 cup	buttermilk	250 mL
2 cups	granulated sugar	500 mL
1 tsp	baking soda	5 mL
1/2 cup	butter or margarine (butter preferred)	125 mL
1/8 tsp	salt	0.5 mL
2 1/2 cups	pecans, in large pieces	625 mL
1 tsp	vanilla extract	5 mL

Soft Pecan Pralines (page 68) do not contain any acid, but they do contain large quantities of corn syrup, cream and butter or margarine, all of which are known to reduce the size of crystals. Therefore, we know that Soft Pecan Pralines may also be creamier than most traditional praline recipes.

Ingredients for Soft Pecan Pralines

2 cups	granulated sugar	500 mL
1/3 cup	light (white) corn syrup	75 mL
2/3 cup	heavy or whipping (35%) cream	150 mL
Pinch	salt	Pinch
2 cups	pecans, in large pieces	500 mL
1/4 cup	butter or margarine	60 mL
1/2 tsp	vanilla extract	2 mL

Ruth's Angel Pralines (page 67) do not contain any acid; plus the recipe calls for relatively low amounts of cream and butter. If we think about sugar and what affects its crystallization, we know that this combination of ingredients is likely to produce sugary, traditional pralines.

Ingredients for Ruth's Angel Pralines

1 cup	granulated sugar	250 mL
1 cup	packed light brown sugar	250 mL
1/2 cup	half-and-half (10%) cream	125 mL
1/4 tsp	salt	1 mL
2 tbsp	butter or margarine	30 mL
1 cup	pecans, in large pieces	250 mL

Eventually, analyzing recipes becomes second nature as we learn which candies we like and which ingredients will produce them.

Duplicating Lost Recipes

The purpose of including a wide variety of similar candies is to help cooks locate cherished recipes that may have been lost from one generation to the next. Often, the first step to finding a recipe similar to the one lost is to write down everything remembered about the candy.

For example, if you are trying to duplicate your mother's delicious date roll, what do you remember about the way she cooked? Did she like easy recipes that just involved mixing a few ingredients together in a bowl or was she an old-fashioned candy maker who let candies simmer slowly on the stove?

Do you remember any special processes she may have used, such as hand beating or kneading? People often comment that their mothers kept date roll candy rolled in a damp towel, which is a sure sign that they are trying to duplicate an old-fashioned, slow-cooked date roll rather than a quick date roll. Any little tidbit of information, such as "Mom always cooked in an old iron skillet," can be a clue.

Did the candy have cherries, marshmallows, pineapple or other unusual ingredients that could lead you to the recipe? Do you remember it having a brown sugar flavor or was it just brown in color? For example, most date rolls are some shade of brown, but recipes that contain brown sugar often have a strong brown sugar taste. Candies containing melted, caramelized sugar also have a distinctive flavor, though it is a milder flavor than that of brown sugar.

Do you remember your mother using corn syrup in candies, cookies or other kinds of recipes? If so, then it is likely that the recipe you want contains corn syrup because candy makers often follow patterns.

What kind of texture did the candy have? Was it sugary or smooth? By reading about The Science of Candy Making (page 13), it may be easier to determine the kinds of ingredients that can produce the texture you remember.

Once you have gathered every bit of information available about the candy you want to duplicate, select a few recipes to try. If you still do not have an exact match, consider modifying a near match by adjusting a few ingredients, using the information in The Science of Candy Making. For example, adding corn syrup often makes a candy smoother, and light cream or evaporated milk produces a richer candy than milk. A dry candy can often be made creamier by adding a little extra butter after cooking and cocoa powder or unsweetened chocolate can usually be increased or decreased as desired. The amount of sugar in a recipe can often be modified slightly, though this may depend upon the particular recipe or type of candy being made. Ingredients such as salt and vanilla can be added or eliminated and using nuts is typically a matter of personal choice.

Problems and Solutions

No matter what problem you encounter in candy making, someone has probably had a similar or worse experience. If your first candy-making attempt is less than successful, do not stop trying. Candy making becomes easier with experience. Most problems can be diagnosed and corrected rather easily.

Candy is too soft, too sticky or like soup

The candy is probably undercooked. Increase the temperature by 1 or 2°F (0.5 to 1°C) next time (or by 3 or 4°F/1.5 to 2°C if the candy was really like thin soup). High humidity could also be a factor, as well as under beating.

Candy is too dry, too brittle or resembles a brick

The candy is probably overcooked. Decrease the temperature by 1 or 2°F (0.5 to 1°C) next time (or by 3 or 4°F/1.5 to 2°C if you could use it to break a window). Also consider the cooking pot used. Even if you followed all instructions, cooking in a lightweight pot can ruin a batch of candy.

Candy is too grainy

A number of factors contribute to graininess. If you followed all directions, then the most likely causes are (1) you stirred too vigorously, (2) the candy was cooked too rapidly at too high a temperature or (3) the sugar crystals were not removed from the sides of the pan. See Basic Things to Know (page 6) and The Science of Candy Making (page 13). Also know that some candies are just grainier than others due to the ingredients used in the recipe. An example is Pumpkin Fudge (page 162).

Candy is too dark, would not cook properly and texture is incorrect

The saucepan or kettle used for cooking can make the difference between a good batch of candy and a "strange" one. Most candies should be cooked in a heavyweight pan made of a material such as aluminum, not in pans made of lightweight stainless steel. Candies cooked in stainless-steel pots often cook too quickly, causing them to scorch. If the heat is reduced to accommodate the stainless-steel pan, then the candy may cook so slowly that the sugar caramelizes.

Also check to see that the stove's heating element is working properly. The removable metal elements in electric burners can become old and worn, causing them to conduct heat unevenly or improperly.

What to Do with Candy Failures

These are some interesting ideas other candy makers have shared about what they did with less-than-perfect candy.

If the candy is too soft and undercooked, stir in some confectioner's sugar before turning it into the pan. Another thought is to roll the candy into balls and then roll the balls into coconut or chopped nuts.

When a friend had chocolate soup instead of fudge, she sprinkled a layer of coconut in the bottom of several small disposable dishes, poured her soup on top and served it with a spoon. Her son thought it was so good that he asked her to make more.

Another friend crumbled scorched toffee into small bits and added them to chocolate chip cookie dough. She said the cookies were delicious.

White Cherry Fudge

(See recipe, page 164 for detailed step-by-step instructions.)

1

Bring the sugar, sour cream, milk, butter, corn syrup and salt to a boil.

2

Insert the candy thermometer.

3

Cook, stirring constantly, to 238°F (114°C).

4

Remove from the heat.

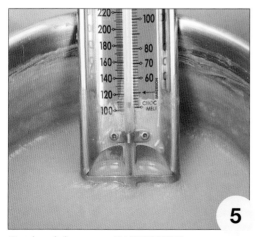

5

Cool to lukewarm (110°F/43°C).

6

Add the vanilla.

continued…

A.

White Cherry Fudge *(continued)*

(See recipe, page 164 for detailed step-by-step instructions.)

7

Beat by hand until the candy begins to lose its gloss and hold its shape.

8

Quickly stir in the walnuts and cherries.

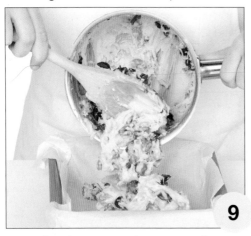

9

Immediately turn into the prepared pan.

10

Pat or press the candy into the pan, if needed.

11

Cut the cooled candy into squares.

12

Store in an airtight container.

B.

Charlotte's Extra-Good, Extra-Wicked Fudge

(See recipe, page 123 for detailed step-by-step instructions.)

Bring the sugar, milk and butter to a boil.

Insert the candy thermometer.

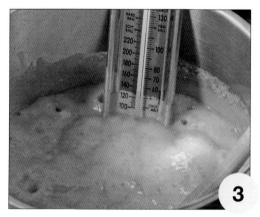

Cook, stirring constantly, to 236°F (113°C).

Remove from the heat. Stir in the chocolate chips milk chocolate and marshmallow creme.

Stir in the nuts and vanilla.

Pour into the prepared pan and smooth top.

C.

Lollipops

(See recipe, page 57 for detailed step-by-step instructions.)

1

Bring the sugar, corn syrup and water to a boil.

2

Cover and cook 2 to 3 minutes to dissolve sugar crystals on the sides of the pan.

3

Insert the candy thermometer and cook to 300°F (149°C).

4

Remove from the heat. Quickly stir in the coloring and flavoring.

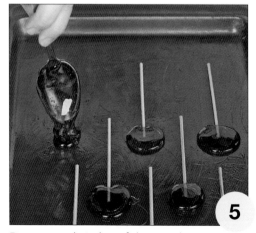

5

Drop round circles of the candy mixture onto the prepared baking sheet.

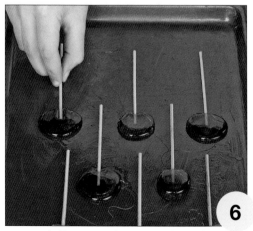

6

Press a lollipop stick into each circle.

D.

Holiday Divinity

(See recipe, page 84 for detailed step-by-step instructions.)

Beat the egg whites until very stiff peaks form.

Cook the sugar, corn syrup, water and salt to 248°F (120°C).

Turn the mixer to medium-high speed and gradually pour half the hot syrup over the egg whites.

Turn the electric mixer to medium-high speed and gradually pour the remaining hot syrup over the top of the candy mixture.

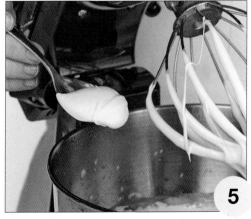

Beat with the electric mixer until the candy becomes slightly dull and holds its shape.

Quickly drop the candy onto the waxed paper using the tip of a buttered spoon.

E.

Almond Butter Toffee

(See recipe, page 50 for detailed step-by-step instructions.)

1

Bring the butter, sugar and water to a boil.

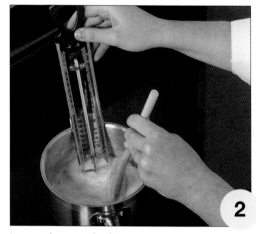

2

Insert the candy thermometer.

3

Cook, stirring constantly, to 300°F (149°C).

4

Stir in the chopped almonds and vanilla.

5

Add the baking soda.

6

Pour onto the prepared baking sheet and spread in a thin layer.

F.

7

Melt half the chocolate chips in the top of a double boiler.

8

Spread the melted chocolate on one side of the cooled toffee.

9

Sprinkle the side coated with melted chocolate with chopped almonds.

10

Turn the toffee over and repeat steps 7 through 9 to coat the other side of the toffee.

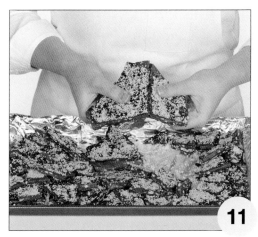

11

Break into pieces.

12

Store in an airtight container.

G.

Molasses Taffy

(See recipe, page 107 for detailed step-by-step instructions.)

1 Cook the granulated and brown sugars, molasses and water to 272°F (133°C).

2 Add the butter, baking soda and salt.

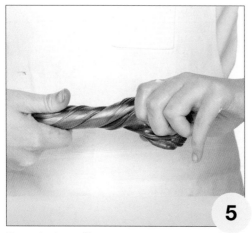

3 Pour onto the prepared baking sheet and cool just until the candy can be handled.

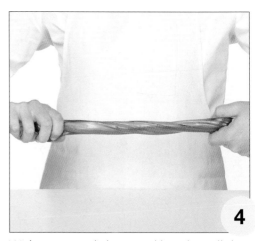

4 With generously buttered hands, pull the taffy until it is firm and golden brown.

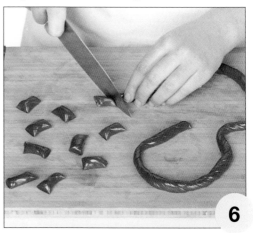

5 Stretch the taffy into a rope, twisting the rope.

6 Cut into 1-inch (2.5 cm) lengths.

H.

Caramel Pecan Roll

(See recipe, page 98 for detailed step-by-step instructions.)

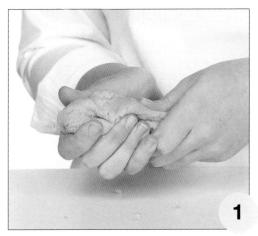

1

Knead the cream candy filling between hands until smooth and creamy.

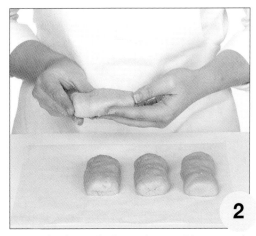

2

Form the kneaded candy into 4 logs, each about 4 inches (10 cm) long.

3

Cut the cooled caramel into 4 equal rectangles.

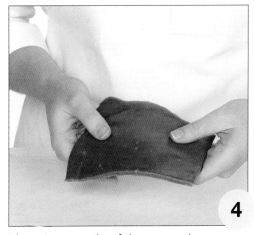

4

Place 1 rectangle of the caramel on waxed paper.

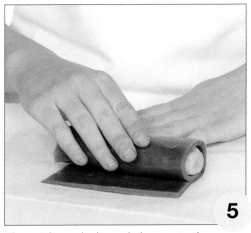

5

Place 1 kneaded candy log onto the caramel. Wrap up into a cylinder.

6

Roll the caramel-wrapped cylinder in the pecans.

Luscious Raspberry-Fudge Truffles

(See recipe, page 220 for detailed step-by-step instructions.)

Shape the mixture into balls ¾ inch (2 cm) in diameter.

Melt the chocolate candy coating over hot, but not boiling water.

Dip the balls in the melted chocolate.

Drop on waxed paper and let stand until firm.

Decorate with White Chocolate Drizzle.

Store in an airtight container in the refrigerator.

J.

Ultra-Creamy Fondant

(See recipe, Bonbons variation, page 204 for detailed step-by-step instructions.)

Blend the butter, corn syrup, flavoring, salt and food coloring with a wooden spoon. **1**

Gradually add the confectioner's (icing) sugar. **2**

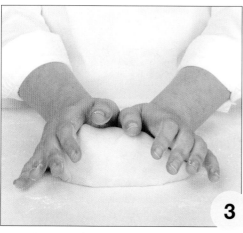

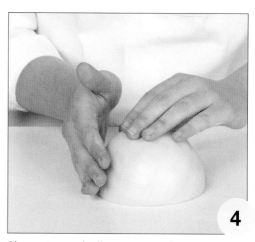

Knead by hand until the mixture is smooth. **3**

Shape into a ball or a mound. **4**

Pinch off small pieces of the fondant and shape into balls ¾ inch (2 cm) in diameter. **5**

Roll or dip in the coating of choice. **6**

K.

Stages of Cooked Sugar

(See chart, page 11 for more details.)

1

Soft Ball Stage (234°F to 240°F/112°C to 116°C): Soft ball may be formed in cold water but the ball flattens some when picked up.

2

Medium Ball Stage (241°F to 244°F/ 116.5°C to 118°C): Medium ball may be formed in cold water and will be slightly firmer than a soft ball but may still flatten some when picked up.

3

Firm Ball Stage (244°F to 248°F/118°C to 120°C): Firm ball may be formed in cold water and the ball holds its shape unless pressed.

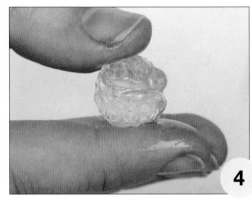

4

Hard Ball Stage (250°F to 265°F/121°C to 129°C): Hard ball may be formed in cold water and the ball can be rolled on a buttered surface and still retain its shape.

5

Soft Crack Stage (270°F to 290°F/132°C to 143°C): Hard threads form as the hot syrup strikes the cold water.

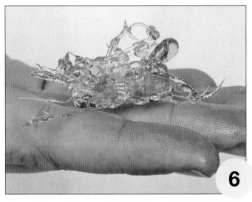

6

Hard Crack Stage (300°F to 310°F/149°C to 154°C): Hard, brittle threads form as the hot syrup strikes the cold water.

L.

Jane's Top 40

With so many delicious candies made from the four basic food groups of sugar, cream, butter and chocolate, choosing my favorites can be impossible. These 40 recipes are some of my top selections for candy makers of all ages and all skill levels for all occasions. Many of the candies on this list are recipes I have enjoyed for many years, with some being recent discoveries that are too good not to mention. (See also Recipes by Skill Level, page 277.)

Novice, Super Simple

Chipper Nutty Fudge (page 268)
Cinnamon Walnut Balls (page 178)
Marvelous Marbled Mints (page 208)

Mom's Peanut Butter Candy (page 269)
Orange-Nut Tea Balls (page 174)

Novice, Easy

Aunt Mary's Turtles (page 199)
Chocolate-Cherry Creams (page 170)
Chocolate-Covered Cherries (page 198)
Coconut Bonbons (page 182)
Crispy Peanut Butter Balls (page 189)
Gourmet Layered Peppermint Bark (page 258)

Humdinger Date Balls (page 179)
Luscious Raspberry-Fudge Truffles (page 220)
Lynda's Gourmet Chocolate Truffles (page 213)
Roasted Cinnamon Pecans (page 224)
Sensational Orange Mint Patties (page 211)

Average

Aunt Lucy's Extra-Buttery Brittle (page 43)
Charlotte's Extra-Good, Extra-Wicked Fudge (page 123)
Chewy, Gooey Caramel Pecan Squares (page 59)
Classic Combo Fudge (page 142)
Cowboy Crunch (page 229)

Katie's Perfect Fudge (page 132)
Lemon–White Chocolate Fudge (page 160)
Lindsay's Luscious Peanut Butter Fudge (page 140)
Marry Me Toffee (page 47)
Pistol Pete Peanut Brittle (page 42)
Twice-as-Tempting Two-Tone Fudge (page 144)

Advanced

Creamy Orange Fudge (page 158)
Delicate Apricot Roll (page 91)
Grace's Walnut Butter Fudge (page 115)
Jolly Good Fudge (page 117)
Mom's Divinity (page 78)
Out-of-This-World Maple Fudge (page 155)

Penuche Nut Roll (page 97)
Perfect Pralines (page 63)
Pineapple Sherbet Fudge (page 160)
Private Collection Fudge (page 113)
Sinfully Rich Buttermilk Fudge (page 152)
White Cherry Fudge (page 164)

Expert

Aunt Bill's Brown Candy (page 28)

Candy Glossary

The glossary includes old-fashioned phrases, such as "butter the size of an egg," to help you update any old family recipes that might be in your recipe collection or ones found in an old cookbook, as well as terms such as "candy coating," used in candy making today.

almond bark A confectionery product similar to candy coating but made with vegetable fats instead of cocoa butter. Almond bark is commonly sold in U.S. grocery stores in imitation chocolate or vanilla flavor. It is available under several brand names and is typically found near baking items such as chocolate chips. Almond bark can also refer to a type of candy made from chocolate or white chocolate and almonds. When almond bark is listed as an ingredient in a recipe, the recipe is referencing the candy-coating product made with vegetable fats.

block chocolate High-quality, gourmet chocolate that is usually cut to order and sold by the pound (gram) from large blocks. It is available from a variety of chocolate manufacturers in many price ranges from high-end grocery stores and specialty stores in some major cities. Those who cannot purchase block chocolate can often substitute the highest quality chocolate available for block chocolate.

brown sugar Granulated sugar combined with molasses to make a soft brown sugar. The darker the color of the brown, the stronger the flavor a product made with it will have.

buttermilk In the days when families churned their own butter, they often used the milky substance drained from freshly churned butter for cooking purposes. This "buttermilk" was a staple in most rural kitchens and was commonly used in place of fresh milk. Today's cooks find buttermilk in the refrigerated section of most grocery stores. Used according

to package directions, dried buttermilk works well in baked goods, but do not use dried buttermilk for candy recipes.

butter the size of an egg Usually in a much older recipe, 4 tbsp (60 mL) butter.

butter the size of a walnut Often found in older recipes, 2 tbsp (30 mL) butter.

candy coating A product containing chocolate or imitation chocolate that is melted and then used to coat the outside of candies such as truffles, bonbons, turtles or other chocolate-covered or chocolate-dipped candies or fruits. It contains a firming agent that allows the chocolate to dry quickly and to a harder shell than regular melted chocolate would produce. Candy coating may be sold as wafers, rounds, chips or squares and is available in dark chocolate, milk chocolate, white chocolate, imitation chocolate and vanilla. Some brands offer a variety of colors, with a few brands offering specialty flavors such as caramel. Candy coating may be found in grocery stores, especially during the holiday season, but the most reliable year-round sources are specialty stores that sell confectionery supplies. If you do not have a specialty store in your area then purchase the candy coating via the Internet. Brand names include Bakels, Baker's, Felchlin, Ghirardelli, Merckens, Nestlé and Wilton, though other brands may be available in your area. The price, quality, taste and firmness of the coating varies by brand.

cherries, candied The same syrup-coated cherries used in most fruitcake recipes. They are available in both red and green colors and are usually sold in clear plastic 4-oz (125 g) or 8-oz (250 g) containers or in bulk food sections of the grocery store. Grocers often display candied cherries in the produce department, in the baking aisle, with dried fruits and nuts and/or with the seasonal fruitcake ingredients. Green candied cherries do not always have the same flavor as red candied cherries; use red candied cherries for the recipes in this book unless otherwise specified. Many grocers carry candied cherries as a seasonal holiday item, sometimes making them difficult to locate for about nine months of the year. Candied cherries may be tightly sealed and refrigerated or frozen for later use.

clabber milk Unpasteurized milk that soured and thickened due to lack of refrigeration. It was used as a beverage and in cooking before refrigeration was common. Possible substitutes for clabber milk might be sour cream, buttermilk, or milk mixed with 1 tsp (5 mL) cider vinegar.

confectioner's (icing) sugar Also known as powdered sugar. Granulated sugar that has been ground into a powder. Cornstarch is added to prevent clumping. If clumps do form, measure the sugar and then sift it before using.

corn syrup Light (white), which is clear and colorless, or dark (golden) corn syrup added to candies to prevent crystallization. The dark syrup is used when a caramel flavor is desired.

cream Cream is available in light (5%) cream, half-and-half (10%), table (18%) cream and heavy or whipping (35%) cream. Whipping cream contains less moisture and has a higher fat content than light (5%) cream or half-and-half (10%) cream.

cream of tartar An acid in powder form added to candies to make them creamier by retarding the formation of large crystals. Other acids sometimes added to candy include lemon juice or vinegar.

cube of margarine or butter Occasionally appearing in old recipes, the equivalent of 1 stick, $\frac{1}{4}$ lb (125 g) or $\frac{1}{2}$ cup (125 mL) of butter or margarine.

evaporated milk Milk from which 60% of the water has been removed. It is typically sold in 5-oz (142 mL) and 12-oz (370 mL) cans. One 5-oz (142 mL) can of evaporated milk contains slightly less than $\frac{2}{3}$ cup (150 mL). One 12-oz (370 mL) can of evaporated milk contains $1\frac{1}{2}$ cups (375 mL). Evaporated milk and sweetened condensed milk are different products and cannot be used interchangeably.

flavored oils Flavored oils such as cinnamon oil, clove oil or anise oil that are much more concentrated than extracts and appear most often in recipes for old-fashioned hard candies. Flavored oils usually come packaged in very small bottles, with cooks measuring them by drops rather than by teaspoons. Oils can often be found in stores that specialize in baking supplies, candy-making supplies or craft items.

glycerin usp A thick, slick liquid usually sold as a skincare product and a common ingredient in skin lotions. It can also be a home remedy for removing difficult stains, such as chocolate, from washable clothing. In candy making, glycerin may be added to fondant recipes to make very soft centers for bonbons. Occasionally, it can appear in other candy recipes such as those for taffy. Most pharmacies sell glycerin in small bottles of about 4 oz (125 g) each for just a few dollars. It is available in craft stores that sell cake and candy-making supplies. You can use leftover glycerin as a skin protectant or softener.

granulated sugar Common white sugar. If a recipe simply calls for sugar, this is the one to use.

homogenized milk Milk in which the size of the fat particles are distributed throughout the milk, staying in suspension. Today most of our milk is both pasteurized and homogenized. Pasteurization destroys any bacteria in the milk and makes it safe for consumption. The cream does not rise to the surface (see Top milk, page 21) as it does in non-homogenized milk.

maple sugar A product derived from maple syrup harvested from sugar maple trees. It can be difficult to locate in grocery stores but can be ordered via the Internet or purchased at farmers' markets and maple syrup farms.

maple syrup Pure maple syrup boiled from the sap from maple trees. It is very expensive so often maple-blended syrups are used. However, pure maple syrup is preferred.

milk See clabber milk, evaporated milk, homogenized milk, rich milk, sweetened condensed milk, sweet milk, top milk, whole milk.

molasses A sweetener made from the juice of the sugar cane. Molasses is available in several different varieties that vary in flavor and different brands use different terms on the label so it can be confusing. For these candy recipes you can use any unsulphured (check the ingredients on the label) mild, light, original, golden, fancy, full-flavor, dark, cooking or baking molasses, keeping in mind, the resulting molasses flavor will be stronger when made with darker, richer molasses. Avoid blackstrap molasses as the flavor is too harsh for these recipes or any that are lower in sugar or calories as the candy will not cook properly.

nuts Often called nutmeats in older recipes, an important ingredient in many candies. The type and quantity of nuts used in candies is often a personal choice, though most recipes that simply call for "nuts" assume the use of either pecans or walnuts. Be sure to buy fresh nuts and keep them in the refrigerator or freezer to prevent them from turning rancid. For most candies, I prefer to buy walnut or pecan halves and break them by hand into smaller pieces rather than chop them in a food processor, for hand breaking produces larger pieces. Fresh nuts are usually far more flavorful than the packaged nuts commonly found with baking ingredients and can make a significant contribution to the flavor of a candy. Avoid using finely chopped nuts available in the supermarket, if possible.

oleo or oleomargarine The original name of the vegetable oil spread that we now know as margarine. In most cases, if a recipe calls for oleo, either margarine or butter may be used.

paraffin wax Sometimes called paraffin, a product that was commonly used to seal jars of homemade jams, jellies and preserves and added to chocolate to make shiny, hard coatings on dipped candies. However, paraffin wax is no longer recommended for use in food. For newer recipes for Chocolate Coatings, see page 185.

pineapple, candied The same chopped, syrup-coated pineapple used in most fruitcake recipes. Grocers often display candied pineapple in the produce department, in the baking aisle, with dried fruits and nuts and/or with the seasonal fruitcake ingredients, or in the bulk food section. Many grocers carry candied pineapple as a seasonal holiday item, sometimes making it difficult to locate for about nine months of the year. Candied pineapple may be tightly sealed and refrigerated or frozen for later use.

powdered sugar See confectioner's (icing) sugar.

rich milk Much like top milk (see page 21), an ambiguous term once used to describe milk that was rich in fat, with exact proportions of cream to milk left open for interpretation. Today's cook can use half-and-half (10%) cream or whole milk with 4% fat.

sea salt Sea salt is a coarse form of salt often used in gourmet cooking. It is usually found near table salt in large grocery stores.

sorghum syrup or pure sorghum A product made from the juice of certain types of sorghum cane. It is sometimes called sorghum molasses, but that term is now used for a combination of sorghum syrup and molasses.

sugar See brown sugar, confectioner's (icing) sugar, granulated sugar, maple sugar, superfine sugar.

summer chocolate coating Another term for candy coating.

superfine sugar Sugar that contains smaller granules than regular granulated sugar. It should not be substituted for the granulated sugar used in recipes in this book.

sweetened condensed milk A thick, highly concentrated form of milk with added sugar and about 60% of the water removed. It is typically sold in 14-oz or 300 mL cans. Sweetened condensed milk and evaporated milk cannot be used interchangeably. One 14-oz or 300 mL can of sweetened condensed milk contains approximately $1\frac{1}{4}$ cups (300 mL).

sweet milk An old term used to describe the fresh, unspoiled table milk that we now buy in grocery stores to pour over our cereal.

top milk An ambiguous term once used to describe the creamy substance that rose to the top of the milk from the family cow or the grocery store before homogenization. As in light cream, the proportion of cream to milk often depended upon what type of milk cow the family owned and who was holding the dipper. Today's cook should use half-and-half (10%) cream for recipes requiring top milk.

vanilla extract Choice of pure vanilla extract or imitation vanilla extract. While gourmet and imported vanilla extracts are now popular with many cooks, logic tells us that previous generations did not have these choices and thus used common brands of vanilla extracts in their candies. In some cases, gourmet or double-strength vanilla extracts may significantly alter the taste of a candy, sometimes overwhelming subtle flavors such as caramelized sugar or chocolate and completely changing the end product. For this reason, I use common brands of vanilla extract, reserving strongly flavored, specialty vanilla extracts for other foods.

whole milk Whole milk is milk containing 3.25 to 4% butterfat. Skim or nonfat milk (except for instant nonfat dry milk) is seldom used in candy making because some fat is needed to produce proper candy texture. Older recipes in particular assume that whole milk will be used, as lower-fat milk was most likely not available at the time the recipe was created. If desired, milk containing 2% butterfat may usually be substituted in recipes requiring whole milk, though the candy may be slightly less rich or less creamy than it would be if whole milk were used.

Dipping Candies in Chocolate

A few years before writing this book, I read an article criticizing some of the older and more common products and techniques used for dipping candies in chocolate. I thought of all the "inferior" homemade candies I have enjoyed the past few decades. Many of these candies relied on melting chocolate with paraffin wax to give the candy a firm outer shell. Though millions of candy makers have used this combination successfully, we must now find other solutions, as paraffin wax is no longer considered safe for human consumption. Fortunately, we can now purchase specially designed chocolate candy coating products that offer the same firming qualities that paraffin wax once provided. For further information on these products, see Chocolate Coatings (page 185). If these products are not available locally, they can be ordered via the Internet.

Most candy makers eventually develop their own blends of chocolate and their own dipping techniques using tools and products that are commonly available. For example, I may combine dark chocolate candy coating with semisweet chocolate or milk chocolate to give my coatings a personal touch; sometimes adjusting the combination to accommodate different types of recipes. Occasionally I dip one type of candy using a specially designed dipping tool and then dip another type of candy using a toothpick. How we go about coating our candies is often a matter of personal preference rather than a steadfast rule.

The focus of this chapter is to describe some of the methods others have used so that new candy makers have a starting point for developing their own techniques. Certainly, those who want to experiment with very high-quality chocolates and professional methods are encouraged to do so. Candy-making supply stores usually offer products, tools and books to help you get started.

Heating Chocolate

Professional chocolatiers heat high-quality chocolates through a process known as tempering, which involves the repeated heating and cooling of the chocolate to very specific temperatures. Tempering is what gives gourmet chocolate candies the beautiful gloss that we associate with luxury. The majority of home candy makers need not worry about tempering as long as they understand one basic fact: Chocolate can burn.

The purpose of melting chocolate in the top of a double boiler over hot water, not boiling water, is to prevent the chocolate from scorching. Chocolate that has been heated too long or at too high a temperature "seizes" and becomes an unsalvageable, grainy mess. Melted chocolate will also seize if a drop of water gets into it. The only way to recover from a seized batch of melted chocolate is to throw it away and start again.

Most candy makers take great care to keep chocolate from overheating because chocolate that has overheated can also lose its gloss. The exceptionally careful candy maker heats water in a pan, removes the pan from the heat and then places the top double boiler pan containing the chocolate over the hot water, stirring until the chocolate has melted. This works best when working with very small amounts of chocolate.

I am not that careful or that patient, usually preferring to place the entire double boiler pan over very low heat, stirring the chocolate until melted. I remove the pan from the heat while dipping my candies, sometimes warming the pan again slightly as the chocolate cools and becomes too thick for coating.

Many people are not as careful or patient as I am, choosing to melt chocolate in the microwave rather than in a double boiler. This must be done with great care, especially if dealing with white chocolate and milk chocolate. The lighter the chocolate, the more easily it burns.

Dipping Methods

One of the easiest and most common methods for dipping candies is to insert a toothpick into the center of the candy, dip the candy into the melted chocolate and then drop it onto waxed paper to dry. Generations of North Americans have successfully used this method, though it does have its drawbacks. The warm chocolate often pools underneath the candy as it dries, meaning that candies such as bonbons or truffles may have a flat bottom rather than being attractive, round balls. The toothpick also leaves a hole in the top of the candy. Dabbing a tiny amount of melted chocolate over the hole is one solution, but it can be time-consuming.

Another method is to drop the candy into the melted chocolate, remove it from the chocolate using either one or two forks and then drop it onto waxed paper to dry. Unfortunately, the forks usually leave imprints on the outer chocolate coating. Though rolling the candy into chopped nuts will cover the imprints, not all of us want nut-coated candies.

When I first began making Chocolate-Dipped Strawberries (page 197), I developed my own method for dipping that eliminates the chocolate pools. Place a plastic colander on waxed paper, turning the colander upside down so that the rounded bottom is upright. Insert a toothpick into the strawberry or candy center, dip it into the melted chocolate and then insert the toothpick into a hole on the colander. The excess chocolate drips off the candy onto the waxed paper rather than pooling underneath the coated ball or berry. Let the candies stand until firm or refrigerate

the colander filled with the candies or berries until the chocolate cools. A large piece of hard foam or similar material could be used in place of the colander.

This homespun method offers a few improvements but is certainly not foolproof. Soft-centered candies such as truffles may fall off the toothpicks, ruining the candies and creating quite a mess. Once the coating is dry and the toothpicks removed, the candies still have holes in them, though at least the holes are at the bottom of the candies instead of on the top. For most candies this may not matter, but in the case of some soft-centered candies, such as Luscious Raspberry-Fudge Truffles (page 220), these holes must be covered with chocolate or the filling will ooze out of the hole.

By far, the best method for dipping fruits or candies is to use specially designed candy dipping tools. These tools are often available at large craft stores or candy-making supply stores for a very reasonable price. While very inexpensive plastic models are available, I prefer a moderately priced, two-piece wood and metal set made by Wilton or a three-piece metal set sold in specialty stores. These sets usually contain at least one or two specially designed forks and a long hollow spoon. One tool is a long two-pronged fork; the other is a long hollow spoon that resembles a flat basket. Drop the ball or the candy into the melted chocolate, slide the hollow spoon or fork underneath it, lift and gently tap the handle on the side of the double boiler to remove the excess chocolate. With a flip of the wrist, turn the candy over and drop it onto waxed paper. The hollow spoon often leaves an attractive swirl pattern on the top of the candy, making it appear professionally dipped. With just a little practice, you will wonder why you did not invest in a set of dipping tools long ago.

Heirloom Candies

Like that bit of handmade lace *found tucked in an old family cedar chest, the recipes in this collection are the legacies of another* generation, each telling a story of the families who once held them dear. They remind us of a different era in our country, a time when traditions passed from father to son, from mother to daughter, rooting each generation in the family history. Homemade candy was often at the center of these traditions, bringing excitement and adventure to everyday lives and marking special occasions with delectable treats.

Families once gathered in the heart of their homes, building fires to warm cold fingers and toes while Granddad told tall tales of bear hunting or sang silly ditties to amuse the children. They would shell fresh nuts scavenged in the woods, skim fresh cream from the pail of cow's milk left cooling in the water well, then marvel as a penny turned over upon Granddad's command. Homemade candy was as common as homespun entertainment, with fiddles, harmonicas and taffy pulls bringing families and communities together for a night of old-fashioned fun.

> Some of the most delicious candies we have today are those once cherished by our grandmothers.

Some of the most delicious candies we have today are those once cherished by our grandmothers. They gave us extraordinary recipes such as Aunt Bill's Brown Candy, Patience Candy or Penuche Nut Roll plus unusual recipes such as Holiday Pineapple Candy and Peanut Butter Cracker Candy, which is far more interesting than it sounds. They reminded us to use damp tea towels to shape date rolls, to remove any sugar crystals from the sides of the pan and to beat divinity until the candy becomes very stiff. They taught us to make brittles and chocolate-topped toffees, to cook Black Walnut Caramels slowly and to be inventive in the combinations we use. They wrapped pecans in rich white cream and coconut in sumptuous orange, mixed peanut butter with cinnamon or apricots and mashed potatoes with confectioner's sugar, delighting us with their novel ideas. They loved hard candies flavored with oils of peppermint, lemon or anise and festive, colorful candies such as Fruit Fancies and the rich, nutty flavor of Perfect Pralines. They dazzled us with Caramel Pecan Roll and brightened our day with Lollipops, showering us with sweet memories we can never forget.

Reminiscent of days gone by, these recipes are the legacies of our grandmothers, now gathered into one rare collection for you to enjoy. Even the most experienced candy makers will find new flavors and new adventures to explore. Many of these candies have brought joy to generation after generation for one simple reason: they truly are superb.

Brown Sugar Candy

3 cups	granulated sugar	750 mL
3 cups	packed light brown sugar	750 mL
1 cup	heavy or whipping (35%) cream	250 mL
½ cup	light (white or golden) corn syrup	125 mL
½ cup	water	125 mL
2 tsp	vanilla extract	10 mL
2 cups	chopped pecans or walnuts (optional)	500 mL

With a strong brown sugar flavor, some may think of this as caramel fudge.

Cook's Notes

Cutting candy becomes much easier with the use of parchment paper. Rather than buttering the pan directly, butter a piece of parchment paper larger than the pan and press it into the bottom and up the sides of the pan, tucking and creasing the paper as needed to create corners, and leaving a generous overhang over the sides of the pan.

The recipe may be reduce by half, cooked in a heavy 3-quart saucepan and poured into a buttered 8- or 9-inch (20 or 23 cm) square pan.

For a similar candy, see Wildcat Brown Sugar Fudge (Variation, page 156).

Skill Level: Advanced

Makes about 6 lbs (3 kg)

- 13- by 9-inch (33 by 23 cm) pan, lined with parchment (see Cook's Notes, left) or buttered
- 5-quart heavy candy kettle or pot
- Candy thermometer

1. In heavy candy kettle over medium heat, bring the granulated and brown sugars, cream, corn syrup and water to a boil, stirring until the sugars dissolve and the mixture begins to boil. Reduce the heat to medium-low. Cover and cook 2 to 3 minutes to dissolve the sugar crystals on the sides of the pan. Remove the lid. Cook slowly, without stirring, over low to medium-low heat to the medium ball stage (242°F/117°C).

2. Remove from the heat. Cool about 1 hour to lukewarm (110°F/43°C).

3. Stir in the vanilla. Beat by hand until the candy loses its gloss and becomes creamy. Stir in the nuts, if desired. Pour into the prepared pan. Cool and cut into squares. Store in an airtight container.

Candy for the Troops

Candy has long been considered the ultimate comfort food, with homemade candy receiving top billing. Some military families have a long-standing tradition of sending homemade candy to family members serving our nation, sending the same candies to their loved ones today that their mothers and grandmothers sent to loved ones 70 years ago.

During World War II, our country rationed sugar so that soldiers on the battlefield could have a sweet reminder of home. The candy packaged in their C rations (now called MREs, or meals ready to eat) was often the highlight of an exhausted GI's day. Sugar rationing in the U.S. lasted a little over five years, ending in June 1947.

Aunt Bill's Brown Candy

6 cups	granulated sugar, divided	1.5 L
2 cups	evaporated milk	500 mL
1/4 tsp	baking soda	1 mL
1/2 cup	margarine	125 mL
1 tsp	vanilla extract	5 mL
2 cups	pecans, in large pieces	500 mL

Skill Level: Expert

Makes about 3 lbs (1.5 kg)

- 13- by 9-inch (33 by 23 cm) pan, lined with parchment (see Cook's Notes, page 27) or buttered
- 5-quart heavy candy kettle or pot
- Candy thermometer

Aunt Bill's Brown Candy is Oklahoma's pride and joy. This wonderful old recipe has circulated throughout my home state for at least 80 years and is rumored to have originated with an Oklahoma pioneer. No one seems to know exactly who Aunt Bill was, but we do know that she made one of the richest, smoothest and most distinctively flavored homemade candies ever tasted.

My mother was the Queen of Aunt Bill's so while the original recipe calls for light cream, I make it exactly as she did by substituting evaporated milk for light cream. The evaporated milk gives a slightly different texture than light cream, and I think Mom's secret ingredient is what made her signature candy so special.

Cook's Notes

Many believe that this recipe requires two cooks, and though it is nice to have an extra set of hands, one experienced candy maker can make this candy alone.

My mother was successful cooking Aunt Bill's to 244°F (118°C). I have better luck cooking it to 246°F (119°C). I do not recommend varying the cooking temperature beyond this 2°F (1°C) range.

1. Place 2 cups (500 mL) of the sugar into a heavy aluminum or cast-iron skillet. Place the remaining 4 cups (1 L) of sugar and milk into heavy kettle.

2. Melt the sugar in the skillet slowly over low heat, stirring constantly to prevent scorching. When fully melted, the caramelized sugar should be a golden brown liquid. (It will take about 30 minutes.)

3. While sugar is melting, cook sugar and milk slowly over low heat, stirring constantly but gently to prevent scorching. (Both the sugar in the skillet and the sugar and milk in the kettle must be stirred simultaneously.) The sugar and milk mixture should reach a slow boil 2 to 3 minutes before the sugar in the skillet is completely melted. If the sugar and milk begins to boil before the sugar in the skillet is almost completely melted, reduce the heat slightly, maintaining a slow, steady boil.

4. Slowly pour the melted sugar into the boiling sugar and milk mixture in a thin stream no larger than a knitting needle, stirring across the bottom of the kettle at all times to prevent the melted sugar from clumping. Any clumps of sugar that form may be dissolved later through cooking and stirring, but the candy is best when no large clumps are allowed to form. If the sugar and milk mixture begins to boil over the sides of the pan while adding the melted sugar, reduce the heat but maintain a slow, steady boil.

5. Cook the combined mixture, stirring slowly but constantly, over low heat to the firm ball stage (246°F/119°C), 35 to 40 minutes.

6. Remove from the heat. Add the baking soda and stir vigorously until the mixture foams and nearly doubles in volume, about 1 minute. Stir in the margarine just until melted. Set the candy away from the heat. Cool 20 minutes.

Cook's Notes

Proper beating is critical to this candy's texture. If in doubt about how to judge when this candy is properly beaten, set a kitchen timer for 20 minutes just as you begin beating. When the timer rings, the candy is usually ready for the pecans.

Strongly flavored or double-strength vanilla extracts can overwhelm the subtle caramelized sugar flavor of this candy and are not recommended. Pure vanilla extract is best, but imitation vanilla extract may also be used.

7. Add the vanilla. Using a sturdy wooden spoon, beat the candy by hand until it is thick and heavy and has a dull appearance, 20 to 25 minutes. Stir in the pecans. Turn into the prepared pan. Cool and cut into squares.

8. Store the candy in an airtight container. If covered and refrigerated, it will stay moist and delicious almost indefinitely.

Recruit a Friend

This recipe requires two hours, and all but 20 minutes is spent stirring or beating the candy by hand. The first 40 minutes can be especially challenging so if you have never tackled a recipe like this, recruit a friend to help. My friend Becky and I made our first batch together nearly 30 years ago, and we remember it as one of the most fun times we ever shared. My mother was still making Aunt Bill's Brown Candy by herself at age 76 and I rarely have a helper, so with a little practice you can make this candy alone.

Golden Butter Nut Candy

7 cups	granulated sugar	1.75 L
2 cups	dark (golden) corn syrup	500 mL
1 cup	butter	250 mL
1	can (12 oz or 370 mL) evaporated milk	1
2 cups	pecans, in large pieces	500 mL

This golden, pecan-packed candy is far more interesting than the ingredients suggest, reminding some of Aunt Bill's Brown Candy (left).

Variation

Nut Candy Loaf: Use 6 cups (1.5 L) granulated sugar. Add 1 tsp (5 mL) vanilla extract to the candy while beating. Use 3 cups (750 mL) walnuts and 1 cup (250 mL) pecans, in large pieces (or add the nuts to taste). Do not add the nuts until after the candy has been beaten and begins to hold its shape.

Skill Level: Advanced

Makes about 6 pounds (3 kg)

- 13- by 9-inch (33 by 23 cm) pan, lined with parchment (see Cook's Notes, page 27) or buttered
- 5-quart heavy candy kettle or pot
- Candy thermometer

1. In heavy candy kettle over medium heat, bring the sugar, corn syrup, butter and milk to a boil, stirring until the sugar dissolves and the mixture begins to boil. Cook, stirring frequently to prevent scorching, at a rolling boil to the high end of the soft ball stage or the medium ball stage (240°F to 242°F/116°C to 117°C), about 17 minutes.

2. Remove from the heat. Stir in the pecans. Beat by hand until the candy becomes creamy and begins to hold its shape, 30 to 40 minutes. Pour into the prepared pan. Cool and cut into squares. Store in an airtight container.

Fresh Buttermilk Candy

2 cups	granulated sugar	500 mL
$2/3$ cup	buttermilk	150 mL
1 tsp	baking soda	5 mL
$1/4$ cup	butter or margarine	60 mL
1 tsp	vanilla extract	5 mL
1 cup	pecans, in large pieces	250 mL

> If you have never had a candy such as this, you are missing one of the richest, most delectable treats invented. This caramel-colored, nut-packed confection has a soft texture and a deep, robust flavor.

Cook's Notes

The buttermilk mixture can scorch very easily, making low heat and stirring a must.

If preferred, the finished candy may be dropped by spoonfuls onto waxed paper rather than poured into a pan.

For candies with a similar flavor, see Sinfully Rich Buttermilk Fudge (page 152), Perfect Pralines (page 63), Texas Pralines (page 64) and Ultra-Creamy Buttermilk Pralines (page 65).

Skill Level: Advanced

Makes about $1\frac{1}{2}$ lbs (750 g)

- 9- by 5-inch (23 by 12.5 cm) loaf pan, lined with parchment (see Cook's Notes, page 35) or buttered
- 5-quart heavy candy kettle or pot
- Candy thermometer

1. In heavy candy kettle over low heat, bring the sugar, buttermilk and baking soda to a boil, stirring constantly to prevent scorching. The mixture will foam rapidly and rise in the kettle when it begins to boil. Cook, stirring constantly to prevent scorching, to the soft ball stage (234°F to 240°F/112°C to 116°C, with 236°F/113°C recommended).

2. Remove from the heat. Add the butter and vanilla. Beat by hand until the candy thickens and loses its gloss. Stir in the pecans. Pour into the prepared pan. Cool and cut into squares. Store in an airtight container.

Storing Candy

Most candies should be stored in an airtight container to keep them fresh. Unless specifically instructed in the recipe, refrigeration is often a matter of personal choice, but generally, most fudges and fudge-like candies should keep at least 1 week at room temperature and at least 1 month, sometimes much longer, if refrigerated. Excessive heat, high humidity, or added ingredients such as fruit may shorten the storage time so it is important to use common sense. If the color or texture of the candy has changed, dispose of it and make a fresh batch.

Sweet Buttermilk Candy

2 cups	granulated sugar	500 mL
1 cup	buttermilk	250 mL
1 tbsp	butter	15 mL
1 cup	chopped pecans	250 mL

This unusual and somewhat crispy candy looks and tastes like sweetened buttermilk.

Cook's Note

For a softer candy with a similar flavor, see Extra-Buttery Buttermilk Fudge (page 151).

- 9- by 5-inch (23 by 12.5 cm) loaf pan, lined with parchment (see Cook's Notes, page 35) or buttered
- 3-quart heavy candy kettle or pot
- Candy thermometer

1. In heavy saucepan over low heat, bring the sugar and buttermilk to a boil, stirring until the sugar dissolves and the mixture begins to boil. Cook, without stirring, to the soft ball stage (234°F to 240°F/112°C to 116°C, with 234°F/112°C recommended).

2. Remove from the heat. Add the butter. Beat by hand until the candy thickens slightly. Add the pecans a few at a time, beating until the candy begins to lose its gloss. Quickly pour into the prepared pan. Cool and cut into squares. Store in an airtight container.

Peanut Butter Cracker Candy

1 cup	granulated sugar	250 mL
1 cup	packed light brown sugar	250 mL
1/3 cup	evaporated milk	75 mL
2 tbsp	butter or margarine	30 mL
2 tbsp	smooth peanut butter	30 mL
1 tsp	vanilla extract	5 mL
24	soda crackers (saltines), finely crushed	24

No one but you will ever guess that this surprisingly delicious, old-time favorite is made with soda crackers.

- 9- by 5-inch (23 by 12.5 cm) loaf pan, lined with parchment (see Cook's Notes, page 35) or buttered
- 2-quart heavy saucepan
- Candy thermometer

1. In heavy saucepan over medium heat, bring the granulated and brown sugars, milk and butter to a boil, stirring until the sugars dissolve and the mixture begins to boil. Cook, stirring frequently to prevent scorching, to the soft ball stage (234°F to 240°F/112°C to 116°C, with 236°F/113°C recommended).

2. Remove from the heat. Stir in the peanut butter, vanilla and cracker crumbs. Beat by hand until the candy begins to thicken and cool, about 5 minutes. Pour into the prepared pan. Cool and cut into squares. Store in an airtight container.

Butterscotch Nut Marshmallows

1½ cups	pecans, finely chopped	375 mL
1½ cups	packed light brown sugar	375 mL
¾ cup	half-and-half (10%) cream or evaporated milk	175 mL
¼ tsp	salt	1 mL
½ tsp	vanilla extract (optional)	2 mL
25 to 35	large marshmallows	25 to 35

> The kid inside you will love these fluffy, white marshmallows coated in rich, gooey butterscotch and crispy chopped nuts.

Cook's Notes

If the butterscotch becomes too stiff to coat the marshmallows, warm it over low heat until the candy reaches the desired consistency.

For smaller-size servings, cut the marshmallows in half before dipping.

Skill Level: Average

Makes 25 to 35 marshmallows

- 1- or 2-quart heavy saucepan
- Candy thermometer

1. Cover a large countertop area or large baking sheet with waxed paper. Place the chopped pecans into a small dish.

2. In a heavy saucepan over low to medium-low heat, bring the sugar, half-and-half and salt to a boil, stirring until the sugar dissolves and the mixture begins to boil. Cook, stirring occasionally to prevent scorching, to the soft ball stage (234°F to 240°F/112°C to 116°C, with 238°F/115°C recommended).

3. Remove from the heat. Stir in the vanilla, if using. Set the saucepan into a pan or sink filled with hot water to keep the butterscotch warm. (Do not allow the hot water to seep into the butterscotch mixture.) Using a fork, toothpick or specially designed dipping tool, dip the marshmallows, one at a time, into the hot butterscotch mixture. Roll the coated marshmallows in the chopped pecans. Place on the waxed paper to cool. Store in an airtight container.

Storing Candy

Most candies should be stored in an airtight container to keep them fresh. Unless specifically instructed in the recipe, refrigeration is often a matter of personal choice, but generally, most fudges and fudge-like candies should keep at least 1 week at room temperature and at least 1 month, sometimes much longer, if refrigerated. Excessive heat, high humidity, or added ingredients such as fruit may shorten the storage time so it is important to use common sense. If the color or texture of the candy has changed, dispose of it and make a fresh batch.

Orange Creams

3 cups	granulated sugar	750 mL
1¼ cups	half-and-half (10%) cream or evaporated milk	300 mL
½ tsp	salt	2 mL
3 tbsp	light (white) corn syrup	45 mL
2 tbsp	freshly grated orange zest	30 mL
2 tbsp	butter	30 mL
1½ cups	sweetened flaked coconut	375 mL

One word comes to mind when I think of this rich, creamy, fudge-like candy: "Yum!" Try adding a little extra orange zest or substituting chopped pecans for the coconut.

Cook's note

The coconut adds moisture to this candy, making it fairly soft. For a firmer candy, cook to a medium ball stage (242°F/117°C).

Skill Level: Advanced

Makes about 1¾ lbs (875 g)

- 8-inch (20 cm) square pan, lined with parchment (see Cook's Notes, page 35) or buttered
- 3-quart heavy saucepan
- Candy thermometer

1. In heavy saucepan over low heat, bring the sugar, half-and-half, salt and corn syrup to a boil, stirring until the sugar dissolves and the mixture begins to boil. Cover and cook 2 to 3 minutes to dissolve the sugar crystals on the sides of the pan. Remove the lid. Cook slowly, stirring occasionally to prevent scorching, over low heat to the soft ball stage (234°F to 240°F/112°C to 116°C, with 240°F/112°C recommended).

2. Remove from the heat. Add the orange zest and butter. Do not stir. Cool to lukewarm (110°F/43°C), 45 minutes to 1 hour.

3. Beat by hand until the candy begins to thicken and lose its gloss. Stir in the coconut. Beat by hand until the candy thickens and is creamy. Pour into the prepared pan. Cool and cut into squares. Store in an airtight container. This candy can be somewhat soft so refrigeration is recommended.

Variation

If preferred, the candy may be shaped into small balls and rolled in additional coconut.

Important Tip

In many recipes, it is important to be prepared for all the steps because timing can be critical. Have all ingredients available and ready to use, and have the pan, baking sheet, or surface prepared before you begin cooking.

Fruit Fancies

3 cups	granulated sugar	750 mL
1 cup	light (white) corn syrup	250 mL
1½ cups	half-and-half (10%) cream	375 mL
½ tsp	salt	2 mL
1 tsp	vanilla extract	5 mL
1 cup	Brazil nuts, cut lengthwise in halves	250 mL
1 cup	walnuts, in large pieces	250 mL
1 cup	pecan halves	250 mL
1 cup	candied cherries, chopped	250 mL
1 cup	candied pineapple, chopped	250 mL

What could be more festive than cherries, pineapple and three kinds of nuts wrapped in a light, creamy candy? This 1950s-style recipe is sure to tickle your fancy and delight your family and friends.

Skill Level: Advanced
Makes about 4 lbs (2 kg)

- 9- by 5-inch (23 by 12.5 cm) loaf pan
- 5-quart heavy candy kettle or pot
- Candy thermometer

1. Line the loaf pan with waxed paper, leaving a 1-inch (2.5 cm) overhang over sides of pan.

2. In heavy candy kettle over medium-low heat, bring the sugar, corn syrup, half-and-half and salt to a boil, stirring until the sugar dissolves and the mixture begins to boil. Cook, stirring occasionally to prevent scorching, to the soft ball stage (234°F to 240°F/112°C to 116°C, with 238°F/114°C recommended).

3. Remove from the heat. Cool 20 minutes.

4. Add the vanilla. Beat by hand until the candy begins to thicken. Stir in the nuts and fruits. Beat by hand until the candy loses its gloss. The mixture will be thick and sticky. Using a wet spoon, pack the candy into the lined loaf pan. Tightly cover with plastic wrap or aluminum foil. Refrigerate 24 hours. The sticky syrup will become firm, creamy and lighter in color after a few hours of refrigeration.

5. Lift the candy from the loaf pan. Cut into ½-inch (1 cm) thick slices. Cut each slice into finger length pieces or cubes. Store in an airtight container.

Nut Cream Loaf

2 cups	granulated sugar	500 mL
½ cup	light (white) corn syrup	125 mL
1 cup	half-and-half (10%) cream	250 mL
1 tbsp	butter or margarine	15 mL
1 tbsp	vanilla extract	15 mL
1 cup	chopped pecans or walnuts	250 mL

The flavor of this vanilla fudge-like candy improves with age as the candy absorbs the nut flavors.

Cook's Note

Cutting candy becomes much easier with the use of parchment paper. Rather than buttering the pan directly, butter a piece of parchment paper larger than the pan and press it into the bottom and up the sides of the pan, tucking and creasing the paper as needed to create corners, and leaving a generous overhang over the sides of the pan.

For similar candies, see Creamy Blonde Fudge (page 163) and Creamy White Fudge (page 163).

Skill Level: Advanced

Makes about 1½ lbs (750 g)

- 9- by 5-inch (23 by 12.5 cm) loaf pan, lined with parchment (see Cook's Notes, left) or buttered
- 3-quart heavy saucepan
- Candy thermometer

1. In heavy saucepan over medium-low to medium heat, bring the sugar, corn syrup and half-and-half to a boil, stirring until the sugar dissolves and the mixture begins to boil. Cook, stirring occasionally to prevent scorching, to the soft ball stage (234°F to 240°F/112°C to 116°C, with 240°F/116°C recommended).

2. Remove from the heat. Add the butter and vanilla. Beat by hand until the candy thickens and loses its gloss. Stir in the nuts. Pour into the prepared pan. Cool and cut into squares. Store in an airtight container.

Storing Candy

Most candies should be stored in an airtight container to keep them fresh. Unless specifically instructed in the recipe, refrigeration is often a matter of personal choice, but generally, most fudges and fudge-like candies should keep at least 1 week at room temperature and at least 1 month, sometimes much longer, if refrigerated. Excessive heat, high humidity, or added ingredients such as fruit may shorten the storage time so it is important to use common sense. If the color or texture of the candy has changed, dispose of it and make a fresh batch.

Three-Nut Candy

3 cups	granulated sugar	750 mL
2 cups	half-and-half (10%) cream	500 mL
1 cup	light (white or golden) corn syrup	250 mL
2 cups	walnuts, in large pieces or halves	500 mL
2 cups	pecans, in large pieces or halves	500 mL
2 cups	Brazil nuts, in large pieces or halves	500 mL
1 tsp	vanilla extract	5 mL

Only mildly sweet, this is a candy for those who love nuts. Try substituting your favorite combination of nuts for those listed, keeping the proportions the same.

Cook's Notes

The basic recipe used for this candy is very similar to the recipe for Fruit Fancies (page 34), but this version produces very different results. This candy has twice as many nuts as Fruit Fancies, plus a darker color and a much deeper nut flavor because the nuts are cooked with the candy.

The recipe may be reduced by half and cooked in a 3-quart pan.

Skill Level: Advanced

Makes about 4½ lbs (2.25 kg)

- 13- by 9-inch (33 by 23 cm) pan or two 9- by 5-inch (23 by 12.5 cm) loaf pans
- 5-quart heavy candy kettle or pot
- Candy thermometer

1. Line pan(s) with waxed paper or foil, leaving a 1-inch (2.5 cm) overhang over the sides of the pan. Butter the lining generously or spray with nonstick spray.

2. In heavy candy kettle over medium-low heat, bring the sugar, half-and-half, corn syrup and walnuts, pecans and Brazil nuts to a boil, stirring until the sugar dissolves and the mixture begins to boil. Cover and cook 2 to 3 minutes to dissolve the sugar crystals on the sides of the pan. Remove the lid. Cook, stirring gently only a few times to prevent scorching, over low to medium-low heat to the soft ball stage (234°F to 240°F/112°C to 116°C, with 236°F/113°C recommended), 30 to 40 minutes.

3. Remove from the heat. Cool about 5 minutes.

4. Add the vanilla. Beat by hand until the candy begins to stiffen. The candy will be sticky. Using a wet spoon, pack the candy into the prepared pan(s). Cover tightly with plastic wrap or aluminum foil. Let ripen at room temperature 24 hours.

5. Lift the candy from the pan. Peel off the lining. Wrap the entire block of candy in aluminum foil and store, covered. Cut into paper thin slices as needed. The beaten candy may also be cut into squares, but each piece must be individually wrapped in plastic wrap. To cut into individual pieces, place the block of candy on a cutting board. Using a sharp knife and a sawing motion, cut the block into 1-inch (2.5 cm) strips and then cut each strip into squares. Wrap each piece in plastic wrap and store in an airtight container.

Pralines-in-a-Pan

2 cups	granulated sugar	500 mL
1 cup	milk (see Cook's Notes, below)	250 mL
2 tbsp	butter or margarine	30 mL
2 tbsp	light (white) corn syrup	30 mL
1/4 tsp	salt	1 mL
1/4 tsp	baking soda	1 mL
1 cup	chopped pecans	250 mL
1 tsp	vanilla extract	5 mL

Originally known as Pecan Candy, this recipe tastes so much like pralines that it earned a new name. One easy way to serve this golden brown pecan candy is to break it into pieces somewhat like a bark.

Cook's Notes

Generally, it is best to use milk with minimum 2% fat for candies because the additional fat content helps produce a creamy texture. If preferred, experiment with lower fat milks to see if you notice a difference.

If preferred, this candy may be dropped by spoonfuls onto waxed paper, creating individual praline-type candies.

Skill Level: Advanced

Makes about 1 1/2 lbs (750 g)

- 8-inch (20 cm) square pan, buttered
- 5-quart heavy candy kettle or pot
- Candy thermometer

1. In heavy candy kettle over low heat, bring the sugar, milk, butter, corn syrup, salt and baking soda to a boil, stirring until the sugar dissolves and the mixture begins to boil. The mixture will foam rapidly and rise in the kettle when it begins to boil. Stir in the pecans. Cook, stirring occasionally to prevent scorching, over low heat to the soft ball stage (234°F to 240°F/112°C to 116°C, with 236°F/113°C recommended).

2. Remove from the heat. Add the vanilla. Beat by hand until the candy thickens and begins to hold its shape. Pour into the prepared pan. Cool and cut into squares or break into serving-size pieces similar to a bark. Store in an airtight container.

Patience Candy

3 cups	granulated sugar, divided	750 mL
¼ tsp	baking soda	1 mL
scant	milk, divided	scant
2 cups		500 mL
¼ cup	butter	60 mL
¾ to	chopped pecans (optional)	175 to
1 cup		250 mL
	Confectioner's (icing) sugar (optional)	

This charming old recipe from my hometown newspaper immediately conjures up images of a sweet grandmother carefully writing her favorite recipe for a young bride. I smile every time I read the original instructions. "Take a large pan so candy will not boil over. Put 1 cup granulated sugar in pan and place over fire; stir constantly until melted and brown like syrup. After all is melted, slowly stir in 1 cup (scant) sweet milk, in which has been dissolved a pinch of soda the size of a bean. Do not get scared, but stir and boil until smooth. Then add a second cup of sweet milk (scant), 2 cups of sugar and butter the size of an egg. Boil until the candy forms a soft ball. Remove from fire and beat until the candy starts to grain. Add nuts if you wish. May be rolled in confectioner's sugar or poured. This candy is very delicious and worth your patience."

My thanks to Tom Muchmore and the *Ponca City News* for allowing me to share this gem.

Makes 1½ to 2 lbs (750 g to 1 kg)

- 8-inch (20 cm) square pan, buttered
- Large heavy aluminum skillet
- Candy thermometer

1. In a large heavy aluminum skillet over low to medium-low heat, slowly melt 1 cup (250 mL) of the sugar, stirring constantly to prevent scorching. While the sugar is melting, dissolve the baking soda into 1 scant cup (250 mL) of the milk.

2. When the sugar is fully melted to a brown liquid, slowly stir the milk-soda mixture into the melted sugar. The mixture will foam rapidly and rise in the skillet as it begins to boil. Cook, stirring constantly, until the mixture is smooth.

3. Slowly add the remaining 1 scant cup (250 mL) of milk, remaining 2 cups (500 mL) of sugar and butter. Cook, stirring constantly, to the soft ball stage (234°F to 240°F/112°C to 116°C, with 234°F/112°C recommended).

4. Remove from the heat. Beat by hand until the candy is thick and loses its gloss. Add the pecans, if desired. The candy may be formed into a log and rolled in confectioner's sugar or poured into a buttered pan. Cool and slice as needed or cut into squares. Store in an airtight container.

Important Tip

In many recipes, it is important to be prepared for all the steps because timing can be critical. Have all ingredients available and ready to use, and have the pan, baking sheet, or surface prepared before you begin cooking.

Holiday Pineapple Candy

3 cups	granulated sugar	750 mL
2 tbsp	light (white) corn syrup	30 mL
1 cup	canned crushed pineapple with juice	250 mL
24	large marshmallows	24
2 tbsp	butter	30 mL
1 tsp	vanilla extract	5 mL
1½ cups	pecans, in large pieces	375 mL

This delicately flavored, ultra-sweet confection has been at the center of one hometown family's holiday tradition since the 1930s, with the recipe being passed from one generation to the next.

Cook's Note

The original recipe contained 3 cups (750 mL) pecans. The quantity may be adjusted to personal tastes.

Skill Level: Average

Makes about 1½ lbs (750 g)

- 8-inch (20 cm) square pan, lined with parchment (see Cook's Notes, page 35) or buttered
- 2-quart heavy saucepan
- Candy thermometer

1. In heavy saucepan over medium-low heat, bring the sugar, corn syrup and pineapple to a boil, stirring until the sugar dissolves and the mixture begins to boil. Cook, stirring frequently to prevent scorching, to the soft ball stage (234°F to 240°F/112°C to 116°C, with 238°F/115°C recommended).

2. Remove from the heat. Add the marshmallows, butter and vanilla. Let stand until the marshmallows are partially melted, about 3 minutes. Stir the candy until the marshmallows are completely melted and the mixture is well blended. Stir in the pecans. Pour into the prepared pan. Cool and cut into squares. Store in an airtight container in the refrigerator.

Variation

Hawaiian Pineapple Candy: Substitute 2 cups (500 mL) granulated sugar and 1 cup (250 mL) packed light brown sugar for the 3 cups (750 mL) granulated sugar.

Pineapple Cremes

1 cup	granulated sugar	250 mL
$\frac{1}{2}$ cup	packed light brown sugar	125 mL
$\frac{1}{4}$ cup	half-and-half (10%) cream	60 mL
$\frac{1}{8}$ tsp	salt	0.5 mL
$\frac{1}{2}$ cup	well-drained canned crushed pineapple	125 mL
2 tbsp	butter or margarine	30 mL
12	large marshmallows	12
$\frac{1}{2}$ tsp	vanilla extract or lemon juice	2 mL
$\frac{1}{2}$ cup	chopped pecans (optional)	125 mL

Brown sugar and half-and-half give this candy a darker color and heavier texture than Holiday Pineapple Candy (page 39), making this recipe somewhat similar to light brown fudge.

Skill Level: Advanced

Makes about 1 lb (500 g)

- 9- by 5-inch (23 by 12.5 cm) loaf pan, lined with parchment (see Cook's Notes, page 35) or buttered
- 1- to 2-quart heavy saucepan
- Candy thermometer

1. In heavy saucepan over medium-low heat, bring the granulated and brown sugars, half-and-half, salt and pineapple to a boil, stirring until the sugar dissolves and the mixture begins to boil. Cook, stirring occasionally to prevent scorching, to the firm ball stage (244°F to 248°F/118°C to 120°C, with 244°F/118°C recommended).

2. Remove from the heat. Add the butter and the marshmallows, stirring only until blended. Cool to lukewarm (110°F/43°C), 30 to 45 minutes.

3. Add the vanilla. Beat by hand until creamy. Stir in the pecans, if using. Pour into the prepared pan. Cool and cut into squares. Store in an airtight container.

St. Patty's Pineapple Candy

3 cups	granulated sugar	750 mL
$\frac{1}{2}$ cup	half-and-half (10%) cream	125 mL
2 tbsp	light (white) corn syrup	30 mL
1	can (8-oz/227 mL) crushed pineapple with juice	1
3 tbsp	butter or margarine	45 mL
	Few drops green food coloring	

What better way to celebrate St. Patty's Day than with a batch of this pineapple-packed green candy?

Cook's Note

For a similar candy, see The Preacher's Pineapple Fudge (page 161).

Skill Level: Advanced

Makes about $1\frac{1}{2}$ lbs (750 g)

- 9- by 5-inch (23 by 12.5 cm) loaf pan, lined with parchment (see Cook's Notes, page 35) or buttered
- 3-quart heavy saucepan
- Candy thermometer

1. In heavy saucepan over medium-low heat, bring the sugar, half-and-half, corn syrup, pineapple with juice and butter to a boil, stirring until the sugar dissolves and the mixture begins to boil. Cook, stirring occasionally to prevent scorching, to the soft ball stage (234°F to 240°F/112°C to 116°C with 236°F/113°C recommended).

2. Remove from the heat. Stir in green food coloring. Beat by hand until the candy thickens and begins to lose its gloss. Pour into the prepared pan. Cool and cut into squares. Store in an airtight container.

Sour Cream Candy

½ cup	sour cream	125 mL
2 cups	packed light brown sugar	500 mL
2 tbsp	butter or margarine	30 mL
1 tsp	vanilla extract	5 mL
	Few grains of salt	
1 cup	chopped pecans (optional)	250 mL

> Ultra-rich and creamy, this fudge-like brown-sugar candy retains a hint of sour cream.

Cook's Note

If preferred, the beaten candy may be dropped by spoonfuls onto waxed paper.

Makes about 1 lb (500 g)

- 9- by 5-inch (23 by 12.5 cm) loaf pan, lined with parchment (see Cook's Notes, page 35) or buttered
- 2-quart heavy saucepan
- Candy thermometer

1. In heavy saucepan over medium-low heat, bring the sour cream and sugar to a boil, stirring until the sugar dissolves and the mixture begins to boil. Cook, stirring occasionally to prevent scorching, to the soft ball stage (234°F to 240°F/112°C to 116°C, with 236°F/113°C recommended).

2. Remove from the heat. Add the butter without stirring. Cool to lukewarm (110°F/43°C), 30 to 45 minutes.

3. Add the vanilla and salt. Beat by hand until the candy loses its gloss and begins to hold its shape. Stir in the nuts, if using. Pour into the prepared pan. Cool and cut into squares if needed. Store in an airtight container.

Cutting into Perfect Squares and Special Shapes

Cutting candy becomes much easier with the use of parchment paper. Rather than buttering the pan directly, butter a piece of parchment paper larger than the pan and press it into the bottom and up the sides of the pan, tucking and creasing the paper as needed to create corners, and leaving a generous overhang over the sides of the pan. Pour the candy into the parchment-lined pan. Once the candy has cooled, use the parchment to lift the entire block of candy out of the pan. Place the block of candy on a cutting board and use a long, serrated knife to cut straight, uniform rows of the candy, and then cut the rows into squares. For a special presentation, cut the block of candy into diamonds, triangles or other shapes, as desired.

The parchment paper method is optional, but over the years I have found it much easier than cutting candy in the pan, and it saves my pans from deep scratches left by sharp knives. At times I have shipped large blocks of candy to friends and family with the candy still wrapped in the parchment paper and then wrapped again in foil wrap. It simplifies shipping and allows others to cut the candy as they choose.

Pistol Pete Peanut Brittle

2 cups	granulated sugar	500 mL
1 cup	light (white or golden) corn syrup	250 mL
½ cup	water	125 mL
1 tsp	salt	5 mL
2 cups	raw unsalted peanuts	500 mL
2 tbsp	butter or margarine	30 mL
2 tsp	baking soda	10 mL
1 tsp	vanilla extract	5 mL

This classic peanut brittle recipe is a personal favorite and was one of many candy recipes perfected in the Oklahoma A&M (now Oklahoma State University) test kitchen in the early 1950s. I named it for the OSU mascot in honor of my mother, who loved all things related to OSU, especially Pistol Pete. This version of a well-known favorite is thin, porous and crunchy just as classic peanut brittle should be. Add your own touch by adding coconut or by substituting pecans for peanuts.

Skill Level: Average

Makes about 2 lbs (1 kg)

- 2 large baking sheets, buttered
- 5-quart heavy candy kettle or pot
- Candy thermometer

1. In heavy candy kettle over medium heat, bring the sugar, corn syrup, water and salt to a boil, stirring until the sugar dissolves and the mixture begins to boil. Cover and cook 3 minutes to dissolve the sugar crystals on the sides of the pan. Remove the lid. Cook, without stirring, to 260°F (127°C).

2. Stir in the peanuts and butter. Cook, stirring occasionally to prevent the peanuts from settling on the bottom of the pan, to the hard crack stage (300°F/149°C).

3. Remove from the heat. Add the baking soda and vanilla without stirring, allowing the mixture to foam rapidly. Gently stir just until blended (too much stirring will cause this candy to become dense rather than porous). Quickly pour onto the baking sheets. Cool and break into pieces. Store in an airtight container.

Variations

Pistol Pete Coconut Peanut Brittle: Add ½ cup (125 mL) sweetened flaked coconut when adding the vanilla and baking soda.

Pistol Pete Pecan Brittle: Substitute 2 cups (500 mL) pecans in large pieces for the peanuts.

Aunt Lucy's Extra-Buttery Brittle

3 cups	raw unsalted peanuts, almonds, cashews, pecans, walnuts, macadamia nuts or pine nuts	750 mL
2 cups	granulated sugar	500 mL
1 cup	light (white or golden) corn syrup	250 mL
½ cup	water	125 mL
1 cup	butter	250 mL
1 tsp	baking soda	5 mL

My aunt sent me this recipe many years ago with a note saying, "Extra buttery," but she forgot to say, "Extra good." Do not be surprised if friends tell you this is the best brittle they ever tasted. This recipe produces a thin, crisp, nonporous brittle with a smooth texture similar to toffee.

Cook's Notes

This candy may be cooked in a 3-quart heavy saucepan but must be watched carefully to prevent the mixture from boiling over the sides of the pan.

Because raw, unsalted cashews can be difficult to locate, roasted, salted cashews may be substituted. If roasted cashews are used, cook the candy mixture slightly longer to 285°F (140°C) or 290°F (143°C) before adding the cashews so that the nuts are not roasted again during cooking.

Skill Level: Average

Makes about 2½ lbs (1.25 kg)

- 2 large baking sheets, buttered
- 5-quart heavy candy kettle or pot
- Candy thermometer

1. If using large nuts, cut or break the nuts into smaller pieces.

2. In heavy candy kettle over medium heat, bring the sugar, corn syrup and water to a boil, stirring until the sugar dissolves and the mixture begins to boil. When the mixture reaches a full, rolling boil, stir in the butter until melted. Reduce the heat slightly to medium-low, maintaining a medium boil. Cook, stirring frequently, to the soft crack stage (280°F/138°C).

3. Stir in the nuts. Cook, stirring frequently, to the hard crack stage (300°F/149°C).

4. Remove from the heat. Stir in the baking soda until well blended. Quickly pour the mixture onto the prepared baking sheets, spreading evenly across both pans. If desired, use two forks or the back the spoon to spread the candy into an extra thin layer. Cool and break into pieces. Store in an airtight container.

Munchabuncha Peanut Brittle

1 cup	granulated sugar	250 mL
1 cup	light (white or golden) corn syrup	250 mL
1 tbsp	water	15 mL
2 cups	raw unsalted peanuts or pecans	500 mL
1 tsp	baking soda	5 mL

This version is thicker and more porous than some brittle recipes, giving it extra crunch appeal. I did not know how much I liked peanut brittle until I began munching on a bunch of this stuff, hence the name. I could also call it Munchacruncha because it's impossible to eat this candy quietly.

Cook's Note

Be sure to store candies such as brittles and toffees in airtight containers and away from sources of moisture such as air conditioner vents. In extremely humid conditions these candies can absorb moisture and become somewhat soft, losing the crunch appeal that we expect.

Skill Level: Average

Makes about 1½ lbs (750 g)

- Large baking sheet, buttered
- 3-quart heavy saucepan
- Candy thermometer

1. In heavy saucepan over medium to medium-high heat, bring the sugar, corn syrup and water to a boil, stirring until the sugar dissolves and the mixture begins to boil. Cook, without stirring, to the soft crack stage (280°F/138°C).

2. Stir in the peanuts. Cook, stirring occasionally to prevent the peanuts from settling on the bottom of the pan, to the hard crack stage (300°F/149°C).

3. Remove from the heat. Gently stir in the baking soda until well blended. Pour onto the prepared baking sheet. Cool and break into pieces. Store in an airtight container.

Farmers' Market Peanut Brittle

1½ cups	granulated sugar	375 mL
½ cup	light (white or golden) corn syrup	125 mL
2 tbsp	water	30 mL
1½ cups	raw unsalted peanuts	375 mL
½ tsp	salt	2 mL
1½ tbsp	butter or margarine	22 mL
1 tsp	baking soda	5 mL

The friendly folks at the local farmers' market are always glad to share a few of their favorite recipes, such as this one for extra thin peanut brittle.

Skill Level: Average

Makes about 1½ lbs (750 g)

- Large baking sheet, buttered
- 2-quart heavy saucepan
- Candy thermometer

1. In heavy saucepan over medium-high heat, bring the sugar, corn syrup and water to a boil, stirring until the sugar dissolves and the mixture begins to boil. Cook, without stirring, to the soft crack stage (280°F/138°C).

2. Stir in the peanuts. Cook, stirring occasionally to prevent the peanuts from settling on the bottom of the pan, to the hard crack stage (300°F/149°C).

3. Remove from the heat. Add the salt, butter and baking soda, stirring until well mixed. Pour onto the prepared baking sheet. Using the back of a wooden spoon, a flat metal spatula or two forks, spread or pull the mixture into a very thin layer until the brittle is so thin that you can almost see through it. Cool and break into pieces. Store in an airtight container.

Reece's Microwave Peanut Brittle

1 cup	granulated sugar	250 mL
1 tsp	salt	5 mL
½ cup	light (white or golden) corn syrup	125 mL
1 cup	raw unsalted peanuts	250 mL
1 tbsp	butter or margarine	15 mL
1 tsp	vanilla extract	5 mL
1 tsp	baking soda	5 mL

Nothing beats my neighbor's microwave candy for speed, ease and taste, all features appreciated by today's grandmothers.

Skill Level: Novice, Easy

Makes about 1 lb (500 g)

- Large baking sheet, buttered
- 2-quart microwave-safe bowl

1. In microwave-safe bowl, stir together the sugar, salt, corn syrup and peanuts. Microwave, on High, uncovered, for 4 minutes. Stir the candy and turn the dish.

2. Microwave on High 4 minutes. Stir in the butter and vanilla.

3. Microwave on High 1 to 1½ minutes. Gently stir in the baking soda (the mixture will become light and foamy). Pour onto the prepared baking sheet. Cool and break into pieces. Store in an airtight container.

Almond Brittle

2 cups	granulated sugar	500 mL
1/2 cup	light (white or golden) corn syrup	125 mL
1/3 cup	water	75 mL
1/4 tsp	salt	1 mL
3 tbsp	butter or margarine	45 mL
1 1/4 cups	halved or coarsely chopped blanched almonds	300 mL
1 tsp	vanilla extract	5 mL

With this brittle being only mildly sweet and smooth as glass, nut lovers will be "nuts" for this candy because most of the flavor comes from the almonds, which roast during cooking.

Skill Level: Average

Makes about 1 1/2 lbs (750 g)

- 2 large baking sheets, buttered
- 3-quart heavy saucepan
- Candy thermometer

1. In heavy saucepan, combine the sugar, corn syrup, water, salt and butter. Bring to a boil over medium to medium-high heat, stirring until the sugar dissolves and the mixture begins to boil. Stir in the almonds and bring to a second boil. Cook, stirring frequently, to the hard crack stage (300°F/149°C).

2. Remove from the heat. Quickly stir in the vanilla. Pour onto the prepared baking sheets. Cool and break into pieces. Store in an airtight container.

Variation
Try substituting pecans for the almonds.

Toffees

Marry Me Toffee

2 to 2½ cups	chopped toasted almonds, divided	500 to 625 mL
6	bars (each 1.55 oz/44 g) milk chocolate (9.3 oz/264 g total)	6
1 lb	good-quality butter (do not use margarine)	500 g
2 cups	granulated sugar	500 mL
3 tbsp	water	45 mL
1 tsp	vanilla extract	5 mL

I first tasted my signature candy in the late 1980s when my neighbor Julie gave me a bag for Christmas. I knew after the first bite that I had to have this recipe. Since then, I have made several hundred batches of this mouthwatering toffee for people all over the country, and almost everyone agrees that it is one of the most delicious and addictive candies they have ever tasted. This buttery, chocolate-topped candy is particularly popular with men, hence the name.

Cook's Notes

See When Butter Separates (page 49).

This candy is extra delicious when made with toasted almond topping sold in ice cream specialty stores.

Remember to use high-quality ingredients because the better the butter, the better the toffee.

It takes about 45 minutes to make this candy. The recipe may be doubled and cooked in a 5-quart heavy candy kettle or large pot.

Skill Level: Average

Makes about 2¼ lbs (1.125 kg)

- Large baking sheet
- Small to medium baking sheet
- 3-quart heavy saucepan
- Candy thermometer

1. Scatter about half of the almonds over the 2 baking sheets, dividing proportionately between the 2 sheets. Reserve the remaining almonds for the topping. Break the chocolate bars into pieces and set aside.

2. In a heavy 3-quart saucepan over medium to medium-high heat, bring the butter, sugar and water to a boil, stirring until the sugar dissolves and the mixture begins to boil. Cook, stirring constantly, to the hard crack stage (300°F/149°C).

3. Remove from the heat. Quickly stir in the vanilla. Immediately pour a thin layer of hot toffee over the almonds on the baking sheets. (The toffee will not completely cover the baking sheets.) Immediately place the chocolate pieces on top of the hot toffee (the chocolate will melt within a few minutes).

4. Using a flat metal spatula or a knife, spread the melted chocolate in an even layer over the toffee.

5. Sprinkle with the reserved almonds, lightly pressing the almonds into the chocolate with the palms of your hands. Let stand until the chocolate is firm. The toffee may be cooled in the refrigerator or freezer, if preferred. Break into pieces. Store in an airtight container at room temperature or in the refrigerator or in the freezer, as desired. Do not store in a container with other candies.

English Toffee

1 cup	butter (do not use margarine)	250 mL
1 cup	granulated sugar	250 mL
2 tbsp	water	30 mL
1 tbsp	light (white or golden) corn syrup	15 mL
¾ cup	finely chopped walnuts or toasted almonds	175 mL
4 to 8 oz	sweet chocolate (preferably German's by Baker's), semisweet chocolate or milk chocolate, melted	125 to 250 g

> Just a tablespoon of corn syrup makes this traditional English toffee extra smooth.

The Candy Dance

Nothing can tell of America's continued love of homemade candy quite like the story of the Candy Dance. In 1919, the ladies of the tiny community of Genoa, Nevada, held a dance and passed out homemade candy to raise funds for community streetlights. The Candy Dance was such an overwhelming success that they made it an annual event. In the 1970s, the Candy Dance became a two-day affair when organizers added an arts and crafts show. Held in late September, attendance at the annual Candy Dance has steadily risen over the years, with thousands of visitors pouring into this small community to sample the candy and join in the fun. Volunteers make up to 4,000 pounds (1,814 kg) of candy in the weeks preceding the event, most of which is sold during the first day.

Makes about 1¼ lbs (625 g)

- Large baking sheet, lined with foil, then buttered or sprayed with nonstick spray
- 2-quart heavy saucepan
- Candy thermometer

1. In heavy saucepan over low to medium-low heat, slowly melt the butter, being careful not to allow it to burn. Stir in the sugar and cook, stirring constantly, until the mixture begins to bubble. Remove from the heat temporarily. Stir in the water and corn syrup, mixing well. Return to the heat and cook, stirring as needed to prevent scorching, to the hard crack stage (300°F/149°C).

2. Remove from the heat. Stir in the nuts. Immediately pour the hot mixture onto the prepared baking sheet, spreading into a thin layer with the back of a spoon. Cool at room temperature.

3. Spread 4 oz (125 g) melted chocolate over the toffee. Let stand until the chocolate is firm. If desired, turn the coated toffee over and spread 4 oz (125 g) melted chocolate on other side. Let stand until the chocolate is firm. Break into pieces. Store in an airtight container in the refrigerator.

Variation

Nut-Topped English Toffee: If desired, additional chopped or ground nuts may be sprinkled on top of the warm chocolate. Without these nuts, the candy must remain refrigerated or the chocolate coating may become soft and somewhat sticky.

One-in-a-Million Toffee

$\frac{1}{2}$ to $\frac{3}{4}$ cup	chopped pecans	125 to 175 mL
6	bars (each 1.55 oz/44 g) milk chocolate (9.3 oz/264 g total)	6
1 lb	butter (do not use margarine)	500 g
2 cups	granulated sugar	500 mL
1 to $1\frac{1}{2}$ cups	very finely chopped pecans	250 to 375 mL

Professional toffee tasters have named this pecan toffee as a worthy opponent to my signature candy, Marry Me Toffee (page 47), with a few, including my own brother, hinting that this candy might even be better.

- 15- by 10-inch (38 by 25 cm) jelly roll pan
- 3-quart heavy saucepan
- Candy thermometer

1. Scatter the chopped pecans across jelly roll pan. Break the chocolate bars into pieces.

2. In heavy saucepan over medium heat, bring the butter and sugar to a boil, stirring until the sugar dissolves and the mixture begins to boil. Cook, stirring constantly, to the hard crack stage (300°F/149°C).

3. Remove from the heat. Quickly pour a thin layer of hot toffee over the pecans in the jelly roll pan. Immediately place the chocolate pieces on top of the hot toffee. (The chocolate will melt within a few minutes.)

4. Using a flat metal spatula or knife, spread the melted chocolate in an even layer over the toffee. Sprinkle with the very finely chopped pecans. Let stand until the chocolate is firm. Place a sheet of waxed paper over the cooled toffee and break into pieces using a small hammer. Store in an airtight container.

When Butter Separates

Occasionally when cooking toffee, the butter may separate from the sugar. I have mostly eliminated the problem by cooking at just under medium-high heat and by always starting with cold ingredients and letting the butter and sugar melt together. Other causes are not stirring enough while cooking, or stirring too quickly; rapidly changing heat settings during cooking; and using low quality butter. Using salted butter helps prevent separation.

If the butter separates during cooking, you can try to salvage the candy by adding $\frac{1}{4}$ to $\frac{1}{2}$ cup (60 to 125 mL) very hot water, stirring in 1 tbsp (15 mL) at a time until the mixture blends again. Be careful not to let the hot candy splatter on you. The other solution is to discard the separated mixture and start again, cooking at a little higher temperature the next time. If the butter separates and creates small pools of liquid as you pour the cooked toffee onto the baking sheets, use a paper towel to absorb the extra butter before adding the chocolate topping. If it creates large pools of liquid on top of the toffee, absorb the moisture with a paper towel and do not try to finish the recipe with chocolate topping. Instead break up the candy into small chips and add to ice cream or cookie dough.

Almond Butter Toffee

½ cup	butter (do not use margarine)	125 mL
1 cup	granulated sugar	250 mL
1 tbsp	water	15 mL
½ cup	chopped toasted almonds	125 mL
½ tsp	vanilla extract	2 mL
¾ tsp	baking soda	3 mL
1 to 1½ cups	semisweet chocolate chips, divided	250 to 375 mL
¼ cup	ground or additional finely chopped toasted almonds	60 mL

This unusual toffee recipe contains baking soda, giving it an extra crunchy texture.

Cook's Notes

For step-by-step photographs of making toffee, see color pages F and G.

See When Butter Separates (page 49).

Skill Level: Average

Makes about 1¼ lbs (625 mL)

- Large baking sheet, lined with foil, then buttered or sprayed with nonstick spray
- 2-quart heavy saucepan
- Candy thermometer
- Double boiler

1. In heavy saucepan over medium heat, bring the butter, sugar and water to a boil, stirring until the sugar dissolves and the mixture begins to boil. Cook, stirring constantly, to the hard crack stage (300°F/149°C).

2. Remove from the heat. Stir in the chopped almonds and vanilla. Add the baking soda. When the candy foams, immediately pour it onto the prepared baking sheet and spread in a thin layer about ¼ inch (0.5 cm) thick. Cool.

3. In the top pan of a double boiler over hot, but not boiling water, melt half of the chocolate chips, stirring until smooth. Spread the chocolate on one side of the cooled toffee, then sprinkle with half of the finely chopped almonds. Let stand until the chocolate is firm. Melt the remaining chocolate chips using the same method. Turn the toffee and spread the uncoated side with chocolate. Sprinkle with the remaining nuts. Let stand until the chocolate is firm. Break into pieces. Store in an airtight container.

Storing Candy

Most candies should be stored in an airtight container to keep them fresh. Unless specifically instructed in the recipe, refrigeration is often a matter of personal choice, but generally, most fudges and fudge-like candies should keep at least 1 week at room temperature and at least 1 month, sometimes much longer, if refrigerated. Excessive heat, high humidity, or added ingredients such as fruit may shorten the storage time so it is important to use common sense. If the color or texture of the candy has changed, dispose of it and make a fresh batch.

Butternut Toffee

1/2 cup	butter (do not use margarine)	125 mL
1 cup	granulated sugar	250 mL
1/2 tsp	salt	2 mL
1/4 cup	water	60 mL
3/4 cup	finely chopped walnuts, divided	175 mL
1 cup	semisweet chocolate chips, melted	250 mL

> With a mild walnut taste and a rich, dark chocolate topping, this candy often becomes the toffee of choice. The recipe also contains half the butter of some toffee recipes.

Skill Level: Average

Makes about 1 lb (500 g)

- Large baking sheet, buttered
- 2-quart heavy saucepan
- Candy thermometer

1. In heavy saucepan over medium heat, bring the butter, sugar, salt and water to a boil, stirring until the sugar dissolves and the mixture begins to boil. Cook, stirring constantly, to the hard crack stage (300°F/149°C).

2. Remove from the heat. Stir in 1/2 cup (125 mL) of the walnuts. Immediately pour the hot mixture onto the prepared baking sheet, spreading into a thin layer with the back of a spoon. Cool.

3. Spread the melted chocolate over the toffee. Sprinkle with the remaining walnuts. Let stand until the chocolate is firm. Break into pieces. Store in an airtight container.

Butter Pecan Toffee

1 lb	butter (do not use margarine)	500 g
2 cups	granulated sugar	500 mL
2 tsp	light (white or golden) corn syrup	10 mL
1/2 cup	water	125 mL
2 cups	chopped pecans	500 mL
12 oz	milk chocolate chips	375 g

> Everyone will want samples of this delicious toffee, shared by my cousin Susan's friend Donna, of Huntsville, Arkansas.

Cook's Note

See When Butter Separates (page 49).

Skill Level: Average

Makes about 2 1/4 lbs (1.125 kg)

- 2 baking sheets, lined with foil
- 3-quart heavy saucepan
- Candy thermometer

1. In heavy saucepan over medium heat, bring the butter, sugar, corn syrup and water to a boil, stirring until the sugar dissolves and the mixture begins to boil. Cook, stirring constantly, to just below the hard crack stage (295°F/146°C).

2. Remove from the heat. Stir in the pecans. Pour in a thin layer onto the prepared baking sheets. Sprinkle the chocolate chips over the hot mixture and let stand a few minutes to melt. Using a knife or spatula, spread the melted chocolate across the toffee in an even layer. Let stand until the chocolate is firm. Break into pieces. Store in an airtight container in the refrigerator.

Buttercrunch Candy

6	bars (each 1.55 oz/44 g) milk chocolate (9.3 oz/264 g total)	6
1 lb	butter, softened (do not use margarine)	500 g
2 cups	granulated sugar	500 mL
1 cup	finely chopped pecans, divided	250 mL

Finally, a candy that we can burn! The slightly scorched flavor of this special toffee may remind you of a Heath candy bar.

Skill Level: Average

Makes about 2 lbs (1 kg)

- Large baking sheet
- 3-quart heavy saucepan
- Candy thermometer

1. Break the milk chocolate bars into pieces.

2. In heavy saucepan, cream the butter and sugar together until well blended. Cook, stirring constantly, over medium-high to high heat to the hard crack stage (300°F/149°C). Allow the candy to cook slightly past the hard crack stage, to about 303°F (150°C) or until it appears slightly scorched.

3. Remove from the heat. Stir in $\frac{1}{2}$ cup (125 mL) of the pecans. Immediately pour in a thin layer onto the baking sheet. Immediately place the chocolate pieces on top of the hot toffee. (The chocolate will melt within a few minutes.)

4. Using a flat metal spatula or knife, spread the melted chocolate in an even layer over the toffee. Sprinkle with the remaining pecans, lightly pressing the nuts into the chocolate with the palms of your hands. Let stand until the chocolate is firm. (The candy may be cooled in the refrigerator or freezer if preferred.) Break into pieces. Store in an airtight container at room temperature, in the refrigerator or in the freezer, as desired. Do not store in a container with other candies.

Microwave Toffee

1 cup	chopped pecans, walnuts or toasted almonds, divided	250 mL
1 cup	granulated sugar	250 mL
1/4 cup	water	60 mL
1/2 tsp	salt	2 mL
1/2 cup	butter, thinly sliced (do not use margarine)	125 mL
2	bars (each 1.55 oz/44 g) milk chocolate (3.1 oz/88 g total), coarsely chopped into pieces	2

Though the microwave version may not be as smooth as most traditional toffees, it can certainly satisfy a craving.

- 8-inch (20 cm) square pan, lined with foil

1. Sprinkle half of the nuts evenly across the bottom of the prepared pan.

2. In a medium microwave-safe bowl, combine the sugar, water and salt until well mixed. Add the butter. Microwave on High 3 minutes. Stir. Microwave on High 3 minutes. Stir again. Microwave on High 1 to 5 minutes or until the mixture reaches a light golden brown; watch carefully and stir every 1 to 2 minutes. Pour the browned sugar mixture over the nuts in the pan. Cool.

3. In a small microwave-safe dish, microwave the chocolate on High 30 seconds to 1 minute or until mostly melted; watch carefully so that the chocolate does not burn. Stir until the chocolate is completely melted. Spread over the cooled toffee. Sprinkle with the remaining nuts. Cool and break into pieces. Store in an airtight container.

Old-Fashioned Hard Candies

Glass Candy

2 cups	granulated sugar	500 mL
2 cups	light corn syrup	500 mL
1 tsp	cinnamon oil (see Cook's Note, below)	5 mL
1 tsp	red food coloring	5 mL

A friend once gave me a lovely glass water pitcher tied with a bow and filled with bright red, cinnamon-flavored Glass Candy. Not only was the candy delicious, but it was also a beautiful way to present a glass gift!

Cook's Note

Cinnamon oil may damage plastic measuring spoons; it's better to use metal spoons if possible. Be cautious using flavored oils. The fumes are very strong when added to the hot candy. Turn on the exhaust fan and do not lean over the pan.

Skill Level: Average

Makes about 1 $\frac{1}{2}$ lbs (750 g)

- 2 large baking sheets
- 3-quart saucepan
- Candy thermometer

1. In heavy saucepan over medium heat, bring the sugar and corn syrup to a boil, stirring until the sugar dissolves and the mixture begins to boil. Cook, without stirring, to the hard crack stage (300°F/149°C).

2. Remove from the heat. Quickly stir in the cinnamon oil and food coloring. Pour the hot syrup onto the baking sheets in thin, even layers. Cool at room temperature in a dry location. Break into small pieces. Store in an airtight container.

Old-Fashioned Hard Candies

The candies in this collection are similar to the first candies enjoyed by our ancestors. According to the National Confectioners Association, hard candies made of boiled sugar were gaining popularity with American colonists as early as the 17th century. By the early 1800s, improvements in technology brought this type of candy making into the home, where cooks flavored their candies with lemon, peppermint and other common flavorings. Our tastes have not changed over the years, for who can resist savoring one of these candies for as long as they will last?

Licorice

3 cups	granulated sugar	750 mL
1 cup	water	250 mL
1 cup	light (white) corn syrup	250 mL
1 tsp	anise oil	5 mL
1/4 tsp	black vegetable coloring (see Cook's Note, below)	1 mL

> Unlike the soft, stretchy licorice we ate as kids, this recipe makes the old-fashioned kind of licorice, which is a hard, black candy with licorice flavoring.

Cook's Note
Black vegetable coloring can often be purchased at stores specializing in baking and candy-making supplies.

Skill Level: Average

Makes about 1 1/2 lbs (750 g)

- 2 baking sheets, lined with foil, then butter foil
- 3-quart heavy saucepan
- Candy thermometer

1. In heavy saucepan over medium heat, bring the sugar, water and corn syrup to a boil, stirring until the sugar dissolves and the mixture begins to boil. Cook, without stirring, to 290°F (143°C).

2. Remove from the heat. Quickly stir in the anise oil and the vegetable coloring. Pour the hot syrup onto the baking sheets in thin, even layers. When lukewarm, deeply score the slabs of candy into 1 1/2- by 1-inch (4 by 2.5 cm) bars. When cold, carefully break into pieces along the score lines. Wrap each piece individually in waxed paper.

Hardtack Candy

2 cups	granulated sugar	500 mL
1 cup	water	250 mL
3/4 cup	light (white) corn syrup	175 mL
1/2 tsp	oil flavoring of choice	2 mL
1/2 to 1 tsp	food coloring of choice	2 to 5 mL

> Like many hard candies, this recipe can be flavored and colored any way the cook chooses (see Cook's Notes for suggestions, page 57).

Skill Level: Average

Makes about 1 lb (500 g)

- 13- by 9-inch (33 by 23 cm) metal baking pan or large baking sheet, lined with foil
- 2-quart heavy saucepan
- Candy thermometer

1. In heavy saucepan over medium heat, bring the sugar, water and corn syrup to a boil, stirring until the sugar dissolves and the mixture begins to boil. Cook, without stirring, to the hard crack stage (300°F/149°C).

2. Remove from the heat. Quickly stir in the flavoring and food coloring of choice. Pour the hot syrup into the prepared pan in a thin, even layer. When lukewarm, deeply score the slab of candy into squares or triangles, as desired. When cold, carefully break into pieces along the score lines. Wrap each piece individually in waxed paper. Store at room temperature.

Horehound Candy

¾ cup	boiling water	175 mL
2 tsp	crushed dried horehound	10 mL
1 cup	granulated sugar	250 mL
¼ cup	light (white) corn syrup	60 mL

In the 1920s, my great-grandfather was known for carrying a few pieces of horehound candy in his pocket but keeping his main stash hidden from his 35 grandchildren. When his stash disappeared, he knew that his grandkids were better at playing hide-and-seek than he was.

Cook's Notes

The easiest way to make this recipe is to use two single-serving packets of horehound tea, which usually contain about 1 tsp (5 mL) horehound per bag. Because the horehound is sealed in a tea bag, no straining is needed. Steep the tea bags in ¾ cup (175 mL) boiling water for the number of minutes directed on the tea package (about 3 minutes). If the tea bags are steeped for 10 to 20 minutes as directed above, the candy may develop a bitter taste.

Horehound has a fairly mild and not particularly sweet menthol-type flavor. Most commercial horehound candies contain additional flavoring, such as oil of root beer, to make the candy more interesting. If desired, ¼ to ½ tsp (1 to 2 mL) of flavoring oil may be stirred into this recipe just before pouring the candy onto the baking sheet.

Skill Level: Average

Makes about 8 oz (250 g)

- Large baking sheet, buttered
- Cheesecloth
- 2-quart heavy saucepan
- Candy thermometer

1. Pour the boiling water over the horehound and let stand 10 to 20 minutes. Strain the horehound through a cheesecloth-lined strainer, discarding the horehound and reserving the water.

2. In heavy saucepan, combine the horehound water, sugar and syrup. Cook slowly, without stirring, to the hard crack stage (300°F/149°C). Pour onto the prepared baking sheet. Cut into squares before it hardens. Store in an airtight container.

Horehound

Horehound, sometimes spelled hoarhound, is a flowering plant that grows wild along the roadsides in Europe. Early settlers brought horehound to North America, planting it near homesteads. Today we find dried, crushed horehound in health food stores that specialize in herbs or herbal teas. Sometimes called "soldier's tea," horehound has been used in cough remedies for centuries. Thanks to Kansas State University, I can share this interesting old recipe.

Lollipops

2 cups	granulated sugar	500 mL
2/3 cup	light (white) corn syrup	150 mL
1 cup	water	250 mL
1/2 tsp	food coloring of choice	2 mL
1/2 tsp	oil flavoring of choice	2 mL

To liven up your lollipops, try decorating them with a few multicolored sprinkles while the candy is still warm.

Cook's Notes

For step-by-step photographs, see color page D.

Tint candy with a color to complement the flavor. For example, use green food coloring with oil of lime and yellow food coloring for oil of lemon.

Some suggested flavorings are wintergreen oil, peppermint oil, cinnamon oil, clove oil and anise oil.

Skill Level: Advanced

Makes about 12

- 2 large baking sheets, buttered
- 2-quart heavy saucepan
- Candy thermometer
- Lollipop sticks

1. In heavy saucepan over medium heat, bring the sugar, corn syrup and water to a boil, stirring until the sugar dissolves and the mixture begins to boil. Cover and cook 2 to 3 minutes to dissolve the sugar crystals on the sides of the pan. Remove the lid. Cook, without stirring, to the hard crack stage (300°F/149°C).

2. Remove from the heat. Quickly add the coloring and flavoring, stirring only until mixed. Let the candy cool for about 5 minutes or until starting to thicken. To check if it's ready, spoon a small amount onto the prepared baking sheet. It should flow and spread slowly rather than spreading very quickly to a thin disc. Once the candy is ready, quickly drop from the tip of a large spoon onto the prepared baking sheet, making certain the drops are round. Press a lollipop stick into the edge of each lollipop before it hardens. If desired, spoon a little more of the candy on top of the stick to cover. Press any decorations into the lollipop at the same time. Loosen the lollipops from the pan before they get too cold or they will crack. To store, wrap the cooled lollipops in cellophane or waxed paper.

Dorothy's Never-Fail Caramels

2 cups	granulated sugar	500 mL
1 cup	packed light brown sugar	250 mL
1 cup	light (white or golden) corn syrup	250 mL
1 cup	half-and-half (10%) cream	250 mL
1 cup	milk	250 mL
1 cup	butter	250 mL
4 tsp	vanilla extract	20 mL

Hometown friend Dorothy often used this recipe to teach home economics students about candy making. If teenagers can make these caramels, you can, too.

Cook's Note

Cutting candy becomes much easier with the use of parchment paper. Rather than buttering the pan directly, butter a piece of parchment paper larger than the pan and press it into the bottom and up the sides of the pan, tucking and creasing the paper as needed to create corners, and leaving a generous overhang over the sides of the pan.

Skill Level: Average

Makes about 2 lbs (1 kg)

- 13- by 9-inch (33 by 23 cm) pan, lined with parchment (see Cook's Note, left) or generously buttered
- 5-quart heavy candy kettle or pot
- Candy thermometer

1. In heavy candy kettle over medium heat, bring the granulated and brown sugars, corn syrup, half-and-half, milk and butter to a boil, stirring until the sugars dissolve and the mixture begins to boil. Reduce the heat to medium low. Cook, stirring constantly, to the firm ball stage (244°F to 248°F/118°C to 120°C, with 248°F/120°C recommended).

2. Remove from the heat. Stir in the vanilla. Pour into the prepared pan. Cool and cut into squares. Individually wrap each piece in plastic wrap or waxed paper. Store in an airtight container.

Variation

Dorothy's Never-Fail Caramels with Pecans: Add 2 cups (500 mL) pecans in large pieces with the vanilla.

Chewy, Gooey Caramel Pecan Squares

2 cups	granulated sugar	500 mL
1 cup	packed light brown sugar	250 mL
1	can (12 oz or 370 mL) evaporated milk	1
1 cup	heavy or whipping (35%) cream	250 mL
1½ cups	light (white or golden) corn syrup	375 mL
1 cup	butter (do not use margarine)	250 mL
¼ tsp	salt	1 mL
2½ cups	pecans, in large pieces	625 mL
½ tsp	vanilla extract	2 mL

This outrageously delicious candy is richer than an oil baron.

Skill Level: Average

Makes about 3 lbs (1.5 kg)

- 15- by 10-inch (18 by 25 cm) jelly roll pan, buttered
- 5-quart heavy candy kettle or pot
- Candy thermometer

1. In heavy candy kettle over medium-low heat, bring the granulated and brown sugars, milk, cream, corn syrup, butter and salt to a boil, stirring until the sugars dissolve and the mixture begins to boil.

2. Cover and cook 2 to 3 minutes to dissolve the sugar crystals on the sides of the pan. Remove the lid. Cook slowly, stirring occasionally to prevent scorching, over medium-low heat to the soft ball stage (234°F to 240°F/112°C to 116°C, with 238°F/114°C recommended), about 40 minutes.

3. Remove from the heat. Add the pecans and vanilla extract, stirring only to blend. Pour into the prepared pan. Cool and cut into squares. Wrap each square individually in plastic wrap. Store in an airtight container.

Storing Candy

Most candies should be stored in an airtight container to keep them fresh. Unless specifically instructed in the recipe, refrigeration is often a matter of personal choice, but generally, most fudges and fudge-like candies should keep at least 1 week at room temperature and at least 1 month, sometimes much longer, if refrigerated. Excessive heat, high humidity, or added ingredients such as fruit may shorten the storage time so it is important to use common sense. If the color or texture of the candy has changed, dispose of it and make a fresh batch.

Black Walnut Caramels

3/4 cup	finely chopped black walnuts	175 mL
2 cups	pecans, in large pieces	500 mL
2 1/2 cups	granulated sugar	625 mL
3/4 cup	light (white) corn syrup	175 mL
1/2 cup	butter (do not use margarine)	125 mL
1/4 tsp	cream of tartar	1 mL
2 1/2 cups	whole milk, divided (see Cook's Notes, below)	625 mL
1 tsp	vanilla extract	5 mL

Attention, black walnut lovers: Get ready for the best caramel of your life. Black walnuts are a native North American nut with a pronounced flavor. They are available in some supermarkets, farmers' markets and by mail order.

Cook's Notes

Generally, it is best to use milk with minimum 2% fat for candies because the additional fat content helps produce a creamy texture. If preferred, experiment with lower fat milks to see if you notice a difference.

These are firm caramels and hold their shape well.

This recipe takes about 1 1/2 hours to complete, but caramel lovers will say it is worth it.

Skill Level: Advanced
Makes about 2 1/2 lbs (1.25 kg)

- 13- by 9-inch (33 by 23 cm) pan, lined with parchment (see Cook's Note, page 58) or buttered
- 5-quart heavy candy kettle or pot
- Candy thermometer

1. Sprinkle the black walnuts across the bottom of the prepared pan. Sprinkle the pecans over the walnuts.

2. In heavy candy kettle over medium-low heat, combine the sugar, corn syrup, butter, cream of tartar and 1 cup (250 mL) of the milk, stirring until the sugar dissolves. Cook, stirring constantly, 15 minutes. (The mixture should reach the boiling point 7 or 8 minutes into cooking.) Add 1/2 cup (125 mL) of milk. Cook, stirring constantly, 15 minutes.

3. Add 1/2 cup (125 mL) of milk. Cook, stirring constantly, 10 minutes. Add the remaining 1/2 cup (125 mL) of milk. Cook, stirring constantly, to the high end of the soft ball stage (240°F/116°C).

4. Remove from the heat. Gently add the vanilla, stirring as little as possible. Pour the hot caramel mixture over the nuts in the pan. Cool and cut into squares. Individually wrap each piece in plastic wrap. Store in an airtight container.

Variation

The black walnuts give this candy a strong and distinctive flavor. If preferred, the black walnuts may be decreased or omitted and replaced with walnuts or additional pecans. You can use up to a total of 3 cups (750 mL) nuts.

Chocolate Caramels

1 cup	butter or margarine	250 mL
1 lb	light brown sugar	500 g
1 cup	light (white or golden) corn syrup	250 mL
1	can (14 oz or 300 mL) sweetened condensed milk	1
2 oz	unsweetened chocolate, very finely chopped	60 g
1½ tsp	vanilla extract	7 mL

The only thing better than a smooth, creamy caramel is a smooth, creamy chocolate caramel.

Makes about 2¼ lbs (1.125 kg)

- 9-inch (23 cm) square pan, lined with parchment (see Cook's Note, page 58) or buttered
- 3-quart heavy saucepan
- Candy thermometer

1. In heavy saucepan over medium heat, melt the butter. Stir in the brown sugar and corn syrup, blending well. Gradually stir in the milk, mixing well. Stir in the chocolate. Cook, stirring frequently to prevent scorching, to the firm ball stage (244°F to 248°F/118°C to 120°C, with 246°F/119°C recommended).

2. Remove from the heat. Stir in the vanilla. Pour into the prepared pan. Cool and cut into squares. Individually wrap each piece in plastic wrap. Store in an airtight container.

Honey Walnut Caramels

1 cup	half-and-half (10%) cream or evaporated milk	250 mL
1 cup	honey	250 mL
2 tsp	all-purpose flour	10 mL
½ tsp	salt	2 mL
¼ cup	butter or margarine	60 mL
1 tsp	vanilla extract	5 mL
1 cup	chopped walnuts	250 mL

The use of honey in place of sugar makes these caramels less sweet than most candies. Use good-quality honey because the honey is what adds the flavor.

Makes about 1 lb (500 g)

- 8- by 4-inch (20 by 10) inch or 9- by 5-inch (23 by 12.5 cm) loaf pan, lined with parchment (see Cook's Note, page 58) or buttered
- 1- to 2-quart heavy saucepan
- Candy thermometer

1. In heavy saucepan over medium heat, combine the half-and-half, honey, flour and salt, stirring to dissolve the sugar and any lumps that form from the flour. Add the butter. Bring to a boil over medium heat, stirring constantly until the mixture begins to boil. Cook, stirring frequently, to the firm ball stage (244°F to 248°F/118°C to 120°C, with 248°F/120°C recommended).

2. Remove from the heat. Stir in the vanilla and walnuts. Pour into the prepared pan. Cool and cut into squares. Individually wrap each piece in plastic wrap. Store in an airtight container.

Clusters, Patties and Pralines

Peanut Patties

2½ cups	granulated sugar	625 mL
1 cup	half-and-half (10%) cream	250 mL
⅔ cup	light (white) corn syrup	150 mL
Pinch	salt	Pinch
2½ cups	raw peanuts	625 mL
2 tbsp	butter or margarine	30 mL
1 tsp	vanilla extract	5 mL
4 to 6 drops	red food coloring	4 to 6 drops

> Those who love red peanut patties will want to try this creamy version.

Cook's Note

If preferred, these peanut patties may be dropped into small buttered muffin tins.

Skill Level: Advanced

Makes about 45

- 4- to 5-quart heavy candy kettle or pot
- Candy thermometer

1. Cover a large countertop area or 2 large baking sheets with waxed paper.

2. In heavy kettle over medium-low to medium heat, bring the sugar, half-and-half, corn syrup and salt to a boil, stirring until the sugar dissolves and the mixture begins to boil. Stir in the peanuts. Cook, stirring frequently to prevent scorching, to the medium ball stage (242°F/117°C).

3. Remove from the heat. Add the butter, vanilla and food coloring. Beat by hand until the candy thickens, looks opaque and holds its shape. Quickly drop by spoonfuls onto the waxed paper. Cool. Store in an airtight container.

Microwave Peanut Patties

2 cups	granulated sugar	500 mL
½ cup	light (white) corn syrup	125 mL
½ cup	half-and-half (10%) cream	125 mL
1½ cups	raw peanuts	375 mL
2 tbsp	butter	30 mL
1 tsp	vanilla extract	5 mL
	Few drops red food coloring	

> This microwave version of peanut patties is slightly easier to cook than the traditional version but still requires some hand beating.

Cook's Note

Half-and-half makes a creamier candy but milk may be substituted.

Skill Level: Average

Makes about 36

1. Cover a large countertop area or 2 large baking sheets with waxed paper.

2. In a medium microwave-safe bowl, combine the sugar, corn syrup and half-and-half. Microwave on High 3 minutes. Stir in the peanuts. Microwave on High 4½ minutes. Stir the mixture. Microwave on High 4½ minutes.

3. Remove the bowl from the microwave. Stir in the butter and vanilla. Stir in a few drops of red food coloring, as desired. Beat by hand until the candy is creamy and holds its shape. Quickly drop by spoonfuls onto the waxed paper. Cool. Store in an airtight container.

Perfect Pralines

1 cup	buttermilk	250 mL
2 cups	granulated sugar	500 mL
1 tsp	baking soda	5 mL
1/2 cup	butter or margarine (butter preferred)	125 mL
1/8 tsp	salt	0.5 mL
2 1/2 cups	pecans, in large pieces	625 mL
1 tsp	vanilla extract	5 mL

These semi-smooth, melt-in-your-mouth nut clusters are a personal favorite. The buttermilk makes them extra rich and the pecans are slightly soft because they are cooked along with the candy. These pralines are a little darker than most, so don't be surprised if your friends think they are eating chocolate.

Cook's Notes

The candy may be cooked in a 6-quart kettle but is likely to boil over the sides of the pan if not very carefully watched.

If the candy becomes too stiff to drop, stir in a few drops of half-and-half (10%) cream, evaporated milk or milk until the candy is smooth.

Skill Level: Advanced

Makes about 30 pralines

- 8-quart heavy candy kettle or pot
- Candy thermometer

1. Cover a large countertop area or large baking sheet with waxed paper.
2. In heavy kettle over medium-low heat, bring the buttermilk, sugar and baking soda to a boil, stirring constantly. The mixture will foam rapidly and rise in the kettle as it begins to boil. Boil, stirring constantly, for 7 minutes.
3. Stir in the butter, salt and pecans. Cook, stirring constantly, to the soft ball stage (234°F to 240°F/112°C to 116°C, with 236°F/113°C recommended).
4. Remove from the heat. Stir in the vanilla. Beat by hand until the candy is thick and creamy. Quickly drop by spoonfuls onto the waxed paper. Cool. Store in an airtight container.

Prizewinning Pralines

2 cups	packed light brown sugar	500 mL
1 cup	granulated sugar	250 mL
3 tbsp	light (white or golden) corn syrup	45 mL
1⅓ cups	milk (see Cook's Notes, page 60)	325 mL
⅓ cup	butter or margarine	75 mL
2 tsp	vanilla extract	10 mL
2 to 2½ cups	pecans, in large pieces	500 to 625 mL

These golden brown nut clusters are creamier than traditional pralines.

Cook's Note

If the candy becomes too stiff to drop, stir in a few drops of half-and-half (10%) cream, evaporated milk or milk until the candy is smooth.

Skill Level: Advanced

Makes about 40

- 4- to 5-quart heavy candy kettle or pot
- Candy thermometer

1. Cover a large countertop area or 2 large baking sheets with waxed paper.

2. In heavy kettle over medium heat, bring the brown and granulated sugars, corn syrup and milk to a boil, stirring until the sugars dissolve and the mixture begins to boil. Reduce the heat to medium low. Cook, stirring occasionally to prevent scorching, to the soft ball stage (234°F to 240°F/112°C to 116°C, with 236°F/113°C recommended).

3. Remove from the heat. Add the butter without stirring. Cool slightly, about 10 minutes.

4. Add the vanilla. Beat by hand until the candy thickens and loses its gloss. Stir in the nuts. Quickly drop by spoonfuls onto the waxed paper. Cool. Store in an airtight container.

Texas Pralines

1 cup	buttermilk	250 mL
2 cups	granulated sugar	500 mL
1 tsp	baking soda	5 mL
1 tbsp	butter or margarine	15 mL
1 tsp	vanilla extract	5 mL
2 cups	pecan pieces or halves	500 mL

The nuts in this candy are extra crispy because they are added after the candy is cooked.

Cook's Note

If the candy becomes too stiff to drop, place the kettle back on the burner for a few seconds and stir, continuing to drop the candies when the mixture softens again.

Skill Level: Advanced

Makes about 30

- 8-quart heavy candy kettle or pot
- Candy thermometer

1. Cover a large countertop area or a large baking sheet with waxed paper.

2. In heavy kettle over medium heat, bring the buttermilk, sugar and baking soda to a boil, stirring until the sugar dissolves and the mixture begins to boil. The mixture will foam rapidly and rise in the kettle as it begins to boil. Cook, stirring constantly, to the soft ball stage (234°F to 240°F/112°C to 116°C, with 236°F/113°C recommended).

3. Remove from the heat. Add the butter, vanilla and pecans. Beat by hand until the candy is thick and creamy. Quickly drop by spoonfuls onto the waxed paper. Cool. Store in an airtight container.

Ultra-Creamy Buttermilk Pralines

1 cup	buttermilk	250 mL
3 cups	granulated sugar	750 mL
1 tsp	baking soda	5 mL
¾ cup	light (white or golden) corn syrup	175 mL
⅛ tsp	salt	0.5 mL
2 cups	pecan pieces or halves	500 mL
1 tsp	vanilla extract	5 mL
1 tbsp	margarine	15 mL

With a flavor similar to Perfect Pralines (page 63) and Texas Pralines (page 64), this recipe is a good choice for those who prefer candies containing corn syrup.

Cook's Note

If the candy becomes too stiff to drop, stir in a few drops of half-and-half (10%) cream, evaporated milk or milk until the candy is smooth.

Skill Level: Advanced

Makes about 38

- 8-quart heavy candy kettle or pot
- Candy thermometer

1. Cover a large countertop area or 2 large baking sheets with waxed paper.

2. In a heavy kettle over medium heat, bring the buttermilk, sugar, baking soda, corn syrup and salt to a boil, stirring until the sugar dissolves and the mixture begins to boil. The mixture will foam rapidly and rise in the kettle as it begins to boil. Cook, stirring constantly, to the soft ball stage (234°F to 240°F/112°C to 116°C, with 236°F/113°C recommended).

3. Remove from the heat. Stir in the pecans, vanilla and margarine. Beat by hand until the candy is thick and creamy. Quickly drop by spoonfuls onto the waxed paper. Cool. Store in an airtight container.

New Orleans Roasted Pecan Pralines

1¹⁄₂ cups	pecans, in large pieces	375 mL
1¹⁄₂ cups	granulated sugar	375 mL
³⁄₄ cup	packed light brown sugar	175 mL
²⁄₃ cup	milk (see Cook's Notes, below)	150 mL
6 tbsp	butter	90 mL
1 tsp	vanilla extract	5 mL

Anyone who has eaten New Orleans's famous "prahleens" will be happy to have my cousin Margaret's authentic recipe for these traditional sugary candies from a New Orleans cooking school. Be bold; try one of the unusual flavors.

Cook's Notes

If using waxed paper, protect the countertop by placing newspaper or parchment paper underneath the waxed paper so that hot wax from the paper does not transfer onto the countertop.

Generally, it is best to use milk with minimum 2% fat for candies because the additional fat content helps produce a creamy texture. If preferred, experiment with lower fat milks to see if you notice a difference.

Skill Level: Advanced

Makes 25 to 30

- Preheat oven to 275°F (140°C)
- 3-quart heavy saucepan
- Candy thermometer

1. Spread the pecans in a shallow pan. Bake in preheated oven for 20 to 25 minutes or until the pecans are slightly browned and the smell of roasted pecans permeates the room.

2. Cover a large countertop area or a large baking sheet with buttered waxed paper (see Cook's Notes, left), buttered foil or parchment paper.

3. In saucepan, combine the granulated and brown sugars and milk, stirring to dissolve the sugar. Add the butter and roasted pecans. Bring to a boil over medium heat, stirring constantly. Cook, stirring constantly, to the soft ball stage (234°F to 240°F/112°C to 116°C, with 238°F/114°C recommended).

4. Remove from the heat. Add the vanilla. Beat by hand until the candy thickens and becomes creamy and cloudy and the pecans stay suspended in the mixture. Quickly drop by spoonfuls onto the buttered paper or foil. Cool. Store in an airtight container.

Variations

Flavored and Spiced Pralines: Add 1 tsp (5 mL) of your favorite flavoring, such as coffee or brandy or ¹⁄₂ to 1 tsp (2 to 5 mL) of your favorite spice, such as ground ginger or nutmeg, to the mixture before cooking.

Praline Sauce: Add ¹⁄₂ cup (125 mL) light (white or golden) corn syrup to the mixture before cooking. Follow the directions above but do not drop onto waxed paper. Serve the sauce warm over ice cream or other desserts.

Chocolate-Covered Pralines: Dip the cooled pralines into melted chocolate to coat, placing on waxed paper until the chocolate hardens. See Dipping Candies in Chocolate (page 22) and Chocolate Coatings (page 185) for further instructions and ideas.

Ruth's Angel Pralines

1 cup	granulated sugar	250 mL
1 cup	packed light brown sugar	250 mL
$\frac{1}{2}$ cup	half-and-half (10%) cream	125 mL
$\frac{1}{4}$ tsp	salt	1 mL
2 tbsp	butter or margarine	30 mL
1 cup	pecans, in large pieces	250 mL

Ruth Hoeflin, former dean of home economics at Kansas State University, was known for sending annual greetings to hundreds of friends during her summer break. She always included a few new recipes she discovered that year, such as this one for traditional sugary pralines.

Cook's Note

If the candy becomes too stiff to drop, stir in a few drops of half-and-half (10%) cream, evaporated milk or milk until the candy is smooth.

Skill Level: Advanced

Makes about 24

- 2-quart heavy saucepan
- Candy thermometer

1. Cover a large countertop area or a large baking sheet with waxed paper or foil.

2. In heavy saucepan over medium-low heat, bring the granulated and brown sugars, half-and-half and salt to a boil, stirring until the sugars dissolve and the mixture begins to boil. Cook to 228°F (109°C), stirring gently to prevent scorching. Stir in the butter and pecans. Cook, stirring frequently to prevent scorching, to the soft ball stage (234°F to 240°F/112°C to 116°C, with 236°F/113°C recommended).

3. Remove from the heat. Cool 5 minutes.

4. Beat by hand until the candy is slightly thickened. (The candy coats the nuts but does not lose its gloss.) Quickly drop by spoonfuls onto the waxed paper. Cool. Store in an airtight container.

Important Tip

In many recipes, it is important to be prepared for all the steps because timing can be critical. Have all ingredients available and ready to use, and have the pan, baking sheet, or surface prepared before you begin cooking.

Soft Pecan Pralines

2 cups	granulated sugar	500 mL
1/3 cup	light (white) corn syrup	75 mL
2/3 cup	heavy or whipping (35%) cream	150 mL
Pinch	salt	Pinch
2 cups	pecans, in large pieces	500 mL
1/4 cup	butter or margarine	60 mL
1/2 tsp	vanilla extract	2 mL

Heavy cream makes these pralines unusually soft and light in color.

Cook's Note
If the candy becomes too stiff to drop, stir in a few drops of half-and-half (10%) cream, evaporated milk or milk until the candy is smooth.

Skill Level: Advanced

Makes about 35

- 3-quart heavy saucepan
- Candy thermometer

1. Cover a large countertop area or 2 large baking sheets with waxed paper.

2. In heavy saucepan over medium-low heat, bring the sugar, corn syrup, cream and salt to a boil, stirring until the sugar dissolves and the mixture begins to boil. Cover and cook 2 to 3 minutes to dissolve the sugar crystals on the sides of the pan. Remove the lid. Cook, stirring only as needed to prevent scorching, to the soft ball stage (234°F to 240°F/112°C to 116°C, with 238°F/114°C recommended).

3. Remove from the heat. Add the pecans, butter and vanilla. Beat by hand until the candy thickens and becomes creamy. Quickly drop by spoonfuls onto the waxed paper. Cool. Store in an airtight container.

Creamy Pecan Pralines

2 cups	granulated sugar	500 mL
3/4 tsp	baking soda	4 mL
1 cup	half-and-half (10%) cream or evaporated milk	250 mL
1 1/2 tbsp	butter	22 mL
2 cups	pecan halves	500 mL

It is extremely rare to find baking soda in a candy recipe that does not also contain buttermilk.

Cook's Note
If the candy becomes too stiff to drop, stir in a few drops of half-and-half (10%) cream, evaporated milk or milk until the candy is smooth.

Skill Level: Advanced

Makes about 30

- 5-quart heavy candy kettle or pot
- Candy thermometer

1. Cover a large countertop area or 2 large baking sheets with waxed paper.

2. In heavy kettle, combine the sugar and baking soda, mixing well. Stir in the half-and-half. Bring to a boil over medium heat, stirring until the sugar dissolves and the mixture begins to boil. The mixture will foam rapidly and rise in the kettle as it begins to boil. Reduce the heat to medium low. Cook, stirring occasionally to prevent scorching, to the soft ball stage (234°F to 240°F/112°C to 116°C, with 238°F/114°C recommended).

3. Remove from the heat. Add the butter and pecan halves. Beat by hand until the candy is thick and creamy. Quickly drop by spoonfuls onto the waxed paper. Cool. Store in an airtight container.

Caramel-Pecan Pralines

2½ cups	granulated sugar, divided	625 mL
1 cup	evaporated milk	250 mL
2 tbsp	butter or margarine	30 mL
Pinch	salt	Pinch
1 tsp	vanilla extract	5 mL
2 cups	pecans, in large pieces	500 mL

> These rich, sugary brown pralines have a distinctive flavor that only caramelized sugar can give.

Cook's Notes

These pralines can "sugar" within a few days. To help avoid this, let the candy cool about 20 minutes before beating.

If the candy becomes too stiff to drop, stir in a few drops of half-and-half (10%) cream, evaporated milk or milk until the candy is smooth.

Skill Level: Expert

Makes about 40

- 5-quart heavy candy kettle or pot
- Candy thermometer

1. Cover a large countertop area or 2 large baking sheets with waxed paper.

2. In a small heavy saucepan or skillet over low heat, slowly melt ½ cup (125 mL) of the sugar, stirring constantly to prevent scorching.

3. In heavy kettle over medium-low heat, combine the remaining 2 cups (500 mL) of sugar and the milk. While the sugar slowly melts in the saucepan or skillet, slowly bring the sugar-milk mixture to a gentle boil, gently stirring to prevent scorching.

4. When sugar is fully melted and caramelized, slowly pour it into the kettle containing the boiling sugar-milk mixture, stirring constantly to prevent the caramelized sugar from clumping on the bottom of the kettle. Cook, stirring constantly to prevent scorching, to the soft ball stage (234°F to 240°F/112°C to 116°C, with 236°F/113°C recommended).

5. Remove from the heat. Add the butter, salt and vanilla. Beat by hand until the candy begins to thicken. Stir in the pecans. Quickly drop by spoonfuls onto the waxed paper. Cool. Store in an airtight container.

Variation

Evaporated milk gives the candy a richer texture, but milk may be substituted.

Love Me Pralines

1½ cups	granulated sugar	375 mL
½ cup	packed light brown sugar	125 mL
3 tbsp	light (white or golden) corn syrup	45 mL
½ cup	half-and-half (10%) cream	125 mL
6	large marshmallows	6
2 tbsp	butter or margarine	30 mL
1 tsp	vanilla extract	5 mL
1½ cups	pecans, in large pieces	375 mL

When I was testing recipes for this book, it was not unusual to see me toting candy samples wherever I went. On the day that I took a few of these marshmallow-smooth pralines to a group of dentists, I had a rather unforgettable message from a dentist I had never met. "Tell her I love her," he said. It is amazing how easily candy makers make friends.

Cook's Note

If the candy becomes too stiff to drop, stir in a few drops of half-and-half (10%) cream, evaporated milk or milk until the candy is smooth.

Skill Level: Advanced

Makes about 32

- 2-quart heavy saucepan
- Candy thermometer

1. Cover a large countertop area or 2 large baking sheets with waxed paper or buttered foil.

2. In heavy saucepan over medium heat, bring the granulated and brown sugars, corn syrup and half and-half to a boil, gently stirring until the sugars dissolve and the mixture begins to boil. Cover and cook 2 to 3 minutes to dissolve the sugar crystals on the sides of the pan. Remove the lid. Cook, stirring occasionally to prevent scorching, to the soft ball stage (234°F to 240°F/112°C to 116°C, with 236°F/113°C recommended).

3. Remove from the heat. Add the marshmallows and butter, stirring until melted. Add the vanilla and pecans. Beat by hand until the candy begins to stiffen. Quickly drop by spoonfuls onto the waxed paper. Store in an airtight container.

Butterscotch-Pecan Pralines

1	package (3.5-ounce/100 g or 2/3 cup/150 mL) butterscotch pudding mix (not instant)	1
1 cup	granulated sugar	250 mL
1/2 cup	packed light brown sugar	125 mL
1/2 cup	evaporated milk	125 mL
1 tbsp	butter	15 mL
1/2 tsp	vanilla extract (optional)	2 mL
1 1/2 cups	pecans, in large pieces	375 mL

When my cousin Patti told me that butterscotch-flavored pralines were all the rage in Austin, I enjoyed telling her that this scrumptious candy has been around since we were kids.

Makes about 18 to 24

- 2-quart heavy saucepan
- Candy thermometer

1. Cover a large countertop area or a large baking sheet with waxed paper.

2. In heavy saucepan over medium-low heat, bring pudding mix, sugars, milk and butter to a boil, gently stirring until sugars dissolve and mixture begins to boil. Cook, stirring occasionally to prevent scorching, to the soft ball stage (234°F to 240°F/112°C to 116°C, with 234°F/112°C recommended or 236°F/113°C for a firmer praline).

3. Remove from heat. Add vanilla, if using, and pecans. Beat by hand until candy is creamy and begins to thicken. Quickly drop by spoonfuls onto waxed paper (see Cook's Note, page 70). Cool. Store in an airtight container.

Maple-Pecan Pralines

2 cups	confectioner's (icing) sugar	500 mL
1/2 cup	evaporated milk	125 mL
1 cup	pure maple syrup, preferably good quality	250 mL
Pinch	salt	Pinch
1 tbsp	butter or margarine	15 mL
1 tsp	vanilla extract	5 mL
1 to 1 1/2 cups	pecans, in large pieces	250 to 375 mL

A hint of maple flavoring makes these smooth pralines made with confectioner's sugar hard to beat.

Cook's Note

To reduce the beating time, add the butter, vanilla and pecans without stirring. Let the candy cool slightly, about 5 minutes, before beating.

Makes about 30

- 3-quart heavy saucepan

1. Cover a countertop area or 2 large baking sheets with waxed paper or buttered foil.

2. In heavy saucepan over medium heat, bring the sugar, milk, maple syrup and salt to a boil, stirring until the sugar dissolves and the mixture begins to boil. Cook, stirring occasionally to prevent scorching, to the soft ball stage (234°F to 240°F/112°C to 116°C, with 236°F/113°C recommended). For softer pralines, cook to 234°F (112°C).

3. Remove from the heat. Add the butter, vanilla and pecans. Beat by hand until the candy is opaque and creamy. Quickly drop by spoonfuls onto the waxed paper or foil. Cool. Store in an airtight container.

Evelyn's Maple Pralines

2 cups	granulated sugar	500 mL
⅔ cup	half-and-half (10%) cream	150 mL
1 cup	pure maple syrup	250 mL
2 cups	pecans, in large pieces	500 mL

These ultra-smooth, light-colored pralines were a family friend's favorite. For exceptional flavor, use good-quality maple syrup.

Cook's Notes

For softer pralines, cook to 236°F (113°C).

The cooked candy may be removed from the heat and cooled slightly before beating, about 5 minutes, to reduce the beating time.

This candy sets in the pan very quickly. If the candy becomes too stiff to drop, stir in a few drops of half-and-half (10%) cream, evaporated milk or milk until the candy is smooth.

Skill Level: Advanced

Makes about 30

- 3-quart heavy saucepan
- Candy thermometer

1. Cover a large area of the countertop or 2 large baking sheets with waxed paper.

2. In heavy saucepan over medium heat, bring the sugar, half-and-half and maple syrup to a boil, stirring until the sugar dissolves and the mixture begins to boil. Cook, stirring occasionally to prevent scorching, to the soft ball stage (234°F to 240°F/112°C to 116°C, with 238°F/114°C recommended).

3. Remove from the heat. Beat by hand until the candy thickens and becomes creamy. Stir in the pecans. Quickly drop by spoonfuls onto the waxed paper. Cool. Store in an airtight container.

Storing Candy

Most candies should be stored in an airtight container to keep them fresh. Unless specifically instructed in the recipe, refrigeration is often a matter of personal choice, but generally, most fudges and fudge-like candies should keep at least 1 week at room temperature and at least 1 month, sometimes much longer, if refrigerated. Excessive heat, high humidity, or added ingredients such as fruit may shorten the storage time so it is important to use common sense. If the color or texture of the candy has changed, dispose of it and make a fresh batch.

Molasses Pralines

2 cups	packed light brown sugar	500 mL
1/2 cup	hot water	125 mL
2 tbsp	molasses (see Glossary, page 20)	30 mL
1 tbsp	butter or margarine	15 mL
1 to 1 1/2 cups	pecans, in large pieces	250 to 375 mL

These dark, nontraditional, almost bittersweet pralines are included for those trying to duplicate a lost praline recipe containing molasses.

Cook's Note

Either mild flavor (fancy) or full flavor (dark) molasses may be used.

Makes about 30

- 3-quart heavy saucepan
- Candy thermometer

1. Cover a large countertop area or a large baking sheet with waxed paper.

2. In heavy saucepan over medium heat, bring the sugar, water and molasses to a boil, stirring until the sugar dissolves and the mixture begins to boil. Cook, stirring only as needed to prevent the candy from boiling over the sides of the pan, to the soft ball stage (234°F to 240°F/112°C to 116°C, with 236°F/113°C recommended).

3. Remove from the heat. Add the butter. Beat by hand until the candy begins to thicken. Stir in the pecans. Quickly drop by spoonfuls onto the waxed paper. Cool. Store in an airtight container.

Coconut Pralines

2 cups	packed light brown sugar	500 mL
1 cup	granulated sugar	250 mL
1 cup	water	250 mL
1 tsp	cider vinegar	5 mL
1 tbsp	butter or margarine	15 mL
2 cups	sweetened flaked coconut	500 mL

Light brown and ultra sugary, these praline-like candies contain coconut, instead of nuts.

Cook's Notes

Half-and-half (10%) cream or evaporated milk may be substituted for the water in this recipe, but the brown sugar will still give the pralines a very sugary texture.

For firmer pralines, cook to 238°F (114°C).

Skill Level: Advanced

Makes about 50

- 2-quart heavy saucepan
- Candy thermometer

1. Cover a large countertop area or 2 large baking sheets with waxed paper.

2. In heavy saucepan over medium heat, bring the brown and granulated sugars, water and vinegar to a boil, stirring until the sugar dissolves and the mixture begins to boil. Cook, stirring only a few times to prevent scorching, to the soft ball stage (234°F to 240°F/112°C to 116°C, with 236°F/113°C recommended).

3. Remove from the heat. Add the butter. Cool about 5 minutes to reduce the beating time. Add the coconut. Beat by hand until the candy begins to thicken and hold its shape. Quickly drop by spoonfuls onto the waxed paper. Cool. Store in an airtight container.

Mexican Orange Drops

3 cups	granulated sugar, divided	750 mL
1 cup	evaporated milk	250 mL
	Grated zest of 2 oranges	
¼ cup	orange juice	60 mL
¼ tsp	salt	1 mL
1 cup	pecans, in large pieces	250 mL

Surprise your guests by serving these chewy orange-flavored pralines at your next Mexican dinner party.

Cook's Notes

Boiling water may be substituted for the orange juice, but the orange juice gives a better flavor.

If preferred, the candy may be beaten without cooling to lukewarm, but the cooling period reduces the beating time.

The beaten candy may be pressed into a well-buttered 8- or 9-inch (20 or 23 cm) square pan, cooled and then cut into squares.

If the candy becomes too stiff to drop, stir in a few drops of half-and-half (10%) cream, evaporated milk or milk until the candy is smooth.

- 3-quart heavy saucepan
- Candy thermometer

1. Cover a large countertop area or 2 large baking sheets with waxed paper. Spray with nonstick spray.

2. In heavy saucepan over medium-low heat, slowly melt 1 cup (250 mL) of the sugar, stirring constantly to prevent scorching. While the sugar is melting, in another very heavy saucepan or in the top pan of a double boiler pan over hot, but not boiling water, heat the milk until it is very hot. Do not allow the milk to boil. Heat the orange juice in the microwave until boiling.

3. When the sugar has fully melted into a rich, brown liquid, slowly stir the boiling orange juice into the sugar, being careful that the hot mixture does not splatter. Slowly stir the hot milk into the sugar-orange juice mixture, stirring until the mixture is blended.

4. Gradually add the remaining 2 cups (500 mL) of sugar and the salt, stirring until the sugar dissolves. Bring to a boil over medium-low heat. Cover and cook 2 to 3 minutes to dissolve the sugar crystals on the sides of the pan. Remove the lid. Cook slowly over low or medium-low heat, without stirring, to the soft ball stage (234°F to 240°F/112°C to 116°C, with 236°F/113°C recommended). Just before the candy reaches the desired temperature, gently stir in the orange zest.

5. Remove from the heat. Cool to lukewarm (110°F/43°C), 45 minutes to 1 hour.

6. Beat by hand until the candy thickens and loses its gloss. Stir in the pecans. Quickly drop by spoonfuls onto the waxed paper. Cool. Store in an airtight container.

Mexican Candy

3 cups	granulated sugar, divided	750 mL
1½ cups	evaporated milk	375 mL
	Grated zest of 2 oranges	
Pinch	salt	Pinch
½ cup	butter	125 mL
1 cup	pecans, in large pieces	250 mL

This very interesting recipe for orange-flavored candy is almost a cross between Mexican Orange Drops (page 74) and Aunt Bill's Brown Candy (page 28).

Cook's Notes

If preferred, after stirring in the nuts, the candy may be poured onto a buttered platter or into a buttered 8- or 9-inch (20 or 23 cm) square pan and cut into squares when cool.

If the candy becomes too stiff to drop, stir in a few drops of half-and-half (10%) cream, evaporated milk or milk until the candy is smooth.

Skill Level: Expert

Makes about 36 pieces

- 4- to 5-quart heavy candy kettle or pot
- Candy thermometer

1. Cover a large countertop area or 2 large baking sheets with waxed paper. Spray with nonstick spray.

2. In kettle over low heat, slowly melt 1 cup (250 mL) of the sugar, stirring constantly to prevent scorching. While the sugar is melting, in a very heavy saucepan or in the top pan of a double boiler pan over hot, but not boiling water, heat the milk until it is very hot. Do not allow the milk to boil.

3. When the sugar has fully melted into a rich, brown liquid, slowly stir the hot milk into the melted sugar, being careful that the hot mixture does not splatter. Stir until the mixture is blended.

4. Gradually add the remaining 2 cups (500 mL) of sugar, stirring until the sugar dissolves. Bring to a boil over medium-low heat. Cook, stirring frequently to prevent scorching, to the firm ball stage (244°F/118°C to 248°F/120°C, with 246°F/119°C recommended).

5. Remove from the heat. Stir in the zest, salt and butter. Cool 20 minutes.

6. Beat by hand until the candy is creamy and loses its gloss. Stir in the nuts. Quickly drop by spoonfuls onto the waxed paper. Cool. Store in an airtight container.

Mexican Pecan Candy

2 cups	granulated sugar	500 mL
1 cup	water	250 mL
1 1/2 cups	pecan halves	375 mL

These traditional Mexican candies are a very sugary form of American pralines.

Cook's Note

If the candy becomes difficult to drop, add a drop or two of hot water, stirring until well blended.

Skill Level: Advanced

Makes about 18

- 2-quart heavy saucepan
- Candy thermometer

1. Cover a large countertop area or a large baking sheet with waxed paper.
2. In heavy saucepan over medium heat, bring the sugar, water and pecans to a boil, stirring until the sugar dissolves and the mixture begins to boil. Cook, stirring occasionally to prevent the nuts from settling on the bottom of the pan, to the soft ball stage (234°F to 240°F/112°C to 116°C, with 236°F/113°C recommended).
3. Remove from the heat. Cool slightly, about 10 minutes. Beat by hand until the mixture thickens and becomes difficult to beat. Quickly drop by spoonfuls onto the waxed paper. Cool. Store in an airtight container.

Nut Cream Drops

1 1/2 cups	granulated sugar	375 mL
1/4 cup	milk	60 mL
2 tbsp	light (white or golden) corn syrup	30 mL
Pinch	salt	Pinch
1 tsp	vanilla extract	5 mL
1/2 cup	chopped walnuts, pecans or sweetened flaked coconut	125 mL

Those needing a quick sugar fix will be glad to know that they can make these rich little drops in about 15 minutes.

Skill Level: Advanced

Makes about 24

- 1- to 2-quart heavy saucepan
- Candy thermometer

1. Cover a large countertop area or a large baking sheet with waxed paper.
2. In heavy saucepan over medium-low to medium heat, bring the sugar, milk, corn syrup and salt to a boil, stirring until the sugar dissolves and the mixture begins to boil. Cook, stirring frequently to prevent scorching, to the soft ball stage (234°F to 240°F/112°C to 116°C, with 236°F/113°C recommended).
3. Remove from the heat. Stir in the vanilla and nuts. Beat by hand until the candy is thick and creamy and begins to lose its gloss. Quickly drop by spoonfuls onto the waxed paper. Cool. Store in an airtight container.

Variation

For a richer candy, substitute half-and-half (10%) cream for the milk.

Coconut Haystacks

3/4 cup	packed light brown sugar	175 mL
3/4 cup	evaporated milk	175 mL
6 tbsp	light (white or golden) corn syrup	90 mL
2 tbsp	butter	30 mL
3 cups	sweetened flaked coconut	750 mL

These light brown coconut haystacks may be nothing like the coconut haystacks that you might buy in a candy store, but they may be a favorite of coconut lovers. Nut lovers might like to toss a few chopped pecans into the candy before dropping it onto waxed paper.

Cook's Notes

For a similar candy that is chocolate coated, see Chocolate-Covered Haystacks (page 194).

If preferred, the butter may be added after the candy is cooked to make the candy slightly softer and creamier.

See Chocolate-Covered Haystacks (page 194).

Skill Level: Average

Makes about 36

- 1- to 2-quart heavy saucepan
- Candy thermometer

1. Cover a large countertop area or 2 large baking sheets with waxed paper.

2. In heavy saucepan over medium heat, bring the sugar, milk, corn syrup and butter to a boil, stirring until the sugar dissolves and the mixture begins to boil. Cook, stirring occasionally to prevent scorching, to the soft ball stage (234°F to 240°F/112°C to 116°C, with 238°F/114°C recommended).

3. Remove from the heat. Stir in the coconut until well blended. Quickly drop by spoonfuls onto the waxed paper. To create the haystacks, dip your fingers into cold water and shape the candy into cones $1\frac{1}{2}$ inches (4 cm) high while the candy is still warm. Cool. Store in an airtight container.

Divinities, Nougats and Similar Candies

Mom's Divinity

2	extra-large or large egg whites	2
2²⁄₃ cups	granulated sugar	650 mL
²⁄₃ cup	light (white) corn syrup	150 mL
¹⁄₂ cup	water	125 mL
1 tsp	vanilla extract	5 mL
²⁄₃ cup	pecans, in large pieces	150 mL

My mother's divinity recipe is one of the few versions of this traditional Southern favorite that calls for cooking the syrup in one stage rather than two. When I asked my mother why she chose this recipe, she jokingly said, "I never wanted to make things more difficult than they had to be!" Like mother, like daughter, because this is my favorite divinity recipe, too. It is one of the easiest classic divinity recipes you will find.

Cook's Notes

Experienced candy makers may prefer to beat the egg whites while the syrup is cooking.

Use 1 less tbsp (15 mL) water on humid days.

Skill Level: Advanced

Makes about 30 to 36 pieces

- 1- to 2-quart saucepan
- Candy thermometer

1. See Tips for Making Divinity (page 79).
2. Cover a large countertop area or a large baking sheet with waxed paper. Butter 2 small spoons.
3. In a large mixing bowl, beat the egg whites with an electric mixer on high speed until the whites form very stiff peaks, but not so long that they lose their gloss and become dry.
4. In saucepan over medium-high heat, bring the sugar, corn syrup and water to a boil, stirring just until the sugar dissolves and the mixture begins to boil. Cook, without stirring, to the hard ball stage (260°F/127°C).
5. Remove the syrup from the heat. Turn the electric mixer to medium-high speed and beat the egg whites again while gradually pouring the hot syrup in a thin stream over the top of the egg whites. Continue beating while adding the vanilla. Beat with the electric mixer until the candy becomes slightly dull and holds its shape when dropped from a spoon. If the candy becomes too stiff to beat with an electric mixer, finish beating by hand.
6. Stir in the pecans by hand. Quickly drop the candy onto the waxed paper using the tip of a buttered spoon. Cool. Store in an airtight container at room temperature.

Important Tip

In many recipes, it is important to be prepared for all the steps because timing can be critical. Have all ingredients available and ready to use, and have the pan, baking sheet, or surface prepared before you begin cooking.

Tips for Making Divinity

Divinity is not a difficult candy to make but does have three failure points. If any one of these steps is not completed accurately, the divinity will not hold its shape.

- The egg whites must be properly beaten.
- The syrup must be properly cooked.
- The combined mixture must be properly beaten.

The egg whites should be beaten until they form very stiff peaks. This means that when the beaters are lifted from the egg whites, the tips should stand up straight. If the tops curl to one side, beat the egg whites 1 to 2 minutes longer and then stop the mixer and lift the beaters again. Knowing exactly when the egg whites are ready usually requires stopping the mixer and checking their progress several times during beating. As soon as the egg whites stand in very stiff peaks, stop beating.

Though old-time candy makers know how to test divinity syrup by dropping it into cold water, the best way to know when the syrup is properly cooked is to use a candy thermometer.

The combined egg white–syrup mixture must be beaten until the candy holds its shape when dropped from a spoon. As one cousin put it, "Beat that stuff until the mixer begins to smoke." While it is not necessary to damage the mixer's motor, divinity does need to be beaten until it cools and stiffens, which is quite a bit longer than most people think. If a test candy spreads even slightly on the waxed paper after being dropped from a spoon, the candy has not been beaten long enough. Properly beaten divinity is usually so stiff that it is difficult to stir by hand.

Easy Divinity

1	jar (7 oz/198 g) marshmallow creme	1
2 cups	granulated sugar	500 mL
1/2 cup	water	125 mL
Pinch	salt	Pinch
1 tsp	vanilla extract	5 mL
1/2 cup	chopped pecans	125 mL

This mock divinity recipe is a delicious treat for those who do not want to take the time to beat the egg whites required for classic divinity.

Cook's Note

Once the cooked syrup and marshmallow creme are well blended, place the bowl in the freezer for 1 to 2 minutes to help the mixture cool and thicken. This step reduces the stirring time.

Skill Level: Average

Makes 18 to 20 pieces

- 1-quart saucepan
- Candy thermometer

1. Cover a countertop area or a large baking sheet with waxed paper. Spray with nonstick spray, if desired. Butter 2 small spoons.

2. Spoon the marshmallow creme into a heatproof bowl.

3. In saucepan over medium-high heat, bring the sugar, water and salt to a boil, stirring just until the sugar dissolves and the mixture begins to boil. Cook, without stirring, to the hard ball stage (250°F/121°C).

4. Remove the syrup from the heat. Gradually pour the hot syrup over the marshmallow creme in the bowl, stirring the marshmallow creme while adding the syrup. Stir by hand until the mixture begins to cool and stiffen.

5. Stir in the vanilla and pecans. Quickly drop the candy onto the waxed paper using the tip of a buttered spoon. Cool. Store in an airtight container at room temperature.

Down-Home Divinity

Part 1

3	extra-large or large egg whites	3
3 cups	granulated sugar	750 mL
1 cup	light (white) corn syrup	250 mL
3/4 cup	water	175 mL

Part 2

1 cup	granulated sugar	250 mL
1/2 cup	water	125 mL
1 tsp	vanilla extract	5 mL
2 cups	pecans, in large pieces	500 mL

> While two of my aunts agreed that this classic, two-step recipe was a favorite, they did not agree on what to do with the candy once it was cooked. Aunt Mary preferred to pack it into a buttered pan and cut it into squares, but Aunt Erma insisted that proper Southern divinity must be dropped from the tip of a buttered spoon. I agree with Erma but both methods work.

Cook's Notes

Experienced candy makers may prefer to beat the egg whites while Part I of the syrup is cooking.

The heat settings in this recipe were those my aunts used. Both syrups may be cooked over medium-high heat rather than medium-low heat if preferred.

If preferred, the divinity may be turned into a buttered 13- by 9-inch (33 by 23 cm) pan and cut into squares when firm.

- Heavy-duty electric stand mixer
- 2-quart saucepan
- Candy thermometer

1. See Tips for Making Divinity (page 79).

2. *To make Part 1:* Cover a large countertop area or 2 large baking sheets with waxed paper. Butter 2 small spoons.

3. In a large mixing bowl, beat the egg whites with a heavy-duty electric mixer on high speed until the egg whites form very stiff peaks, but not so long that they lose their gloss and become dry.

4. In saucepan over medium-low heat, bring the sugar, corn syrup and water to a boil, stirring just until the sugar dissolves and the mixture begins to boil. Cook, without stirring, to the hard ball stage (265°F/129°C).

5. Remove the syrup from the heat. Turn the electric mixer to medium-high speed and beat the egg whites again while gradually pouring the hot syrup in a thin stream over the top of the egg whites. Leave the mixer on while placing Part 2 over the heat, turning the mixer off when the mixture is well blended.

6. *To make Part 2:* In a very small saucepan over medium-low heat, bring the sugar and water to a boil, stirring just until the sugar dissolves and the mixture begins to boil. Cook, without stirring, to the hard ball stage (265°F/129°C).

7. Remove the syrup from the heat. Turn the electric mixer to medium-high speed and gradually pour the hot syrup over the top of the candy mixture, beating constantly. Continue beating while adding the vanilla. Beat with the electric mixer until the candy becomes slightly dull and holds its shape when dropped from a spoon.

8. Stir in the pecans by hand. Quickly drop the candy onto the waxed paper using the tip of a buttered spoon. Cool. Store in an airtight container at room temperature.

Sweetheart Divinity

5 cups	granulated sugar	1.25 L
1½ cups	light (white) corn syrup	375 mL
1½ cups	water	375 mL
2	extra-large or large egg whites	2
1 tsp	vanilla extract	5 mL
2 cups	coarsely chopped walnuts	500 mL

If you are sweet on sweets, this is the divinity recipe for you. It contains more sugar than any other divinity recipe in this collection.

Cook's Note

It is not essential to blend the sugar, syrup and water mixture in a separate bowl and leave several hours before making this recipe, but it is interesting to see the different ways that divinity can be made.

A Southern Favorite

In the early days, making divinity was quite a project. Not only did candy makers have to judge the syrup by look and by feel, but they also had to beat both the egg whites and the candy by hand until stiff. Those who owned modern handheld rotary beaters were considered the lucky ones.

With candy thermometers and electric mixers, divinity is now relatively simple to make. It remains a perennial favorite, with some loving the taste and some loving the tradition. Whether you make divinity in one step or two or prefer nuts or candied cherries, this collection will have y'all coming back for more.

Skill Level: Advanced

Makes about 60 pieces

- Heavy-duty electric stand mixer
- 3- to 4-quart saucepan
- Candy thermometer

1. See Tips for Making Divinity (page 79).
2. In a large mixing bowl, combine the sugar, corn syrup and water, stirring until well blended. Let the mixture stand at room temperature several hours or overnight if possible, stirring often. (See Cook's Note, left)
3. Cover a large countertop area or 2 large baking sheets with waxed paper. Butter 2 small spoons.
4. In a large mixing bowl, beat the egg whites with a heavy-duty electric stand mixer on high speed until the egg whites form very stiff peaks, but not so long that they lose their gloss and become dry.
5. Transfer the sugar mixture to saucepan. Bring the sugar mixture to a boil over medium-high heat, stirring just until the sugar dissolves and the mixture begins to boil. Cover and cook 2 minutes to dissolve the sugar crystals on the sides of the pan. Remove the lid. Cook, without stirring, to the firm ball stage (244°F/118°C).
6. Remove the syrup from the heat. Turn the electric mixer to medium-high speed and beat the egg whites again while gradually pouring half of the hot syrup over the top of the egg whites. Leave the mixer on while returning the remaining syrup to the heat, turning the mixer off when the mixture is well blended.
7. Cook the remaining syrup, without stirring, to the hard ball stage (260°F/127°C).
8. Remove the syrup from the heat. Turn the electric mixer to medium-high speed and gradually pour the remaining hot syrup over the top of the candy mixture, beating constantly. Continue beating while adding the vanilla. Beat with the electric mixer until the candy becomes slightly dull and holds its shape when dropped from a spoon.
9. Stir in the walnuts by hand. Quickly drop the candy onto the waxed paper using the tip of a buttered spoon. Cool. Store in an airtight container at room temperature.

Classic Divinity

2	extra-large or large egg whites	2
2 cups	granulated sugar	500 mL
1/2 cup	light (white) corn syrup	125 mL
1/2 cup	water	125 mL
1/8 tsp	salt	0.5 mL
1 tsp	vanilla extract	5 mL
1/2 cup	pecans, in large pieces	125 mL

Classic Divinity has the least amount of sugar of any of the divinity recipes in this collection. Try one of the fun variations.

Cook's Note

If preferred, the divinity may also be turned into a buttered pan and cut into squares when firm.

Variations

Chocolate Marbled Divinity: Substitute 3/4 cup (175 mL) semisweet chocolate chips for the nuts. The chocolate will melt as it is added to the candy mixture, creating a marbled effect.

Cherry Divinity: Reduce the amount of chopped pecans to 1/3 cup (75 mL). Stir in 1/3 cup (75 mL) well-drained, finely chopped maraschino cherries with the nuts. If preferred, use 1/3 cup (75 mL) sweetened flaked coconut or coarsely chopped walnuts in place of the pecans.

Orange Divinity: Stir in 3/4 cup (175 mL) chopped orange jelly candy slices or candied orange peel before dropping the pieces.

Makes 30 to 36 pieces

- Heavy-duty electric stand mixer
- 2-quart saucepan
- Candy thermometer

1. See Tips for Making Divinity (page 79).
2. Cover a large countertop area or a large baking sheet with waxed paper. Butter 2 small spoons.
3. In a large mixing bowl, beat the egg whites with a heavy-duty electric mixer on high speed until the egg whites form very stiff peaks, but not so long that they lose their gloss and become dry.
4. In saucepan over medium heat, bring the sugar, corn syrup, water and salt to a boil, stirring just until the sugar dissolves and the mixture begins to boil. Cover and cook 2 to 3 minutes to dissolve the sugar crystals on the sides of the pan. Remove the lid. Cook, without stirring, to the soft ball stage (234°F/112°C).
5. Remove the syrup from the heat. Turn the mixer to medium-high speed and beat the egg whites again while gradually pouring one-third of the hot syrup over the top of the egg whites. Leave the mixer on while returning the remaining syrup to the heat, turning the mixer off when the mixture is well blended.
6. Cook the remaining syrup, without stirring, to the soft crack stage (272°F/133°C).
7. Remove the syrup from the heat. Turn the electric mixer to medium-high speed and gradually pour the remaining hot syrup over the top of the candy mixture, beating constantly. Continue beating while adding the vanilla. Beat with the electric mixer until the candy becomes slightly dull and holds its shape when dropped from a spoon.
8. Stir in the pecans by hand. Quickly drop onto the waxed paper using the tip of a buttered spoon. Cool. Store in an airtight container at room temperature.

Louisiana Double Divinity Delight

4	extra-large or large egg whites	4
1/8 tsp	salt	0.5 mL
6 cups	granulated sugar	1.5 L
1 cup	light (white) corn syrup	250 mL
4 cups	water	1 L
1 tbsp	vanilla extract	15 mL
2 cups	chopped pecans	500 mL

> Occasionally, one of my cousins goes astray and finds a recipe that she thinks is better than her mother's. Such is the case with my cousin Margaret, whose mother helped make Down-Home Divinity (page 80), a family institution. Margaret's supersized, one-step divinity recipe is a sure winner, especially when entertaining large crowds down on the bayou.

Cook's Notes

Because of the volume of this recipe, it is essential to use a heavy-duty electric stand mixer such as a KitchenAid to beat the candy. Lighter models of electric mixers may not be able to manage this recipe without causing damage to the motors.

This divinity has a slightly softer center than recipes that cook the syrup to a higher temperature.

Skill Level: Advanced

Makes 70 to 90 small pieces

- 4- to 5-quart candy kettle or pot
- Candy thermometer

1. See Tips for Making Divinity (page 79).

2. Cover a large countertop area with newspapers or heavy brown wrapping paper to protect it from the heat and wax. Place waxed paper on top of the newspapers and spray with nonstick spray. Butter 2 small spoons.

3. In a large mixing bowl, beat the egg whites and salt with a heavy-duty electric mixer on high speed until the egg whites form very stiff peaks, but not so long that they lose their gloss and become dry.

4. In kettle over high heat, bring the sugar, corn syrup and water to a boil, stirring just until the sugar dissolves and the mixture begins to boil. Cook, without stirring, to the hard ball stage (250°F/121°C). Watch the thermometer closely; the temperature increases rapidly during the last 5°F (2°C) of cooking.

5. Remove the syrup from the heat. Turn the electric mixer to medium-high speed and beat the egg whites again while gradually pouring the hot syrup in a thin stream into the center of the egg whites. Beat with the electric mixer until the candy becomes slightly dull, stiffens and holds its shape when dropped from a spoon. When properly beaten, the mixture will look as if it has wrinkles in it and the wrinkles will lay flat and hold their shape.

6. Stir in the vanilla and nuts by hand. Quickly drop the candy onto the waxed paper using the tip of a buttered spoon. Cool. Store in an airtight container at room temperature.

Holiday Divinity

2	extra-large or large egg whites	2
2½ cups	granulated sugar	625 mL
½ cup	light (white) corn syrup	125 mL
½ cup	water	125 mL
¼ tsp	salt	1 mL
1 tsp	vanilla extract	5 mL
1 cup	coarsely chopped walnuts or pecans	250 mL
¼ cup	chopped candied cherries	60 mL
¼ cup	chopped candied pineapple	60 mL

This recipe puts a new twist on an old favorite by adding colorful candied fruits.

Cook's Note

For step-by-step photographs of making divinity, see color page E.

Skill Level: Advanced

Makes 30 to 36 pieces

- Heavy-duty electric stand mixer
- 1- to 2-quart saucepan
- Candy thermometer

1. See Tips for Making Divinity (page 79).

2. Cover a large countertop area or a large baking sheet with waxed paper. Butter 2 small spoons.

3. In a large mixing bowl, beat the egg whites with a heavy-duty electric stand mixer on high speed until the egg whites form very stiff peaks, but not so long that they lose their gloss and become dry.

4. In saucepan over medium-high heat, bring the sugar, corn syrup, water and salt to a boil, stirring just until the sugar dissolves and the mixture begins to boil. Cook, without stirring, to the firm ball stage (248°F/120°C).

5. Remove the syrup from the heat. Turn the electric mixer to medium-high speed and beat the egg whites again while gradually pouring half of the hot syrup over the top of the egg whites. Leave the mixer on while returning the remaining syrup to the heat, turning the mixer off when the mixture is well blended.

6. Cook the remaining syrup, without stirring, to the soft crack stage (272°F/133°C).

7. Remove the syrup from the heat. Turn the electric mixer to medium-high speed and gradually pour the remaining hot syrup over the top of the candy mixture, beating constantly. Continue beating while adding the vanilla. Beat with the electric mixer until the candy becomes slightly dull and holds its shape when dropped from a spoon.

8. Stir in the nuts and candied cherries and pineapple by hand. Quickly drop the candy onto the waxed paper using the tip of a buttered spoon. Cool. Store in an airtight container at room temperature.

Rainbow Divinity

2	extra-large or large egg whites	2
3 tbsp	strawberry-, cherry- or lime-flavored gelatin powder, about $1/2$ of 1 (3-ounce/85 g) package	45 mL
3 cups	granulated sugar	750 mL
$3/4$ cup	light (white) corn syrup	175 mL
$3/4$ cup	water	175 mL
Pinch	salt	Pinch
1 tsp	vanilla extract	5 mL
1 cup	chopped pecans	250 mL
$3/4$ cup	sweetened flaked coconut, tinted, if desired (see Cook's Notes, below) or $1/2$ cup (125 mL) chopped candied cherries (optional)	175 mL

> Every time I think of this recipe, I have visions of white-gloved ladies in pillbox hats carrying fluffy pastel candies to the church social. This fruit-flavored never-fail divinity recipe was popular in the 1960s and early 1970s.

Cook's Notes

To tint the coconut, place the coconut in a small plastic bag and sprinkle lightly with water. Add a few drops of food coloring to the bag. Seal the bag and shake well.

Because this recipe contains gelatin, this candy cools and sets very quickly, especially once the nuts and coconut are added. As a result, the best-looking candies are usually the first to be dropped. If preferred, do not stir the nuts and coconut into the candy. Instead, sprinkle these ingredients on the tops of the candies to decorate, lightly pressing them into the candies before they cool.

Skill Level: Advanced

Makes about 45 pieces

- Heavy-duty electric stand mixer
- 2-quart saucepan
- Candy thermometer

1. See Tips for Making Divinity (page 79).

2. Cover the countertop or 2 large baking sheets with waxed paper. Butter 2 spoons.

3. In a large mixing bowl, beat the egg whites with a heavy-duty electric stand mixer on high speed until the egg whites form very stiff peaks, but not so long that they lose their gloss and become dry. Gradually add the gelatin, beating constantly while adding. Beat until well blended; the mixture will be thin.

4. In saucepan over medium-high heat, bring the sugar, corn syrup, water and salt to a boil, stirring just until the sugar dissolves and the mixture begins to boil. Cook, without stirring, to the hard ball stage (250°F/121°C).

5. Remove the syrup from the heat. Turn the electric mixer to medium-high speed and beat the egg whites again while gradually pouring the hot syrup in a thin stream over the top of the egg white–gelatin mixture. Continue beating while adding the vanilla. Beat with the electric mixer until the candy holds its shape when dropped from a spoon.

6. Stir in the pecans and coconut or cherries, if using, by hand. Quickly drop from a buttered spoon onto waxed paper. Cool. Store in an airtight container at room temperature.

Sea Foam Candy

1	extra-large or large egg white	1
2 cups	packed light brown sugar	500 mL
$\frac{1}{2}$ cup	water	125 mL
$\frac{1}{2}$ tsp	vanilla extract	2 mL
$\frac{1}{2}$ cup	pecans, in large pieces	125 mL

Sea Foam Candy is a form of divinity made with brown sugar rather than granulated sugar. With a darker color and heavier texture than classic white divinity, this candy also carries a distinctive brown sugar flavor. Though few Southerners seem to be familiar with this candy, a New Jersey native told me that it was a part of her mother's holiday tradition.

Skill Level: Advanced
Makes about 36 pieces

- 1-quart saucepan
- Candy thermometer

1. See Tips for Making Divinity (page 79).
2. Cover a large countertop area or a large baking sheet with waxed paper. Butter 2 spoons.
3. In a small mixing bowl, beat the egg white with an electric mixer on high speed until the egg white forms very stiff peaks, but not so long that it loses its gloss and becomes dry.
4. In saucepan over medium-high heat, bring the sugar and water to a boil, stirring just until the sugar dissolves and the mixture begins to boil. Cook, without stirring, to the hard ball stage (250°F/121°C).
5. Remove the syrup from the heat. Turn the electric mixer to medium-high speed and beat the egg white again while gradually pouring the hot syrup in a thin stream over the top of the egg white. Continue beating while adding the vanilla. Beat with the electric mixer until the candy becomes slightly dull and holds its shape when dropped from a spoon. Do not overbeat this candy or it may become dry.
6. Stir in the pecans by hand. Quickly drop the candy onto the waxed paper using the tip of a buttered spoon. Cool. Store in an airtight container at room temperature.

Dainty Mint Puffs

1	extra-large or large egg white	1
1¹/₂ cups	granulated sugar	375 mL
2 tbsp	light (white) corn syrup	30 mL
¹/₄ cup	water	60 mL
¹/₄ tsp	peppermint or mint extract	1 mL
5	drops food coloring of choice	5

Perfect for a bridal or baby shower, these delightful pastel candies look like small bites of divinity but have a smooth and creamy mint center.

Skill Level: Advanced

Makes about 40 pieces

- 1-quart saucepan
- Candy thermometer

1. See Tips on Making Divinity (page 79).

2. Cover a large countertop area or large baking sheet with waxed paper. Butter 2 small spoons.

3. In a small mixing bowl, beat the egg white with an electric mixer on high speed until the egg white forms very stiff peaks, but not so long that it loses its gloss and becomes dry.

4. In saucepan over medium-high heat, bring the sugar, corn syrup and water to a boil, stirring just until the sugar dissolves and the mixture begins to boil. Cook, without stirring, to the soft ball stage (240°F/116°C).

5. Remove the syrup from the heat. Turn the electric mixer to medium-high speed and beat the egg white again while gradually pouring the hot syrup in a thin stream over the top of the egg white. Continue beating while adding the flavoring and food coloring, dropping the food coloring into the mixture a little at a time. Beat with the electric mixer until the candy becomes slightly dull and holds its shape when dropped from a spoon.

6. Quickly drop the candy onto waxed paper from the tip of a spoon, making pieces no larger than 1 inch (2.5 cm) in diameter. Cool. Store in an airtight container at room temperature.

Marshmallows

¼ cup	confectioner's (icing) sugar (approx.)	60 mL
2 tbsp	unflavored gelatin powder	30 mL
¾ cup	cold water	175 mL
2 cups	granulated sugar	500 mL
½ cup	hot water	125 mL
¾ cup	light (white) corn syrup	175 mL
	Few grains salt	
1 tsp	vanilla extract	5 mL
2 cups	confectioner's (icing) sugar (approx.), or finely chopped pecans or walnuts or sweetened flaked coconut for rolling	500 mL

Use your imagination and creativity to turn this treasured old recipe into any size, shape and color of marshmallows that you desire. Just add a little food coloring and pull out the cookie cutters, because the possibilities are endless.

Cook's Note

A 13- by 9-inch (33 by 23 cm) pan produces marshmallows about ¾-inch (2 cm) tall. For extra-tall marshmallows, use a 9-inch (23 cm) square pan. If preferred, the marshmallow mixture may be dropped by spoonfuls into a large pan generously coated with confectioner's sugar or into small molds generously dusted with confectioner's sugar. If using this method, work very quickly so that the marshmallow mixture does not set in the bowl.

Skill Level: Advanced

Makes about 1 lb (500 g) or 50 pieces depending on size

- 13- by 9-inch (33 by 23 cm) pan
- 1-quart saucepan
- Candy thermometer
- Heavy-duty electric stand mixer

1. Generously dust pan with confectioner's sugar. Using the back of a spoon, spread the sugar across the bottom and sides of the pan until the bottom surface is completely covered, using slightly more sugar if necessary.

2. In a small bowl, combine the gelatin and cold water, stirring to blend. Set aside.

3. In saucepan over medium heat, bring the granulated sugar, hot water, corn syrup and salt to a boil, stirring until the sugar dissolves and the mixture begins to boil. Cook, without stirring, to the soft ball stage (234°F to 240°F/112°C to 116°C, with 236°F/113°C recommended).

4. Remove from the heat. Stir in the gelatin mixture. Pour the combined mixture into a large mixing bowl. Using a heavy-duty electric stand mixer, beat the mixture on medium-high speed until it holds its shape, blending in the vanilla while beating. Pour the marshmallow mixture into the prepared pan. Let stand until firm, about 20 minutes.

5. Using a sharp knife or cookie cutters dipped in hot water, cut into squares, triangles or other shapes. Roll each marshmallow in confectioner's sugar, nuts or coconut, as desired. If using confectioner's sugar, tap the marshmallows lightly to remove the excess sugar. Store in an airtight container.

Variations

For tinted marshmallows, add a few drops of food coloring during beating. For flavored marshmallows, substitute ¾ cup (175 mL) fruit juice for the cold water used to dissolve the gelatin.

If preferred, the marshmallows can be dipped into melted chocolate.

Cherry-Nut Nougat

3	extra-large or large egg whites	3
5 cups	granulated sugar	1.25 L
1 cup	light (white) corn syrup	250 mL
1 cup	water	250 mL
1 cup	chopped walnuts, pecans, hazelnuts or pistachio nuts or sliced toasted almonds	250 mL
1 cup	candied cherries, chopped	250 mL

> Nougat is a chewy, white candy somewhat similar to divinity. This recipe can be adjusted for different tastes by using a variety of nuts or fruits. It is especially tasty when made with almond extract.

Variations

Candied pineapple, candied orange peel, raisins or similar ingredients may be substituted for the cherries.

Cherry-Almond Nougat: For a robust flavor, add 1 tsp (5 mL) pure almond extract to the candy mixture after adding the last of the syrup. Use 1 cup (250 mL) toasted sliced almonds for the nuts.

Skill Level: Advanced

Makes about 2½ lbs (1.25 kg)

- 9- by 5-inch (23 by 12.5 cm) loaf pan or mold
- Heavy-duty electric stand mixer
- 3-quart saucepan
- Candy thermometer

1. See Tips for Making Divinity (page 79).
2. Line loaf pan or mold with waxed paper, leaving a 1- to 2-inch (2.5 to 5 cm) overhang over the sides.
3. In a large mixing bowl, beat the egg whites with a heavy-duty electric stand mixer on high speed until the egg whites form very stiff peaks, but not so long that they lose their gloss and become dry.
4. In saucepan over medium-high heat, bring the sugar, corn syrup and water to a boil, stirring just until the sugar dissolves and the mixture begins to boil. Cook, without stirring, to the soft ball stage (234°F/112°C).
5. Remove the syrup from the heat. Turn the electric mixer to medium-high speed and beat the egg whites again while gradually pouring about 1 cup (250 mL) of the hot syrup over the top of the egg whites. Leave the mixer on while returning the remaining syrup to the heat, turning the mixer off when the mixture is well blended.
6. Cook the remaining syrup, without stirring, to the hard crack stage (300°F/149°C).
7. Remove the syrup from the heat. Turn the electric mixer to medium-high speed and gradually pour the remaining hot syrup over the top of the candy mixture, beating constantly. Beat just until the mixture begins to hold its shape. Do not overbeat or the candy may be dry.
8. Quickly stir in the nuts and cherries by hand. Immediately pack the candy into the lined pan or mold. Tightly cover the pan with plastic wrap or foil. Let the candy stand at room temperature 12 to 24 hours before cutting. The flavor improves if the candy ripens without being exposed to air.
9. To serve, invert the loaf pan or mold onto a cutting board. Remove the waxed paper and slice into pieces about ¾- to 1-inch (2 to 2.5 cm) thick. Cut each slice into cubes or squares. Each piece may be individually wrapped in plastic wrap or waxed paper, if desired. Store in an airtight container at room temperature.

Cowboy Date Roll

3 cups	granulated sugar	750 mL
2 tbsp	light (white) corn syrup	30 mL
$\frac{1}{4}$ tsp	salt	1 mL
$1\frac{1}{4}$ cups	half-and-half (10%) cream or evaporated milk	300 mL
1 cup	pitted dates, chopped or quartered	250 mL
1 cup	chopped pecans	250 mL
10	maraschino cherries, chopped and drained (optional)	10
$\frac{1}{2}$ cup	confectioner's (icing) sugar (optional)	125 mL

If you have not tried date roll candy, this is a good place to start. This semi-smooth version is my favorite of the two date roll recipes my mother used. My father preferred Dad's Date Loaf (page 92) for its more sugary texture.

Cook's Notes

The recipe may be reduced by half and cooked in a heavy 2-quart saucepan.

If the cooked candy is too soft to shape into a roll, work a little confectioner's (icing) sugar into the candy while kneading.

Skill Level: Advanced

Makes about 30 slices

- 3-quart heavy saucepan
- Candy thermometer

1. In heavy saucepan over low heat, bring the sugar, corn syrup, salt and half-and-half to a boil, stirring just until the sugar dissolves and the mixture begins to boil. Cover and cook 3 minutes to dissolve the sugar crystals on the sides of the pan. Remove the lid. Cook very slowly over low heat, without stirring, to the soft ball stage (234°F to 240°F/112°C to 116°C, with 238°F/114°C recommended). Add the dates and cook 1 minute longer, gently stirring to prevent the fruit from sticking together.

2. Remove from the heat. Cool to lukewarm (110°F/43°C), about 1 hour.

3. Dampen a clean dish towel (not terry cloth). Beat the candy by hand until it begins to stiffen. Add the pecans and cherries, if using. Finish beating by hand until creamy.

4. Turn the candy out onto the damp towel. Shape the candy into a roll about $1\frac{1}{4}$ inches (3 cm) in diameter. Wrap the candy in the damp towel and store in the refrigerator, slicing as needed. If desired, roll the candy in confectioner's sugar just before slicing.

Delicate Apricot Roll

3 cups	granulated sugar	750 mL
2 tbsp	light (white or golden) corn syrup	30 mL
1/4 tsp	salt	1 mL
1 cup	evaporated milk	250 mL
1 cup	finely chopped or ground dried apricots	250 mL
1 tsp	vanilla extract	5 mL
1/2 cup	chopped pecans	125 mL
1/2 cup	confectioner's (icing) sugar (optional)	125 mL

With the delicate flavor of apricots wrapped in rich, white cream, it is no wonder that family members say this candy is a favorite.

Cook's Notes

The recipe may be reduced by half and cooked in a heavy 2-quart saucepan.

If the cooked candy is too soft to shape into a roll, work a little confectioner's sugar into the candy while kneading.

Skill Level: Advanced

Makes about 30 slices

- 3-quart heavy saucepan
- Candy thermometer

1. In heavy saucepan over low heat, bring the sugar, corn syrup, salt and milk to a boil, stirring just until the sugar dissolves and the mixture begins to boil. Cover and cook 3 minutes to dissolve the sugar crystals on the sides of the pan. Remove the lid. Cook very slowly over low heat, without stirring, to the soft ball stage (234°F to 240°F/112°C to 116°C, with 238°F/114°C recommended).

2. Remove from the heat. Stir in the apricots and vanilla. Cool to lukewarm (110°F/43°C), about 1 hour.

3. Dampen a clean dish towel (not terry cloth). Beat the candy by hand until it begins to stiffen. Add the pecans. Finish beating by hand until creamy.

4. Turn the candy out onto the damp towel. Shape the candy into a roll about 1 1/4 inches (3 cm) in diameter. Wrap the candy in the damp towel and store in the refrigerator, slicing as needed. If desired, roll the candy in confectioner's sugar just before slicing.

Dad's Date Loaf

2½ cups	granulated sugar	625 mL
1 cup	milk (see Cook's Note, below)	250 mL
8 oz	pitted dates, chopped	250 g
¾ cup	chopped pecans or to taste	175 mL

Oh, how my father loved this sugary date loaf! Without a doubt, his favorite Christmas present came wrapped in a damp tea towel. This is one of two date loaf candies my mother made.

Cook's Note

Generally, it is best to use milk with minimum 2% fat for candies because the additional fat content helps produce a creamy texture. If preferred, experiment with lower fat milks to see if you notice a difference.

Skill Level: Advanced

Makes 25 to 30 slices

- 2-quart heavy saucepan
- Candy thermometer

1. In heavy saucepan over low to medium-low heat, bring the sugar, milk and dates to a boil, stirring until the sugar dissolves and the mixture begins to boil. Cover and cook 2 to 3 minutes to dissolve the sugar crystals on the sides of the pan, lifting the lid a few times to prevent the mixture from boiling over the sides of the pan. Cook, stirring only as needed to prevent scorching, to the soft ball stage (234°F to 240°F/112°C to 116°C, with 236°F/113°C to 238°F/114°C recommended).

2. Remove from the heat. Cool to lukewarm (110°F/43°C), 45 minutes to 1 hour.

3. Dampen a clean dish towel (not terry cloth). Beat the candy by hand until it begins to thicken and hold its shape.

4. Stir in the pecans and turn onto the damp towel. Shape the candy into a roll 2 inches (5 cm) in diameter. Wrap the candy in the damp towel and store in the refrigerator, slicing as needed. This candy will keep several weeks if tightly covered.

Variations

Aunt Erma's Date Loaf: Add ¼ cup (60 mL) light (white or golden) corn syrup when combining the sugar, milk and dates. Complete the recipe as described above.

Old-Fashioned Apricot Roll: Substitute 1 cup (250 mL) finely chopped dried apricots for the dates. Before beginning the recipe, cover the apricots with water and soak for about 30 minutes or until soft. Drain thoroughly. Do not cook the apricots with the sugar and milk. Add the apricots to the beaten candy along with the pecans.

Pioneer Date Loaf

2 cups	granulated sugar	500 mL
2 cups	packed light brown sugar	500 mL
1⅓ cups	milk (see Cook's Note, page 92)	325 mL
2 tbsp	butter or margarine	30 mL
1½ tsp	vanilla extract	7 mL
1 cup	chopped, pitted dates	250 mL
1 cup	chopped pecans (or ½ cup/125 mL each chopped pecans and chopped walnuts)	250 mL

This recipe came to me with the following note: "Stores well if there is any left."

Skill Level: Advanced

Makes 35 to 40 slices

- 3-quart heavy saucepan
- Candy thermometer

1. In a heavy saucepan over low to medium-low heat, bring the granulated and brown sugars and milk to a boil, stirring until the sugars dissolve and the mixture begins to boil. Cover and cook 2 to 3 minutes to dissolve the sugar crystals on the sides of the pan, lifting the lid a few times to prevent the mixture from boiling over the sides of the pan. Cook slowly to 234°F (112°C), stirring only as needed to prevent scorching. Add the butter. Cook, stirring just enough to blend in the butter, to the soft ball stage (234°F to 240°F/112°C to 116°C, with 236°F/113°C to 238°F/114°C recommended).

2. Remove from the heat. Dampen a clean dish towel (not terry cloth). Beat the candy by hand until it begins to thicken and hold its shape.

3. Stir in the vanilla, dates and nuts. Turn onto the damp towel. Shape the candy into a roll 2 inches (5 cm) in diameter. Wrap the candy in the damp towel and store in the refrigerator. Let the candy ripen 24 hours in the refrigerator, if desired, before serving, slicing as needed.

Variations

Five-Cup Date Roll: Omit the butter and vanilla extract. Use 1 cup (250 mL) each of granulated sugar, packed light brown sugar and milk. Cook to 238°F (114°C). Stir the dates and pecans into the beaten candy before shaping it into rolls.

Buttercup Date Roll: Omit the 2 tbsp (30 mL) butter and the vanilla extract. Use 1½ cups (375 mL) each of granulated sugar and packed light brown sugar and 1 cup (250 mL) milk. Cook to 238°F (114°C). Stir 1 tsp (5 mL) butter into the candy while beating. Stir the dates and pecans into the beaten candy before shaping it into rolls.

Delta Date Loaf

3 cups	granulated sugar	750 mL
1 cup	evaporated milk	250 mL
8 oz	pitted dates, chopped	250 g
1/4 cup	butter	60 mL
1 cup	chopped pecans	250 mL
1 tsp	vanilla extract (optional)	5 mL
1/4 tsp	salt (optional)	1 mL

Extra butter makes this date loaf extra special.

- 3-quart heavy saucepan
- Candy thermometer

1. In heavy saucepan over low to medium-low heat, bring the sugar, milk and dates to a boil, stirring until the sugar dissolves and the mixture begins to boil. Cook, stirring only as needed to prevent scorching, to the soft ball stage (234°F to 240°F/112°C to 116°C, with 240°F/116°C recommended).

2. Remove from the heat. Dampen a clean dish towel (not terry cloth). Add the butter, pecans and the vanilla and salt, if using. Beat by hand until the candy begins to thicken and hold its shape. Shape the candy into a roll 2 inches (5 cm) in diameter. Wrap the candy in the damp cloth and store in the refrigerator, slicing as needed.

Dreamy Date Roll

4 cups	granulated sugar	1 L
1	can (12 oz or 370 mL) evaporated milk	1
1/4 cup	butter or margarine	60 mL
1 lb	pitted dates, chopped	500 g
1	jar (7 oz/198 g) marshmallow creme	1
1 tsp	vanilla extract	5 mL
4 cups	chopped pecans	1 L

With a texture similar to fudge, this ultra-creamy candy is a date lover's dream.

- 15- by 10-inch (38 by 25 cm) jelly roll pan, buttered
- 5-quart heavy candy kettle or pot
- Candy thermometer

1. In heavy kettle over medium heat, bring sugar, milk and butter to a boil, stirring until sugar dissolves and mixture begins to boil. Cook, stirring constantly to prevent scorching, to soft ball stage (234°F to 240°F/112°C to 116°C, with 234°F/112°C recommended). Add dates and cook 1 to 2 minutes more, stirring to separate dates.

2. Remove from the heat. Add the marshmallow creme, stirring until well blended. Stir in the vanilla and pecans. Pour into the prepared pan to cool. Tear 3 large sheets of waxed paper.

3. When the candy is cool enough to handle, divide it into 3 portions, placing each portion on a large sheet of waxed paper. Shape the candy into 3 (2-inch/5 cm diameter) rolls. Cover and refrigerate until firm. To serve, bring the rolls to room temperature and slice into 1/2-inch (1 cm) slices. Store in an airtight container.

Granny's Extra-Sweet Date Roll

4 cups	granulated sugar	1 L
1 cup	milk (see Cook's Note, page 92)	250 mL
1 lb	pitted dates, chopped	500 g
1 tbsp	butter	15 mL
1 tsp	vanilla extract	5 mL
1 cup	chopped pecans	250 mL

This old-fashioned, sugary date roll can be made with a kitchen timer rather than a candy thermometer, though checking the temperature with either a candy thermometer or the soft ball test often helps ensure success.

Cook's Note

If desired, an additional 1 cup (250 mL) chopped pecans may be cooked with the candy.

Makes 35 to 40 slices

- 5-quart heavy candy kettle or pot
- Candy thermometer

1. In heavy kettle over low to medium-low heat, bring the sugar, milk, dates, butter and vanilla to a rolling boil, stirring until the sugar dissolves and the mixture begins to boil. Continue to boil, stirring as needed to prevent scorching, 8 minutes or to the soft ball stage (234°F to 240°F/112°C to 116°C, with 238°F/114°C recommended).

2. Remove from the heat. Cool slightly, about 10 minutes. Beat by hand until the candy is thick. Divide the candy into 2 parts; shape into 2 (about 1½-inch/4 cm diameter) rolls. Roll the candy in the pecans. Wrap the candy rolls in waxed paper and chill in the refrigerator 24 hours before serving. Store covered, slicing as needed.

Old-Fashioned Candy Rolls

The mere mention of homemade candy seems to spark fond memories, yet no one type of candy prompts more discussion among my friends than recipes for old-fashioned date rolls. Time and time again, people smile and tell of the special treat that Granny kept hidden in the refrigerator underneath an old, damp towel.

Those longing for Granny's candy can now savor it once again. Whether you are looking for an old favorite or a new one, this collection of date, apricot, pecan and peanut butter rolls is certain to hold something for everyone. Just remember to cook these candies slowly so that they will not become too sugary.

Caramel-Coated Date Roll

Date Roll

2 cups	granulated sugar	500 mL
1 cup	evaporated milk	250 mL
1 tbsp	light (white or golden) corn syrup	15 mL
8 oz	pitted dates, chopped	250 g
1 cup	chopped pecans	250 mL

Caramel Coating

1 lb	soft caramels	500 g
2 tbsp	evaporated milk	30 mL
1½ to 2 cups	chopped pecans	375 to 500 mL

The caramel coating may be used with this date roll recipe or with your own favorite version.

Makes 25 to 30 slices

- 2-quart heavy saucepan
- Candy thermometer

1. *To make the date roll:* In heavy saucepan over low to medium-low heat, bring the sugar, milk and corn syrup to a boil, stirring until the sugar dissolves and the mixture begins to boil. Cook, stirring only as needed to prevent scorching, to the soft ball stage (234°F to 240°F/112°C to 116°C, with 236°F/113°C to 238°F/114°C recommended).

2. Remove from the heat. Cool to lukewarm (110°F/43°C), 45 minutes to 1 hour. Beat the candy by hand until it begins to thicken and hold its shape. Stir in the dates and nuts. Shape the candy into 4 (1½- to 2-inch/4 to 5 cm diameter) rolls. Wrap the rolls in waxed paper and refrigerate until firm.

3. *To make the caramel coating:* In a large heavy skillet over low heat, melt the caramels and milk, stirring until smooth.

4. Spread the pecans onto a sheet of waxed paper.

5. *To coat:* Holding both ends of the chilled rolls with forks, dip the rolls into the hot caramel, rolling to coat. Quickly roll the dipped candy in the pecans. Let the rolls stand on waxed paper until the coating is firm. To store, tightly wrap the rolls in plastic wrap, aluminum foil or waxed paper, slicing as needed. The rolls may be stored in the refrigerator, if desired. Bring the candy to room temperature before slicing and serving.

Butterscotch Nut Marshmallows (page 32)

Fruit Fancies (page 34)

Clockwise from top left: Aunt Lucy's Extra-Buttery Brittle (page 43), Honey-Nut Popcorn (page 231), Lemon Curd Truffles (page 215), Blue Ribbon Turtles (page 200), Candied Citrus Peel (page 247), Lemon Curd Truffles, variation (page 215) and Hall of Fame Chocolate Fudge (page 126)

Marry Me Toffee (page 47)

Lollipops (page 57)

New Orleans Roasted Pecan Pralines (page 66)

Cherry-Nut Nougat (page 89) and Mom's Divinity (page 78)

Clockwise from top left: Glass Candy (page 54), Peppermint Taffy, white & pink variation (page 106), Lollipops (page 57) and Washington State Apple Squares (page 240)

Penuche Nut Roll

2 cups	granulated sugar	500 mL
1 cup	packed light brown sugar	250 mL
$\frac{1}{2}$ cup	light (white or golden) corn syrup	125 mL
1 cup	half-and-half (10%) cream or evaporated milk	250 mL
$1\frac{1}{2}$ cups	finely chopped pecans	375 mL

This recipe found stashed in my mother's collection is just as delicious as I hoped it would be. With a rich, robust, brown sugar flavor and an ultra-creamy texture, it instantly became a new favorite. Thank you, Barbara Younger, for contributing your special recipe to Mom's collection.

Skill Level: Advanced

Makes about $2\frac{1}{2}$ lbs (1.25 kg)

- Heatproof plate or platter, sprayed with nonstick spray
- 3-quart heavy saucepan
- Candy thermometer

1. In heavy saucepan over medium heat, bring the granulated and brown sugars, corn syrup and half-and-half to a boil, stirring just until the sugar dissolves and the mixture begins to boil. Reduce the heat to low. Cover and cook 2 to 3 minutes to dissolve the sugar crystals on the sides of the pan. Remove the lid. Cook over low heat, without stirring, to the soft ball stage (234°F to 240°F/112°C to 116°C, with 236°F/113°C recommended).

2. Remove from the heat. Cool to lukewarm (110°F/43°C), about 1 hour.

3. Beat the candy by hand until it is creamy and begins to hold its shape. Pour onto the prepared plate. Spread the pecans onto a sheet of waxed paper.

4. Divide the candy into 2 to 6 equal portions. As soon as the candy is cool enough to handle, take one portion and knead by hand until the candy is smooth and creamy. (The cooled candy may develop a hard crust and appear to be hopelessly ruined, but it will become creamy with just a few minutes of kneading.) Form the candy into a roll about $1\frac{1}{4}$ inches (3 cm) in diameter. Roll the candy in the chopped pecans. Repeat until all the candy is kneaded, shaped and rolled. Wrap each roll tightly in plastic wrap or foil, slicing as needed. The candy may be stored in the refrigerator, if desired. Bring to room temperature before serving.

Important Tip

In many recipes, it is important to be prepared for all the steps because timing can be critical. Have all ingredients available and ready to use, and have the pan, baking sheet, or surface prepared before you begin cooking.

Caramel Pecan Roll

Caramel

1/2 cup	granulated sugar	125 mL
1/2 cup	packed light brown sugar	125 mL
1/2 cup	light (white or golden) corn syrup	125 mL
1/4 cup	butter	60 mL
1 cup	heavy or whipping (35%) cream, divided	250 mL

Cream Candy Filling

2 cups	granulated sugar	500 mL
1/2 cup	light (white or golden) corn syrup	125 mL
1/2 cup	milk (see Cook's Notes, below)	125 mL
Pinch	salt	Pinch
2 tbsp	butter	30 mL
1 tsp	vanilla extract	5 mL
1 1/4 cups	finely chopped pecans, for coating	300 mL

> This recipe requires a little extra effort, but in the end, you will have a beautiful and delicious candy that will impress the worst of critics.

Cook's Notes

Generally, it is best to use milk with minimum 2% fat for candies because the additional fat content helps produce a creamy texture. If preferred, experiment with lower fat milks to see if you notice a difference.

While the caramel is cooling on the baking sheet and you're making the filling, keep checking the caramel temperature. You want to let it cool to the point where you can easily handle it but make sure it is still pliable. Once you cut it, lift all 4 rectangles at once, using a spatula if necessary to keep the rectangles in one piece, then roll with the filling as directed.

Makes about 2 1/2 lbs (1.25 kg)

- 15- by 10-inch (38 by 25 cm) jelly roll pan, buttered or sprayed with nonstick spray
- 2-quart heavy saucepan
- Heatproof plate or platter, sprayed with nonstick spray
- Candy thermometer

1. *To make the caramel:* In heavy saucepan over medium-low heat, bring the granulated and brown sugars, corn syrup, butter and 1/2 cup (125 mL) of the cream to a boil, stirring until the sugars dissolve and the mixture begins to boil. Slowly stir in the remaining 1/2 cup (125 mL) of cream. Cook, stirring occasionally to prevent scorching, to the firm ball stage (244°F/118°C to 248°F/120°C, with 246°F/119°C recommended).

2. Remove from the heat. Pour the caramel into the prepared pan, spreading in an even layer and making sure that it has straight corners and edges. (This is much easier to do than it sounds.) Let cool at room temperature just until set (see Cook's Notes, left).

3. *To make the filling:* In a clean heavy 2-quart saucepan over medium heat, bring the sugar, corn syrup, milk and salt to a boil, stirring until the sugar dissolves and the mixture begins to boil. Cook, stirring occasionally to prevent scorching, to the soft ball stage (234°F to 240°F/112°C to 116°C, with 238°F/114°C recommended).

4. Remove from the heat. Add the butter and vanilla. Beat by hand until the candy begins to hold its shape. Pour onto the prepared plate.

5. Divide the candy filling into four equal portions. As soon as the candy is cool enough to handle, take one portion and knead between your hands until smooth and creamy. (The cooled candy may develop a hard crust and appear to be hopelessly ruined, but it will become creamy with just a few minutes of kneading.) Form the kneaded candy into a log about 4 inches (10 cm) long.

6. *To assemble:* Cut the cooled caramel into 4 equal rectangles by making a cut in the vertical center of the caramel, then a cut in the horizontal center of the caramel. Place one rectangle on a sheet of waxed paper. Spread the pecans onto another sheet of waxed paper.

7. Place the kneaded candy log at one short end of the caramel rectangle, patting the log until the ends meet the edges the caramel. Roll up, wrapping the caramel around the roll into a cylinder. If, after rolling, a thinner roll is desired, gently stretch the cylinder from the center outward until it is the desired size.

8. Roll the cylinder in the pecans, pressing the nuts into the caramel coating. Wrap up in waxed paper, then tightly in foil.

9. Repeat with the remaining candy filling and caramel. Store wrapped tightly and covered in an airtight container. Slice as needed using a sharp knife and a sawing motion. The candy may be stored in the refrigerator, if desired. Bring to room temperature before serving.

Classic Pecan Roll

2¼ cups	granulated sugar	550 mL
3 tbsp	light (white) corn syrup	45 mL
1 cup	half-and-half (10%) cream	250 mL
1 tsp	vanilla extract	5 mL
1½ to 2 cups	finely chopped pecans	375 to 500 mL

This creamy, light-colored pecan-packed candy will certainly become a favorite with someone in your family, just as it did in mine.

Cook's Note

As an option, do not add the pecans to the candy. Form the candy into 2 long rolls and then roll the candy into the chopped pecans to coat.

Skill Level: Advanced

Makes about 2 lbs (1 kg)

- 3-quart heavy saucepan
- Candy thermometer

1. In heavy saucepan over medium heat, bring the sugar, corn syrup and half-and-half to a boil, stirring until the sugar dissolves and the mixture begins to boil. Cover and cook 2 to 3 minutes to dissolve the sugar crystals on the sides of the pan. Remove the lid. Cook, stirring only a few times to prevent scorching, to the soft ball stage (234°F to 240°F/112°C to 116°C, with 236°F/113°C recommended).

2. Remove from the heat. Cool about 10 minutes to reduce the beating time. Tear 2 large sheets of waxed paper.

3. Beat the candy by hand until it begins to stiffen and hold its shape. Stir in the vanilla and pecans. Divide the mixture into 2 parts, placing each half of the candy onto waxed paper. Form into 2 (about 2-inch/5 cm diameter) rolls and wrap in the waxed paper. Cool at room temperature. To store, wrap the candy rolls tightly in plastic wrap or foil and refrigerate, slicing as needed. If preferred, the sliced candy may be stored in an airtight container.

Peanut Butter–Cinnamon Roll

2 cups	granulated sugar	500 mL
3/4 cup	milk	175 mL
1 tbsp	ground cinnamon, for rolling, divided (approx.)	15 mL
1/4 cup	smooth peanut butter or to taste	60 mL
1/2 tsp	vanilla extract	2 mL

> Peanut butter fans will love this wonderful combination!

Cook's Notes

This recipe can be made in a heavy 2-quart saucepan but may boil over the sides of the pan if not carefully watched.

The candy may appear very dry until it is kneaded. If it is still too dry after kneading, sprinkle a few drops of half-and-half (10%) cream or milk onto the roll and knead until well blended. If the candy is too sticky, add a little confectioner's (icing) sugar during kneading.

Skill Level: Advanced

Makes about 2 lbs (1 kg)

- 3-quart heavy saucepan
- Candy thermometer

1. In heavy saucepan over medium-low to medium heat, bring the sugar and milk to a boil, stirring until the sugar dissolves and the mixture begins to boil. Cover and cook 2 to 3 minutes to dissolve the sugar crystals on the sides of the pan. Remove the lid. Cook, stirring occasionally to prevent scorching, to the soft ball stage (234°F to 240°F/112°C to 116°C, with 236°F/113°C recommended).

2. Remove from the heat. Cool 20 minutes. Tear 2 large sheets of waxed paper. Sprinkle half of the cinnamon on each sheet of waxed paper.

3. Stir the peanut butter and vanilla into the candy. Beat by hand until the candy thickens and loses its gloss. Turn half of the mixture out of the pan onto another sheet of waxed paper. Knead by hand until smooth. Shape into a roll about $1\frac{1}{2}$ inches (4 cm) in diameter; roll the log in cinnamon. Repeat with the remaining candy and cinnamon. Wrap the rolls tightly in plastic wrap or waxed paper. Store in an airtight container, slicing as needed.

Peanut Butter–Apricot Roll

3 cups	granulated sugar	750 mL
1/2 cup	peanut butter	125 mL
1 cup	milk (see Cook's Note, below)	250 mL
1 cup	finely chopped dried apricots	250 mL
1/2 tsp	salt	2 mL
1/2 cup	confectioner's (icing) sugar, for rolling (approx.)	125 mL
2 tsp	vanilla extract	10 mL

This unusual blend of peanut butter and apricots may remind you of another old-time favorite, peanut butter and jelly.

Cook's Note

Generally, it is best to use milk with minimum 2% fat for candies because the additional fat content helps produce a creamy texture. If preferred, experiment with lower fat milks to see if you notice a difference.

Skill Level: Advanced

Makes about 3 lbs (1.5 kg)

- 3- or 4-quart heavy saucepan
- Candy thermometer

1. In heavy saucepan over medium-low heat, bring the sugar, peanut butter, milk, apricots and salt to a boil, stirring until the sugar dissolves and the mixture begins to boil. Cook, without stirring, to the soft ball stage (234°F to 240°F/112°C to 116°C, with 236°F/113°C recommended).

2. Remove from the heat. Cool to lukewarm (110°F/43°C), about 1 hour. Cover a large countertop area with waxed paper; sprinkle lightly with confectioner's sugar.

3. Add the vanilla to the candy. Beat by hand until the candy loses its gloss and begins to hold its shape. Pour onto the sugared waxed paper. Form into 2 (about 1 1/2 inch/4 cm diameter) rolls. Wrap tightly in waxed paper, plastic wrap or foil. Let stand at room temperature until firm. Slice as needed. Store in an airtight container.

Potato Candies

Potato Fondant

2 tbsp	unseasoned mashed potatoes	30 mL
	Few grains salt	
	Few drops vanilla extract or other extract	
1 to 2	drops food coloring	1 to 2
1½ cups	sifted confectioner's (icing) sugar (approx.)	375 mL

Seniors often remember Potato Fondant with great fondness. One woman said that it was a common after-dinner treat when she was a young girl, just as it was when her mother was a child. Each child in the family took turns choosing what color the candy would be and decorating it in creative and unusual ways.

Cook's Note

Omit the salt if using seasoned mashed potatoes leftover from a meal.

Skill Level: Novice, Super Simple

Makes about 1 cup (250 mL)

1. In a small mixing bowl, combine the potatoes, salt and vanilla. Tint the mixture with a small amount of food coloring, if desired. Gradually add the sugar, blending until the mixture has the consistency of fondant (similar to pie dough). Knead the candy by hand until smooth. Use this candy as a fondant for wafers or as a filling.

Variations

Rainbow Wafers: Dust a sheet of waxed paper with confectioner's (icing) sugar. Place the Potato Fondant on the waxed paper; cover with another sheet of waxed paper. Roll the fondant to wafer thinness, about ¼ inch (0.5 cm) thick. Using a cookie cutter, cut the fondant into small, round wafers or into other shapes, as desired. If desired, decorate the tops of each wafer with a whole almond or pecan or walnut half. Let the wafers dry before storing in an airtight container. The wafers will become hard and somewhat brittle.

Nut Creams: Press a small ball of Potato Fondant between 2 pecan or walnut halves. Store in an airtight container.

Stuffed Dates: Remove the seeds from the dates by making a cut along the side. Fill the cavity of each date with a small amount of fondant. Roll the filled dates in granulated sugar. Store in an airtight container.

If desired, a few tbsp (30 mL) of finely chopped nuts or sweetened flaked coconut may be worked into the fondant.

Potato Kisses

½ cup	unseasoned hot mashed potatoes	125 mL
1 tsp	butter or margarine	5 mL
1 lb	confectioner's (icing) sugar, sifted	500 g
½ tsp	almond extract	2 mL
¾ cup + 2 tbsp	sweetened flaked coconut	205 mL

Filled with coconut, these candies are surprisingly delicious.

Skill Level: Novice, Super Simple

Makes about 18

1. Cover a countertop area or a large baking sheet with waxed paper.

2. In a medium mixing bowl, combine the mashed potatoes and butter, mixing well. Gradually add the confectioner's sugar, blending until smooth. Stir in the almond extract and coconut. Drop by spoonfuls onto the waxed paper. Cool. Store in an airtight container.

Variations

Chocolate Spud Buds: Omit the almond extract. Use ⅔ cup (150 mL) hot mashed potatoes and 2 tsp (10 mL) butter. Add 2½ tbsp (37 mL) unsweetened cocoa powder with the confectioner's sugar. Stir in a pinch salt and 1 tsp (5 mL) vanilla extract with the coconut.

Chocolate Tater Tots: Substitute vanilla extract for the almond extract. Press the candy into a small buttered pan. When the candy has cooled, spread 2 to 3 oz (60 to 90 g) melted semisweet chocolate on top of the candy. Cover and refrigerate until the chocolate is firm. Cut into squares.

Chocolate Mash: Omit the almond extract and the coconut. Add 3 to 4 tbsp (45 to 60 mL) unsweetened cocoa powder with the confectioner's sugar. Stir in ½ tsp (2 mL) vanilla extract and 1 cup (250 mL) chopped nuts before dropping the candies onto the waxed paper.

Potato Pinwheels

1	medium cooked potato, peeled, buttered and mashed	1
1 lb	confectioner's (icing) sugar, sifted	500 g
1 tsp	vanilla extract	5 mL
1¼ cups	smooth peanut butter	300 mL
½ cup	chopped pecans, walnuts or peanuts	125 mL

> Peanut butter lovers will love the pinwheels cut from this fondant-wrapped candy roll.

Potato Candies

Once quite popular as an after-dinner treat with our grandparents and great-grandparents, potato candies are now somewhat of a novelty, with only a handful of lucky people knowing how delicious they can be. For another potato candy, try Wacky Potato Fudge (page 135).

Skill Level: Novice, Super Simple

Makes about 2 lbs (1 kg)

1. In a medium mixing bowl, let the potato stand until cool. Gradually add the confectioner's sugar, blending with the potato until the mixture has a consistency similar to pie dough. Stir in the vanilla, blending well. Place the potato dough on a sheet of waxed paper; cover with another sheet of waxed paper. Roll the potato dough into a rectangle the thickness of pie dough, about ¼ inch (0.5 cm) thick.

2. Remove the top layer of the waxed paper. Spread the peanut butter on top of the potato. Sprinkle the nuts on top of the peanut butter layer, gently pressing them into the peanut butter. Beginning at the long side of the rectangle, roll the candy jelly roll fashion. Seal the waxed paper tightly and cover again in foil. Refrigerate overnight. To serve, slice into ¼-inch (0.5 cm) slices. Store tightly wrapped in the refrigerator.

White Taffy

2 cups	granulated sugar	500 mL
1/2 cup	light (white) corn syrup	125 mL
2/3 cup	water	150 mL
1 tsp	vanilla extract	5 mL

Much like hard candy, this very old recipe produces a mild, vanilla-flavored hard taffy that is distinctively different from most commercially available taffies.

Cook's Note

For step-by-step photographs of making taffy, see color page H.

Skill Level: Average

Makes about 1 lb (500 g)

- 15- by 10-inch (38 by 25 cm) jelly roll pan or large heatproof platter, generously buttered
- 2-quart saucepan
- Candy thermometer

1. In saucepan over medium heat, bring the sugar, corn syrup and water to a boil, stirring until the sugar dissolves and the mixture begins to boil. Cook, without stirring, to the hard crack stage, 300°F (149°C).

2. Remove from the heat. Stir in the vanilla. Pour the candy onto the prepared pan. Cool just until the taffy can be handled, 10 to 15 minutes. Do not allow the candy to cool too long or it will harden.

3. With generously buttered hands, pull and stretch the taffy until the candy changes texture and becomes opaque. Stretch the candy into a long rope, twisting the rope as you pull. Using kitchen shears or a sharp knife, cut the rope into small pieces, turning or twisting the rope again after each cut. Wrap each piece of taffy in waxed paper. Store at room temperature.

Peppermint Taffy

2 cups	granulated sugar	500 mL
1 cup	water	250 mL
1 cup	light (white) corn syrup	250 mL
1 tsp	salt	5 mL
$\frac{1}{2}$ tsp	glycerin	2 mL
2 tsp	butter or margarine	10 mL
$\frac{1}{2}$ tsp	peppermint extract	2 mL
$\frac{1}{4}$ to $\frac{1}{2}$ tsp	red food coloring, optional	1 to 2 mL

> Though not as soft as the taffy I loved as a child, this sticky, chewy candy is my favorite of the homemade taffy recipes.

Cook's Notes

For step-by-step photographs of making taffy, see color page H.

Glycerin can be purchased in the pharmacy section of most large grocery stores and in craft stores that sell cake and candy supplies.

Other extracts may be substituted for the peppermint extract and other food colorings may be used in place of red. If preferred, the food coloring may be omitted entirely, leaving the taffy white.

Keep a glass or a bowl filled with cool water nearby while pulling the candy so that you can quickly dip your hands into the water if the hot candy sticks to your fingers.

Skill Level: Average

Makes about 1$\frac{1}{2}$ lbs (750 g)

- 15- by 10-inch (38 by 25 cm) jelly roll pan or large heatproof platter, generously buttered
- 2-quart heavy saucepan
- Candy thermometer

1. In heavy saucepan over medium heat, bring the sugar, water, corn syrup, salt and glycerin to a boil, stirring until the sugar dissolves and the mixture begins to boil. Cook, without stirring, to the mid–hard ball stage, 258°F (126°C).

2. Remove from the heat. Add the butter, peppermint extract and food coloring, if using, stirring until the butter melts and the food coloring is well blended. Pour the hot candy onto the prepared pan. Cool just until the taffy can be handled, 10 to 15 minutes. Do not allow the candy to cool too long or it will set in the pan.

3. With generously buttered hands, pull and stretch the taffy until the candy changes texture and becomes opaque. Stretch it into a long rope, twisting the rope as you pull. Using kitchen shears or a sharp knife, cut the rope into small pieces. Wrap each piece of taffy in waxed paper. Store at room temperature.

Storing Candy

Most candies should be stored in an airtight container to keep them fresh. Unless specifically instructed in the recipe, refrigeration is often a matter of personal choice, but generally, most fudges and fudge-like candies should keep at least 1 week at room temperature and at least 1 month, sometimes much longer, if refrigerated. Excessive heat, high humidity, or added ingredients such as fruit may shorten the storage time so it is important to use common sense. If the color or texture of the candy has changed, dispose of it and make a fresh batch.

Molasses Taffy

½ cup	granulated sugar	125 mL
6 tbsp	packed light brown sugar	90 mL
1 cup	light (fancy) molasses (see Glossary, page 20)	250 mL
½ cup	water	125 mL
2 tbsp	butter or margarine	30 mL
⅛ tsp	salt	0.5 mL
Pinch	baking soda	Pinch

The combination of brown sugar and molasses gives this old-fashioned taffy a robust flavor.

Cook's Note

For step-by-step photographs of making taffy, see color page H.

Skill Level: Average

Makes about 1 lb (500 g)

- 15- by 10-inch (30 by 20 cm) rimmed baking sheet, generously buttered
- 4-quart heavy saucepan
- Candy thermometer

1. In saucepan over medium heat, bring the granulated and brown sugars, molasses and water to a boil, stirring until the sugars dissolve and the mixture begins to boil. Cook to the soft crack stage, 272°F (133°C), stirring frequently to prevent scorching.

2. Remove from the heat. Add the butter, salt and baking soda, stirring just enough to mix well. Pour onto the prepared baking sheet. Cool just until the candy can be handled, for 10 to 15 minutes.

3. With generously buttered hands, pull the taffy until it is firm and lightened to a golden brown color. Stretch it into a rope (or a few ropes), twist and cut into 1-inch (2.5 cm) lengths. Wrap each piece of taffy in waxed paper.

Molasses Foam Taffy

1 cup	granulated sugar	250 mL
1 cup	light (fancy) molasses (see Glossary, page 20)	250 mL
2 tbsp	cider vinegar	30 mL
¼ cup	butter (about the size of an egg)	60 mL
1 tsp	baking soda	5 mL

This unusual old recipe does not require pulling the candy after it is cooked.

Skill Level: Average

Makes about ½ lb (250 g)

- Large baking sheet, buttered
- 5-quart heavy saucepan
- Candy thermometer

1. In saucepan over medium heat, bring the sugar, molasses, vinegar and butter to a boil, stirring until the sugar dissolves and the mixture begins to boil. Cook, without stirring, to the soft ball stage (234°F to 240°F/112°C to 116°C, with 240°F/116°C recommended).

2. Remove from the heat. Add the baking soda. Beat by hand with a wire egg beater or a slotted spoon until the mixture is light and foamy.

3. Pour the mixture onto the prepared baking sheet. Refrigerate until firm. Turn the candy onto waxed paper and break into pieces with a hammer or a mallet. Wrap each piece of taffy in waxed paper. Store at room temperature.

Brown Sugar Taffy

1 cup	packed light brown sugar	250 mL
½ cup	light (white or golden) corn syrup	125 mL
1½ tbsp	butter or margarine	22 mL
1 tbsp	cider vinegar	15 mL

Those who like the robust flavor of brown sugar may prefer this recipe.

Taffy

When it comes to pulling taffy, the more the merrier, for it is important to pull the taffy before the candy hardens and sets. Make a party of it, letting each set of hands take a small amount of candy to stretch, manipulate and shape into a rope. Children can participate with adult supervision, but remember to use caution; hot taffy can burn fingers and hands very quickly.

Cook's Note

For step-by-step photographs of making taffy, see color page H.

Skill Level: Average
Makes about ½ lb (250 g)

- 15- by 10-inch (38 by 25 cm) jelly roll pan or large platter, generously buttered
- 2-quart saucepan
- Candy thermometer

1. In saucepan over medium heat, bring the brown sugar, corn syrup, butter and vinegar to a boil, stirring until the sugar dissolves and the mixture begins to boil. Cook, without stirring, to the hard ball stage, 260°F (127°C).

2. Remove from the heat. Pour the candy onto the prepared pan. Cool just until the taffy can be handled, 10 to 15 minutes. Do not allow the candy to cool too long or it will harden.

3. With generously buttered hands, pull and stretch the taffy until the candy changes texture and becomes opaque. Stretch the candy into a long rope, twisting the rope as you pull. Using kitchen shears or a sharp knife, cut the rope into small pieces, turning or twisting the rope again after each cut. Wrap each piece of taffy in waxed paper. Store at room temperature.

Old-Fashioned Taffy

3/4 cup	granulated sugar	175 mL
1 1/4 cups	light (fancy) molasses	300 mL
1 tbsp	cider vinegar	15 mL
1 tbsp	butter or margarine	15 mL
1/8 tsp	baking soda	0.5 mL
Pinch	salt	Pinch

If you ever wondered what your grandparents or great-grandparents did on their first date, you can imagine that they may have held an old-fashioned taffy pull with a molasses-based recipe such as this one.

- 15- by 10-inch (38 by 25 cm) jelly roll pan or large heatproof platter, generously buttered
- 3-quart saucepan
- Candy thermometer

1. In saucepan, combine the sugar, molasses and vinegar, stirring to mix. Let stand 10 to 20 minutes, stirring occasionally until the sugar dissolves. Bring to a boil over medium-low heat. Cook, without stirring, to 270°F (132°C).

2. Remove from the heat. Stir in the butter, baking soda and salt. Pour into the prepared platter. Cool just until the taffy can be handled, 10 to 15 minutes. Do not allow the candy to cool too long or it will harden.

3. With generously buttered hands, pull and stretch the taffy until the color lightens. Form into a long rope. Using kitchen shears or a sharp knife, cut the rope into small pieces. Wrap each piece of taffy in waxed paper. Store at room temperature.

The Taffy Pull

One day when I was about nine years old, I told my mother how much I loved the taffy sold at the local swimming pool snack bar. A package of taffy cost a nickel in those days and the summer heat made the candy just soft enough that I could tear off a piece and mold it into any shape I wanted before popping it into my mouth. As far as I was concerned, it was the perfect ending to a carefree summer afternoon.

When I told Mom about my love for this taffy, she smiled, stood up from her chair, and said, "We don't have to buy taffy. We can make taffy!" This was news to me, but soon I found myself in the kitchen, watching my mother's magic. She placed her candy pot on the stove, carefully measured and added ingredients and began that calming, lazy stirring motion that seemed to define her personality.

Before long, our homemade taffy was ready to be pulled, stretched and manipulated into a rope. As we stood facing each other with well-buttered hands and a string of hot candy draped between us, she began to tell of her childhood and how families would gather for community taffy pulls as a way to pass the time. "This was in the day before electricity or television," she reminded me, "and we had to make our own fun."

In the end, Mom's stories were just as entertaining as the candy.

Make Mine Fudge

Penuches

Other Fudges

One of the most celebrated romances in history is our enduring love affair with sweet, creamy fudge. This extraordinary confection captured our hearts long ago, enticing us with its flawless silky texture and daring us to resist.

Our passion may be deep dark chocolate, German's by Baker's, milder sweet chocolate or the luxurious taste of velvety white chocolate that so many of us adore. We dream of fudge rich with maple, peanut butter, butterscotch or buttermilk, while others flirt with orange, lemon or gorgeous flecks of tropical pineapple wrapped in thick white cream. We rendezvous with eggnog, spicy pumpkin or brown sugar penuche to find our perfect match, indulging in our love for apricot, cranberry and coffee along the way.

This extraordinary confection captured our hearts long ago, enticing us with its flawless silky texture and daring us to resist.

We welcome the familiar and court the unusual, tossing in sweetened flaked coconut, bright red cherries or freshly shelled pecans as we please, stacking layer upon layer and combining two favorites for those who cannot choose.

We recall the sweet times shared with our favorite homemade candy, knowing that few other romances are as comforting as ours. We thank our grandmothers for their old-fashioned recipes and our mothers for the simpler versions made with marshmallow creme, scanning them all to find our favorite.

Private Collection Fudge

1 cup	milk	250 mL
2 oz	unsweetened chocolate, finely chopped	60 g
3 cups	granulated sugar	750 mL
1/4 cup	light (white or golden) corn syrup	60 mL
1/8 tsp	salt	0.5 mL
1 tsp	cider vinegar	5 mL
2 tbsp	butter	30 mL
1 tsp	vanilla extract	5 mL
1/2 to 1 cup	chopped walnuts or pecans (optional)	125 to 250 mL

> I have been known to hide this extra-sweet, extra-creamy fudge in the back of my refrigerator where only I can find it. The kneaded chocolate rolls make a wonderful gift if you are willing to share.

Skill Level: Advanced

Makes about 2 lbs (1 kg)

- Large platter, buttered
- 3-quart heavy saucepan
- Candy thermometer

1. In heavy saucepan over low heat, combine the milk and chocolate, stirring constantly until the milk is hot and the chocolate is completely melted.

2. Remove from the heat temporarily. Stir in the sugar, corn syrup and salt. Place over medium heat and bring to a boil, stirring just until the sugar dissolves. Reduce the heat to medium low. Cover and cook 2 to 3 minutes to dissolve the sugar crystals on the sides of the pan. Remove the lid. Cook at a slow, steady boil over low or medium-low heat, without stirring, to the soft ball stage (234°F to 240°F/112°C to 116°C, with 238°F/114°C recommended).

3. Remove from the heat. Gently stir in the vinegar. Add the butter without stirring. Cool to lukewarm (110°F/43°C), about 1 hour.

4. Add the vanilla. Beat by hand until the candy begins to thicken and hold its shape. Stir in the nuts, if desired. Pour onto the prepared platter. Cool 20 to 30 minutes or until the candy can be handled without sticking to your hands and then knead by hand for 5 minutes.

5. Shape the candy into 2 (1 1/2-inch/4 cm diameter) rolls or logs. Wrap tightly in plastic wrap. Store, covered, in a cool, dry place or in the refrigerator until ready to serve. To serve, cut into thin slices.

Aunt Erma's Legendary 'Til It's Done Fudge

2 cups	granulated sugar	500 mL
Scant ½ cup	unsweetened cocoa powder	Scant 125 mL
Scant ⅓ cup	light (white or golden) corn syrup	Scant 75 mL
1 cup	half-and-half (10%) cream	250 mL
1 tbsp	butter	15 mL
1 tsp	vanilla extract	5 mL
½ cup	chopped pecans or sweetened flaked coconut (optional)	125 mL

Makes about 1¼ lbs (625 g)

- 9- by 5-inch (23 by 12.5 cm) pan, buttered
- 10- to 12-inch (25 to 30 cm) heavy skillet
- Candy thermometer

1. In heavy skillet over low heat, bring the sugar, cocoa, corn syrup and half-and-half to a boil, stirring until the sugar dissolves and the mixture begins to boil. Cook at a slow, steady boil over low heat, without stirring, to the soft ball stage (234°F to 240°F/112°C to 116°C, with 234°F/112°C recommended).

2. Remove from the heat. Add the butter and vanilla. Beat by hand until the candy begins to hold its shape and feels heavy. Add the pecans, if desired. Pour into the prepared pan. Cool and cut into pieces. Store in an airtight container.

Cook's Note

This fudge has a very deep chocolate flavor. The amount of cocoa may be reduced, if desired.

Storing Candy

Most candies should be stored in an airtight container to keep them fresh. Unless specifically instructed in the recipe, refrigeration is often a matter of personal choice, but generally, most fudges and fudge-like candies should keep at least 1 week at room temperature and at least 1 month, sometimes much longer, if refrigerated. Excessive heat, high humidity, or added ingredients such as fruit may shorten the storage time so it is important to use common sense. If the color or texture of the candy has changed, dispose of it and make a fresh batch.

If you are born into a family overflowing with children, you must find a way to distinguish yourself lest you become lost in a sea of look-alike faces. For my aunt Erma, the eighth of my grandparents' ten children, fame came in the form of fudge. Aunts, uncles and cousins alike declare that Erma's fudge was the best they ever tasted. Coming from a family that produced several dozen outstanding cooks and twice as many critics, this is quite a compliment.

A few years ago, I called Erma's daughter in hopes of learning the secret behind this legendary fudge. This is what my cousin said.

"Take a skillet, put everything in it except the vanilla and cook it."

"How long?" I asked.

"'Til it's done."

Some of us were born with internal timers that ding when fudge is ready. I did not inherit that gene.

Grace's Walnut Butter Fudge

2 cups	granulated sugar	500 mL
6 tbsp	unsweetened cocoa powder	90 mL
3/4 cup	water	175 mL
1/2 cup	butter	125 mL
1 tsp	vanilla extract	5 mL
1/2 to	coarsely chopped walnuts	125 to
1 cup		250 mL

> Grace's fudge is as legendary with hometown friends as Aunt Erma's fudge is with my family. This buttery, chocolate satin candy is worth every step.

Cook's Notes

For a firmer fudge, cook to 238°F (114°C).

Many recipes in this book contain nuts, and in most cases the type of nuts and the quantity is left up to the candy maker. For example, I prefer to use walnuts in fudge, but others prefer pecans. Some people do not want any nuts in their candies, and usually nuts can be omitted entirely without affecting the candy. This is particularly true of fudge.

Skill Level: Advanced

Makes about 1 1/4 lbs (625 g)

- 9- by 5-inch (23 by 12.5 cm) loaf pan, lined with parchment (see Cook's Notes, page 116) or buttered
- 3-quart heavy saucepan
- Candy thermometer

1. Have a medium to large clean, dry mixing bowl available.

2. In heavy saucepan, combine the sugar and cocoa until well blended. Slowly stir in the water. Bring to a boil over low heat, stirring until the sugar dissolves and the mixture begins to boil. Cover and cook 3 minutes to dissolve the sugar crystals on the sides of the pan, lifting the lid a few times to prevent the mixture from boiling over the sides. Remove the lid. Add the butter without stirring. Cook at a slow, steady boil over low heat, without stirring, to the soft ball stage (234°F to 240°F/112°C to 116°C, with 236°F/113°C recommended).

3. Remove from the heat. Pour into a clean, dry mixing bowl without scraping the sides of the saucepan. Cool to lukewarm (110°F/43°C), about 1 hour, without stirring the candy or moving the bowl.

4. Add the vanilla. Beat by hand until the candy begins to thicken and lose its gloss. Immediately stir in the nuts and turn into the prepared pan. (This candy sets very quickly.) Cool and cut into squares. Store in an airtight container.

Old-Fashioned Chocolate Fudges

These classic recipes represent candy making at its finest. Those who can turn out a perfect batch of sweet, creamy, old-fashioned fudge without timers or thermometers are at the top of their craft. Often the secret is slow cooking, plus experience, precision and a great deal of skill. Fortunately, those of us who are fudge challenged can also be experts if we cheat and use a candy thermometer.

Granny's Best Fudge

3 cups	granulated sugar	750 mL
1 cup	milk	250 mL
3 oz	unsweetened chocolate, finely chopped	90 g
½ cup	light (white or golden) corn syrup	125 mL
¼ cup	butter	60 mL
1 tsp	vanilla extract	5 mL
1 cup	pecans, in large pieces (optional)	250 mL

Sweet, creamy and loaded with chocolate, this recipe from our great-grandmothers comes with an old-fashioned hug.

Cook's Notes

Cutting candy becomes much easier with the use of parchment paper. Rather than buttering the pan directly, butter a piece of parchment paper larger than the pan and press it into the bottom and up the sides of the pan, tucking and creasing the paper as needed to create corners, and leaving a generous overhang over the sides of the pan.

For a firmer fudge, cook to 240°F (116°C).

Skill Level: Advanced
Makes about 2 lbs (1 kg)

- 8-inch (20 cm) square pan, lined with parchment (see Cook's Notes, left) or buttered
- 3-quart heavy saucepan
- Candy thermometer

1. In heavy saucepan over medium-low heat, bring the sugar, milk, chocolate and corn syrup to a boil, stirring until the sugar dissolves and the mixture begins to boil. Cover and cook 2 to 3 minutes to dissolve the sugar crystals on the sides of the pan. Cook, without stirring, to the soft ball stage (234°F to 240°F/112°C to 116°C, with 238°F/114°C recommended).

2. Remove from the heat. Add the butter without stirring. Cool 20 minutes. Add the vanilla. Beat by hand until the candy thickens and holds its shape. Stir in the pecans, if desired. Pour into the prepared pan. Cool and cut into squares. Store in an airtight container.

Jolly Good Fudge

²/₃ cup	milk	150 mL
1 oz	unsweetened chocolate, finely chopped	30 g
2 cups	granulated sugar	500 mL
1 tbsp	light (white or golden) corn syrup	15 mL
Pinch	salt	Pinch
2 tbsp	butter	30 mL
1 tsp	vanilla extract	5 mL
1 cup	pecans or walnuts, in large pieces (optional)	250 mL

Sometimes a name says it all and this one is no exception. This soft, medium chocolate fudge is one of my favorites.

Cook's Note

For a darker chocolate fudge, use up to 2 oz (60 g) unsweetened chocolate.

Skill Level: Advanced

Makes 1½ lbs (750 g)

- 9- by 5-inch (23 by 12.5 cm) loaf pan, lined with parchment (see Cook's Notes, page 116) or buttered
- 2-quart heavy saucepan
- Candy thermometer

1. In heavy saucepan, combine the milk and chocolate over low heat, stirring constantly, until the chocolate is completely melted. Stir in the sugar, corn syrup and salt. Bring to a boil over low heat, stirring until the sugar dissolves and the mixture begins to boil. Cover and cook 2 to 3 minutes to dissolve the sugar crystals on the sides of the pan. Remove the lid. Cook at a slow, steady boil over low heat, without stirring, to the soft ball stage (234°F to 240°F/112°C to 116°C, with 236°F/113°C recommended).

2. Remove from the heat. Add the butter without stirring. Cool 20 minutes.

3. Add the vanilla. Beat by hand until the candy thickens, loses its gloss and begins to hold its shape. Stir in the nuts. Pour into the prepared loaf pan. Cool and cut into squares. Store in an airtight container.

Variation

If preferred, 3 to 4 tbsp (45 to 60 mL) unsweetened cocoa powder may be substituted for the unsweetened chocolate. Combine the sugar and cocoa in the saucepan until well blended and then stir in the milk, corn syrup and salt. Cook as directed.

Old-Time Cocoa Fudge

2 cups	granulated sugar	500 mL
¼ cup	unsweetened cocoa powder	60 mL
¼ cup	light (white or golden) corn syrup	60 mL
1 cup	milk	250 mL
3 tbsp	butter	45 mL
1 tsp	vanilla extract	5 mL

If you like traditional fudge with a moderate amount of chocolate flavor, try this classic combination.

Skill Level: Advanced

Makes about 1½ lbs (750 g)

- 9- by 5-inch (23 by 12.5 cm) loaf pan, lined with parchment (see Cook's Note, page 121) or buttered
- 2-quart heavy saucepan
- Candy thermometer

1. In heavy saucepan, combine the sugar and cocoa until well blended. Stir in the corn syrup and milk. Bring to a boil over low heat, stirring until the sugar dissolves and the mixture begins to boil. Cover and cook 2 to 3 minutes to dissolve the sugar crystals on the sides of the pan. Remove the lid. Cook at a slow, steady boil over low heat, without stirring, to the soft ball stage (234°F to 240°F/112°C to 116°C, with 238°F/114°C recommended).

2. Remove from the heat. Add the butter without stirring. Cool to lukewarm (110°F/43°C), 45 minutes to 1 hour.

3. Add the vanilla to the saucepan. Beat by hand until the candy thickens, loses its gloss and begins to hold its shape. Pour into the prepared pan. Cool and cut into squares. Store in an airtight container.

Important Tip

In many recipes, it is important to be prepared for all the steps because timing can be critical. Have all ingredients available and ready to use, and have the pan, baking sheet, or surface prepared before you begin cooking.

Bullet Fudge

2¼ cups	granulated sugar	550 mL
5 tbsp	unsweetened cocoa powder	75 mL
1½ tbsp	light (white or golden) corn syrup	22 mL
½ cup	milk	125 mL
6 tbsp	butter or margarine	90 mL
1 tsp	vanilla extract	5 mL
½ cup	pecans, in large pieces (optional)	125 mL

> This candy cooks more quickly than most old-fashioned fudges. The original recipe called for boiling the candy mixture rapidly for 1 minute, but I prefer to rely on a candy thermometer. Try it both ways and see which method you prefer.

Skill Level: Advanced

Makes about 1¾ lbs (875 g)

- 9- by 5-inch (23 by 12.5 cm) loaf pan, lined with parchment (see Cook's Note, page 121) or buttered
- 2-quart heavy saucepan
- Candy thermometer

1. In heavy saucepan, combine the sugar and cocoa until well blended. Stir in the corn syrup, milk and butter. Bring to a boil over medium heat, stirring until the sugar dissolves and the mixture begins to boil. Continue to boil, stirring occasionally to prevent scorching, to the soft ball stage (234°F to 240°F/112°C to 116°C, with 236°F/113°C recommended), 4 to 5 minutes.

2. Remove from the heat. Cool 20 to 30 minutes. Add the vanilla and pecans, if desired. Beat by hand until the candy thickens, loses its gloss and begins to hold its shape. Pour into the prepared pan. Cool and cut into squares. Store in an airtight container.

Storing Candy

Most candies should be stored in an airtight container to keep them fresh. Unless specifically instructed in the recipe, refrigeration is often a matter of personal choice, but generally, most fudges and fudge-like candies should keep at least 1 week at room temperature and at least 1 month, sometimes much longer, if refrigerated. Excessive heat, high humidity, or added ingredients such as fruit may shorten the storage time so it is important to use common sense. If the color or texture of the candy has changed, dispose of it and make a fresh batch.

Sweet Milk Fudge

1 cup	granulated sugar	250 mL
1 cup	packed light brown sugar	250 mL
1½ tbsp	unsweetened cocoa powder	22 mL
Pinch	salt	Pinch
½ cup	light (white or golden) corn syrup	125 mL
½ cup	milk	125 mL
2 tbsp	butter	30 mL
1 tsp	vanilla extract	5 mL
1 cup	pecans, in large pieces (optional)	250 mL

Few ingredients hint at a recipe's age quite like "sweet milk," meaning the fresh, unspoiled milk that we now take for granted. Even in the 1940s, electricity was not available in many parts of rural America, making fresh milk somewhat rare. Women like my grandmother routinely cooked with buttermilk, canned milk or soured clabber milk, saving precious sweet milk for their children to drink. Only the most special of recipes might be honored with fresh, sweet milk, because it usually involved trudging to a barn and milking an unfriendly cow named Bessie.

One bite of this light chocolate fudge may explain why women were once willing to fend off rain, hail, sleet and snow to make this spectacular candy. The soft, smooth texture is nothing short of divine.

Skill Level: Advanced

Makes about 1½ lbs (750 g)

- 9- by 5-inch (23 by 12.5 cm) loaf pan, lined with parchment (see Cook's Note, page 121) or buttered
- 2-quart heavy saucepan
- Candy thermometer

1. In heavy saucepan over medium heat, bring the granulated and brown sugars, cocoa, salt, corn syrup, milk and butter to a boil, stirring until the sugars dissolve and the mixture begins to boil. Reduce the heat to low or medium low. Cover and cook 2 to 3 minutes to dissolve the sugar crystals on the sides of the pan, lifting the lid a few times to prevent the mixture from boiling over. Remove the lid. Cook at a slow, steady boil over low or medium-low heat, without stirring, to the soft ball stage (234°F to 240°F/112°C to 116°C, with 236°F/113°C recommended).

2. Remove from the heat. Add the vanilla. Beat by hand until the candy thickens and begins to hold its shape. Stir in the pecans, if desired. Pour into the prepared pan. Cool and cut into squares. Store in an airtight container.

Extra-Chocolaty Brown Sugar Fudge

2 cups	granulated sugar	500 mL
2 cups	packed light brown sugar	500 mL
1½ cups	milk	375 mL
¼ cup	light (white or golden) corn syrup	60 mL
4 oz	unsweetened chocolate, finely chopped	125 g
6 tbsp	butter	90 mL
2 tsp	vanilla extract	10 mL
1½ cups	pecans, in large pieces (optional)	375 mL

The combination of brown sugar and an extra dose of chocolate gives this candy a different flavor from many old-fashioned fudges.

Cook's Note

Cutting candy becomes much easier with the use of parchment paper. Rather than buttering the pan directly, butter a piece of parchment paper larger than the pan and press it into the bottom and up the sides of the pan, tucking and creasing the paper as needed to create corners, and leaving a generous overhang over the sides of the pan.

Skill Level: Advanced

Makes about 4 lbs (2 kg)

- 13- by 9-inch (33 by 23 cm) pan, lined with parchment (see Cook's Note, left) or buttered
- 5-quart heavy candy kettle or pot
- Candy thermometer

1. In heavy candy kettle over medium heat, bring the granulated and brown sugars, milk, corn syrup and chocolate to a boil, stirring until the sugars dissolve and the mixture begins to boil. Reduce the heat to medium low. Cover and cook 2 to 3 minutes to dissolve the sugar crystals on the sides of the pan. Remove the lid. Cook, stirring only as needed to prevent scorching, at a slow, steady boil over medium-low heat to the soft ball stage (234°F to 240°F/112°C to 116°C, with 238°F/114°C recommended).

2. Remove from the heat. Add the butter without stirring. Cool to lukewarm (110°F/43°C), about 1 hour.

3. Add the vanilla. Beat by hand until the candy thickens and begins to hold its shape. Stir in the nuts, if desired. Pour into the prepared pan. Cool and cut into squares. Store in an airtight container.

Jo-Joe's Million-Dollar Fudge

2 cups	semisweet chocolate chips (12 oz/375 g)	500 mL
4 oz	sweet chocolate (preferably German's by Baker's), coarsely chopped	125 g
1	jar (7 oz/198 g) marshmallow creme	1
5 cups	granulated sugar	1.25 L
1	can (12 oz or 370 mL) evaporated milk	1
½ cup	butter or margarine	125 mL
3 cups	pecans, in large pieces (optional)	750 mL
1 tsp	vanilla extract (optional)	5 mL

One advantage to being from a huge family is that you have an endless supply of cousins willing to share fabulous recipes. This extra creamy medium chocolate fudge is a favorite with cousins Jo and Joe of Winthrop, Arkansas.

Cook's Note

Cutting candy becomes much easier with the use of parchment paper. Rather than buttering the pan directly, butter a piece of parchment paper larger than the pan and press it into the bottom and up the sides of the pan, tucking and creasing the paper as needed to create corners, and leaving a generous overhang over the sides of the pan.

Skill Level: Average

Makes about 6 lbs (3 kg)

- 13- by 9-inch (33 by 23 cm) pan, lined with parchment (see Cook's Note, left) or buttered
- 5-quart heavy candy kettle or pot
- Candy thermometer

1. In a large mixing bowl, combine the chocolate chips, sweet chocolate and marshmallow creme. Set aside.

2. In heavy candy kettle over medium heat, bring the sugar and milk to a rolling boil, stirring until the sugar dissolves and the mixture begins to boil. Continue to boil rapidly, stirring constantly to prevent scorching, 5 minutes or until the mixture reaches the soft ball stage (234°F to 240°F/112°C to 116°C, with 234°F/112°C to 236°F/113°C recommended).

3. Remove from the heat. Stir in the butter until melted. Pour the hot mixture over the chocolate and marshmallow creme mixture. Stir until the chocolates and marshmallow creme are melted and the mixture is smooth and well blended. Stir in the pecans and vanilla, if desired. Pour into the prepared pan (it will be very tall). Cool and cut into squares. Store in an airtight container.

Important Tip

In many recipes, it is important to be prepared for all the steps because timing can be critical. Have all ingredients available and ready to use, and have the pan, baking sheet, or surface prepared before you begin cooking.

Charlotte's Extra-Good, Extra-Wicked Fudge

4½ cups	granulated sugar	1.125 L
1	can (12 oz or 370 mL) evaporated milk	1
½ cup	butter or margarine	125 mL
2 cups	semisweet chocolate chips (12 oz/375 g)	500 mL
18 oz	milk chocolate bars, chopped (see Cook's Notes, below)	540 g
1	large jar (13 oz/367 g) marshmallow creme	1
3 cups	coarsely chopped walnuts or pecans (optional)	750 mL
1 tsp	vanilla extract	5 mL

When I first began writing this book, I asked people to sample different recipes I planned to include. As one man bit into this extra delicious, extra creamy light chocolate confection, I said, "This is one of my favorite recipes. I got it from my hometown friend Charlotte. She calls it Extra-Good Fudge."

The man quickly shot back, "You should call it extra wicked."

Cook's Notes

For step-by-step photographs, see color page C.

For this amount of chocolate I recently used two 7 oz (210 g) chocolate bars and one 4 oz (125 g) bar for the 18 oz total. Or use 12 bars (each 1.55 oz/44 g).

This is a soft fudge and often cuts best if slightly chilled first. This candy will stay moist and delicious for at least 4 weeks if stored in an airtight container in the refrigerator.

Skill Level: Average

Makes about 7 lbs (3.5 kg)

- 13- by 9-inch (33 by 23 cm) pan, lined with parchment (see Cook's Notes, page 122) or buttered
- 5-quart heavy candy kettle or pot
- Candy thermometer

1. In heavy candy kettle over medium heat, bring the sugar, milk and butter to a rolling boil, stirring until the sugar dissolves and the mixture begins to boil. Continue to boil rapidly, stirring constantly to prevent scorching, until the mixture reaches the soft ball stage (234°F to 240°F/112°C to 116°C, with 236°F/113°C recommended), about 10 minutes.

2. Remove from the heat. Stir in the chocolate chips and milk chocolate until nearly melted. Add the marshmallow creme and stir until the chocolate is completely melted and the mixture is smooth and well blended. If desired, use an electric mixer on medium speed to beat the candy in the kettle 1 to 2 minutes to thoroughly blend the ingredients. Stir in the nuts, if desired, and vanilla. Pour into the prepared pan and smooth top (it will be very tall). Cool and cut into squares. Store in an airtight container.

Marshmallow Chocolate Fudges

Until about the early 1940s, old-fashioned slow-cooked fudge was the only kind of fudge that most people knew to make. Today we have a wonderful selection of quick marshmallow and marshmallow creme–based chocolate fudge recipes that can be made in a matter of minutes. I love to tell friends that I can produce 6 to 7 pounds (3 to 3.5 kg) of melt-in-your-mouth fudge faster than they can bake two dozen cookies.

Aunt Mary's Favorite Fudge

3 cups	semisweet chocolate chips (about 18 oz/540 g)	750 mL
1	jar (7 oz/198 g) marshmallow creme	1
1 cup	butter or margarine	250 mL
1 tsp	vanilla extract	5 mL
4½ cups	granulated sugar	1.125 L
1	can (12 oz or 370 mL) evaporated milk	1
2 cups	pecans, in large pieces (optional)	500 mL

My mother recalled this as the first recipe for marshmallow creme fudge to appear in her kitchen. Her sister Mary came across it while living in California during World War II and said that it was the best fudge she ever tasted. Aunt Mary treated her family to this candy for the next 45 years.

Skill Level: Average

Makes about 5 lbs (2.5 kg)

- 13- by 9-inch (33 by 23 cm) pan, lined with parchment (see Cook's Note, page 122) or buttered
- 5-quart heavy candy kettle or pot
- Candy thermometer

1. In a large mixing bowl, combine the chocolate chips, marshmallow creme, butter and vanilla. Set aside.

2. In heavy candy kettle over medium heat, bring the sugar and milk to a rolling boil, stirring until the sugar dissolves and the mixture begins to boil. Continue to boil rapidly, stirring constantly to prevent scorching, or until the mixture reaches the soft ball stage (234°F to 240°F/112°C to 116°C, with 234°F/112°C recommended).

3. Pour the hot mixture into the bowl over the chocolate and marshmallow creme mixture. Beat 2 minutes with an electric mixer. Stir in the pecans, if desired, and pour into the prepared pan. Cool and cut into squares. Store in an airtight container.

Variation

Ozark Mountain Fudge: For a lighter chocolate fudge, substitute 1 jar (13 oz/367 g) marshmallow creme for the 7 oz (198 g) jar. Add an additional 1 cup (250 mL) pecans.

Margaret's Double Fantasy Fudge

6 cups	granulated sugar	1.5 L
1⅓ cups	evaporated milk	325 mL
1½ cups	butter or margarine	375 mL
4 cups	semisweet chocolate chips (1½ lbs/750 g)	1 L
1	jar (13 oz/367 g) marshmallow creme	1
2 cups	pecans, in large pieces, or more to taste (optional)	500 mL
2 tsp	vanilla extract	10 mL

My cousin Margaret keeps plenty of this medium chocolate fudge on hand to feed her Louisiana friends and neighbors during the holidays.

Cook's Note

If you like small, flat squares then use a bigger pan such as the 13- by 9-inch (33 by 23 cm) one, or for large recipes like Margaret's, use two pans. If you like tall, thick, elegant-looking candy then use smaller pans. I like the tall version myself — it's easier to butter and cut one pan than two and it's easier to store in many containers, plus taller candy has more eye appeal. See also Guide to Selecting Candy Pans, page 6.

Skill Level: Average
Makes about 7 lbs (3.5 kg)

- Two 9-inch (23 cm) square pans, lined with parchment (see Cook's Note, left) or buttered
- 5-quart heavy candy kettle or pot
- Candy thermometer

1. In heavy candy kettle over medium heat, bring the sugar, milk and butter to a rolling boil, stirring until the sugar dissolves and the mixture begins to boil. Continue to boil rapidly, stirring constantly to prevent scorching, 5 minutes or until the mixture reaches the soft ball stage (234°F to 240°F/112°C to 116°C, with 234°F/112°C recommended).

2. Remove from the heat. Stir in the chocolate chips until melted. Add the marshmallow creme and stir until the mixture is smooth and well blended. Stir in the pecans, if desired, and vanilla. Pour into the prepared pans, dividing equally (it will be very tall). Cool and cut into squares. Store in an airtight container in the refrigerator or at room temperature.

Hall of Fame Chocolate Fudge

4½ cups	granulated sugar	1.125 L
1	can (12 oz or 370 mL) evaporated milk	1
¼ cup	butter	60 mL
Pinch	salt	Pinch
2 cups	semisweet chocolate chips (12 oz/375 g)	500 mL
12 oz	sweet baking chocolate (preferably German's by Baker's), coarsely chopped	375 g
1	jar (7 oz/198 g) marshmallow creme	1
2 cups	pecans or walnuts, in large pieces (optional)	500 mL
1 tsp	vanilla extract (optional)	5 mL

An instant hit with friends and family, this wonderfully smooth, deep chocolate fudge is destined for the chocolate lover's hall of fame. Thanks to my cousin Margaret, all of us can now enjoy her friend Ruby's special recipe.

Cook's Note

Cutting candy becomes much easier with the use of parchment paper. Rather than buttering the pan directly, butter a piece of parchment paper larger than the pan and press it into the bottom and up the sides of the pan, tucking and creasing the paper as needed to create corners, and leaving a generous overhang over the sides of the pan.

Skill Level: Average

Makes about 6 lbs (3 kg)

- 13- by 9-inch (33 by 23 cm) pan, lined with parchment (see Cook's Note, left) or buttered
- 5-quart heavy candy kettle or pot
- Candy thermometer

1. In heavy candy kettle over medium heat, bring the sugar, milk, butter and salt to a rolling boil, stirring until the sugar dissolves and the mixture begins to boil. Continue to boil rapidly, stirring constantly to prevent scorching, 6 minutes or until the mixture reaches the soft ball stage (234°F to 240°F/112°C to 116°C, with 236°F/113°C recommended).

2. Remove from the heat. Stir in the chocolate and marshmallow creme until melted and well blended. Add the nuts and vanilla, if desired. Pour into the prepared pan (it will be very tall). Cool and cut into squares. Store in an airtight container.

Important Tip

In many recipes, it is important to be prepared for all the steps because timing can be critical. Have all ingredients available and ready to use, and have the pan, baking sheet, or surface prepared before you begin cooking.

Famous Fudge

3 cups	granulated sugar	750 mL
1 cup	evaporated milk	250 mL
1/2 cup	margarine	125 mL
2 cups	semisweet chocolate chips (12 oz/375 g)	500 mL
1 cup	marshmallow creme	250 mL
1 tsp	vanilla extract	5 mL
1 cup	pecans or walnuts, in large pieces (optional)	250 mL

With a deeper chocolate flavor than many marshmallow creme fudges, it is no wonder this version is such a winner. Just for fun, try substituting almond extract for the vanilla extract and 3/4 cup (175 mL) sliced toasted almonds for the pecans or walnuts.

Skill Level: Average

Makes 2½ to 3 lbs (1.25 to 1.5 kg)

- 13- by 9-inch (33 by 23 cm) or 9-inch (23 cm) square pan, lined with parchment (see Cook's Note, page 126) or buttered
- 5-quart heavy candy kettle or pot
- Candy thermometer

1. In heavy candy kettle over medium heat, bring the sugar, milk and margarine to a rolling boil, stirring until the sugar dissolves and the mixture begins to boil. Cook, stirring constantly to prevent scorching, to the soft ball stage (234°F to 240°F/112°C to 116°C, with 236°F/113°C recommended).

2. Remove from the heat. Stir in the chocolate chips and marshmallow creme until melted and well blended. Add the vanilla and the nuts, if desired. Pour into the prepared pan. Cool and cut into squares. Store in an airtight container.

Five-Minute Fudge

1⅔ cups	granulated sugar	400 mL
⅔ cup	evaporated milk	150 mL
½ tsp	salt	2 mL
1 cup	semisweet chocolate chips or butterscotch chips	250 mL
1½ cups	miniature marshmallows	375 mL
1 tsp	vanilla extract	5 mL

This simple, medium-chocolate fudge can be made using a kitchen timer. Depending on the chips you choose, it can be either chocolate or butterscotch.

Skill Level: Average

Makes about 2 lbs (1 kg)

- 8-inch (20 cm) square pan, lined with parchment (see Cook's Note, page 126) or buttered
- 3-quart heavy saucepan
- Candy thermometer

1. In heavy saucepan over medium heat, bring the sugar, milk and salt to a rolling boil, stirring until the sugar dissolves and the mixture begins to boil. Continue to boil rapidly, stirring constantly to prevent scorching, 5 minutes. (If using a candy thermometer, the temperature should be approximately 226°F/108°C, which is below the soft ball range.)

2. Remove from the heat. Stir in the chocolate chips until melted. Add the marshmallows and stir until the marshmallows melt and the mixture is smooth and well blended. Stir in the vanilla. Pour into the prepared pan. Cool and cut into squares. Store in an airtight container.

Christmas Fudge

2 cups	granulated sugar	500 mL
2/3 cup	evaporated milk	150 mL
1 cup	semisweet chocolate chips	250 mL
10	large marshmallows, quartered	10
1/2 cup	margarine or butter	125 mL
1 tsp	vanilla extract	5 mL
1 cup	pecans or walnuts, in large pieces (optional)	250 mL

By using marshmallows rather than marshmallow creme, this medium chocolate fudge puts one more spin on a classic recipe.

Makes about 1 1/2 lbs (750 g)

- 8-inch (20) square pan, lined with parchment (see Cook's Note, page 126) or buttered
- 3-quart heavy saucepan
- Candy thermometer

1. In heavy saucepan over medium-low heat, bring the sugar and milk to a rolling boil, stirring until the sugar dissolves and the mixture begins to boil. Continue to boil rapidly, stirring constantly to prevent scorching, 6 minutes or until the mixture reaches the soft ball stage (234°F to 240°F/112°C to 116°C, with 234°F/112°C recommended).

2. Remove from the heat. Stir in the chocolate chips until melted. Add the marshmallows, butter and vanilla and stir until the marshmallows melt and the mixture is smooth and well blended. Stir in the nuts, if desired. Pour into the prepared pan. Cool and cut into squares. Store in an airtight container.

Extra-Firm Fudge

2 1/4 cups	granulated sugar	550 mL
1 cup	evaporated milk	250 mL
1/4 cup	butter or margarine	60 mL
16	large marshmallows	16
1/4 tsp	salt	1 mL
1 cup	semisweet chocolate chips	250 mL
1 tsp	vanilla extract	5 mL

Extra chocolaty and extra firm, this recipe adds the marshmallows during cooking.

Cook's Note

This fudge is very firm when cooked to 234°F (112°C). For a slightly softer version, cook to 232°F (111°C) or add a few more marshmallows.

Makes about 2 lbs (1 kg)

- 8-inch (20 cm) square pan, lined with parchment (see Cook's Note, page 126) or buttered
- 5-quart heavy candy kettle or pot
- Candy thermometer

1. In heavy candy kettle over medium heat, bring the sugar, milk, butter, marshmallows and salt to a rolling boil, stirring until the sugar dissolves and the mixture begins to boil. Cook, stirring constantly to prevent scorching, to the soft ball stage (234°F to 240°F/112°C to 116°C, with 234°F/112°C recommended).

2. Remove from the heat. Add the chocolate chips and vanilla and stir until the chocolate is melted and the mixture is smooth and well blended. Pour into the prepared pan. Cool and cut into squares. Store in an airtight container.

Marshmallow Cocoa Fudge

2 cups	granulated sugar	500 mL
2 tbsp	unsweetened cocoa powder	30 mL
1 cup	milk	250 mL
2 tbsp	marshmallow creme	30 mL
1 tsp	vanilla extract	5 mL
½ cup	coarsely chopped pecans or walnuts (optional)	125 mL

> This intriguing recipe combines elements of old-fashioned fudge with marshmallow creme, producing a soft, light chocolate candy that is quite sweet and creamy.

Skill Level: Advanced

Makes about 1½ lbs (750 g)

- 9- by 5-inch (23 by 12.5 cm) loaf pan, lined with parchment (see Cook's Note, page 126) or buttered
- 3-quart heavy saucepan
- Candy thermometer

1. In heavy saucepan over medium heat, combine the sugar and cocoa, stirring until well blended. Stir in the milk. Bring to a rolling boil, stirring until the sugar dissolves and the mixture begins to boil. Cook, stirring frequently to prevent scorching, to the soft ball stage (234°F to 240°F/112°C to 116°C, with 234°F/112°C recommended).

2. Remove from the heat. Add the marshmallow creme and vanilla without stirring. Let cool slightly, about 5 minutes, to reduce the beating time. Beat by hand until the candy thickens, loses its gloss and begins to hold its shape. Stir in the nuts, if desired. Pour into the prepared pan. Cool and cut into squares. Store in an airtight container.

Storing Candy

Most candies should be stored in an airtight container to keep them fresh. Unless specifically instructed in the recipe, refrigeration is often a matter of personal choice, but generally, most fudges and fudge-like candies should keep at least 1 week at room temperature and at least 1 month, sometimes much longer, if refrigerated. Excessive heat, high humidity, or added ingredients such as fruit may shorten the storage time so it is important to use common sense. If the color or texture of the candy has changed, dispose of it and make a fresh batch.

Rocky Road Fudge

40	large marshmallows, divided	40
4 cups	granulated sugar	1 L
1	can (12 oz or 370 mL) evaporated milk	1
2 cups	semisweet chocolate chips (12 oz/375 g)	500 mL
1/4 cup	butter or margarine	60 mL
1 1/2 cups	pecans or walnuts, in large pieces	375 mL
1 tsp	vanilla extract	5 mL

Chunks of marshmallows coated
in chocolate make this fudge
a real kid pleaser.

Cook's Note

Cutting candy becomes much easier with the use of parchment paper. Rather than buttering the pan directly, butter a piece of parchment paper larger than the pan and press it into the bottom and up the sides of the pan, tucking and creasing the paper as needed to create corners, and leaving a generous overhang over the sides of the pan.

Skill Level: Average

Makes about 3 lbs (1.5 kg)

- 9-inch (23 cm) square pan, lined with parchment (see Cook's Note, left) or buttered
- 5-quart heavy candy kettle or pot
- Candy thermometer

1. Using kitchen shears, cut 20 of the marshmallows into quarters. Cover the marshmallows and freeze 1 hour or more. When ready to make the candy, cut the remaining marshmallows in half.

2. In heavy candy kettle over medium heat, bring the sugar and milk to a rolling boil, stirring until the sugar dissolves and the mixture begins to boil. Cook, stirring constantly to prevent scorching, to the soft ball stage (234°F to 240°F/112°C to 116°C, with 234°F/112°C recommended).

3. Remove from the heat. Add the chocolate chips, butter and the room temperature marshmallow halves. Stir until the chocolate chips and marshmallows are melted and the mixture is well blended and slightly thickened.

4. Stir in the nuts, vanilla and frozen quartered marshmallows. Pour into the prepared pan. Cool in the refrigerator 30 minutes to 1 hour. Cut into squares. Store in an airtight container.

Microwave Rocky Road Fudge

1 lb	chocolate almond bark (see page 18) or semisweet chocolate, chopped	500 g
1	can (14 oz or 300 mL) sweetened condensed milk	1
2 tsp	vanilla extract	10 mL
2 cups	miniature marshmallows	500 mL
1 cup	pecans, in large pieces	250 mL

> My cousin Margaret's 5-minute recipe is almost too good to be true. Even the busiest people can find time to make this candy.

Skill Level: Novice, Super Simple

Makes about 2½ lbs (1.25 kg)

- 8-inch (20 cm) square pan, lined with foil

1. In a large microwave-safe bowl, combine the chocolate and the sweetened condensed milk. Microwave on High, uncovered, 1 to 1½ minutes. Stir. Microwave 1 to 1½ minutes or until the chocolate is almost melted.

2. Remove the bowl from the microwave. Stir until the chocolate is completely melted and the mixture is smooth. Stir in the vanilla, marshmallows and pecans, mixing until the marshmallows and nuts are well coated. Spread into the prepared pan. Refrigerate 2 hours or until firm. Lift the candy from the pan and peel off the foil lining. Cut into squares. Store in an airtight container.

Microwave Fudge

3 cups	granulated sugar	750 mL
¾ cup	butter or margarine	175 mL
⅔ cup	evaporated milk	150 mL
2 cups	semisweet chocolate chips (12 oz/375 g)	500 mL
1	jar (7 oz/198 g) marshmallow creme	1
1 tsp	vanilla extract	5 mL
2 cups	pecans or walnuts, in large pieces (optional)	500 mL

> Busy chocoholics will love this quick and easy fudge recipe.

Skill Level: Novice, Easy

Makes about 3 lbs (1.5 kg)

- 9-inch (23 cm) square pan, lined with parchment (see Cook's Note, page 130) or buttered

1. In a large microwave-safe bowl, combine the sugar, butter and milk. Microwave on High, uncovered, 5 to 6 minutes or until the mixture comes to a rolling boil, stirring twice during cooking. Microwave on High 3 minutes, stirring once or twice to prevent the mixture from boiling over the sides of the bowl.

2. Remove the bowl from the microwave. Stir in the chocolate chips until melted. Blend in the marshmallow creme and vanilla, mixing until smooth. Stir in the nuts, if desired. Pour into the prepared pan. Cool and cut into squares. Store in an airtight container.

Katie's Perfect Fudge

3 cups	semisweet chocolate chips (18 oz/540 g)	750 mL
1 cup	butter or margarine, thinly sliced	250 mL
4½ cups	granulated sugar	1.125 L
1	can (12 oz or 370 mL) evaporated milk	1
1 tsp	vanilla extract	5 mL
3 cups	pecans or walnuts, in large pieces (optional)	750 mL

A longtime favorite with my friend Katie, this quick fudge recipe is unlike any other I have seen, cooking much like a marshmallow-based fudge, yet without the marshmallows. If made as directed, this extra-chocolaty, extra-creamy fudge will be perfect every time.

Skill Level: Average

Makes about 5 lbs (2.5 kg)

- 13- by 9-inch (33 by 23 cm) pan, lined with parchment (see Cook's Note, page 130) or buttered
- 5-quart heavy candy kettle or pot

1. In a large mixing bowl, combine the chocolate chips and butter.

2. In heavy candy kettle over medium heat, bring the sugar and milk to a rolling boil, stirring until the sugar dissolves and the mixture begins to boil. Boil rapidly, stirring constantly to prevent scorching, exactly 8½ minutes.

3. Remove from the heat. Pour the hot mixture over the chocolate chips and butter. Stir until the chocolate and butter are melted and the candy is smooth and creamy. Stir in the vanilla and nuts, if desired. Pour into the prepared pan. Refrigerate overnight or until firm. Cut into squares. Store in an airtight container.

Variations

Katie's Chocolate Mint Fudge: Substitute mint chocolate chips for the semisweet chocolate chips. Omit the nuts, if desired.

Katie's Peanut Butter Fudge: Substitute peanut butter chips for the semisweet chocolate chips.

Important Tip

In many recipes, it is important to be prepared for all the steps because timing can be critical. Have all ingredients available and ready to use, and have the pan, baking sheet, or surface prepared before you begin cooking.

Chocolate Cream Cheese Fudge

6 oz	cream cheese, softened	175 g
1 lb	confectioner's (icing) sugar, sifted	500 g
4 oz	unsweetened chocolate, melted	125 g
½ to 1 tsp	vanilla extract, to taste	2 to 5 mL
Pinch	salt (optional)	Pinch

A friend's mother has received so much fame with this buttery, creamy fudge that she keeps the recipe hidden from friends and family in hopes that no one else will learn how to make it.

Cook's Note

If preferred, the cream cheese can be melted in the top of a double boiler over hot but not boiling water. The confectioner's (icing) sugar, melted chocolate, salt and vanilla can then be stirred into the mixture, blending until smooth.

Skill Level: Novice, Easy
Makes about 1 lb (500 g)

- Small pan or dish, buttered

1. In a small mixing bowl, beat the cream cheese by hand or with an electric mixer until it is soft and smooth. Slowly blend in the confectioner's sugar. Add the chocolate, mixing well. Stir in the vanilla and salt, if desired.

2. Press the candy into the prepared pan. Refrigerate until firm, about 15 minutes. Cut into squares. Store in airtight container in the refrigerator.

Variation

Cream Cheese Pecan Fudge: Omit the chocolate. Make as directed, stirring in 1 cup (250 mL) pecans, in large pieces, before pressing the candy into the pan. This candy can be somewhat soft so if you prefer a firmer consistency, stir in a little more confectioner's sugar (about ½ cup/125 mL).

Creamy Two-Chocolate Fudge

2 cups	semisweet chocolate chips (12 oz/375 g)	500 mL
1 cup	milk chocolate chips	250 mL
1	can (14 oz or 300 mL) sweetened condensed milk	1
1 to 2 tsp	vanilla extract, to taste	5 to 10 mL
1 cup	pecans or walnuts, in large pieces (optional)	250 mL

Treat your taste buds to an ultra-creamy sensation with this simple 5-minute recipe.

Skill Level: Average
Makes about 2 lbs (1 kg)

- 8-inch (20 cm) square pan, lined with foil
- 2-quart heavy saucepan

1. In heavy saucepan over low heat, combine the chocolate chips and sweetened condensed milk. Cook over low heat, stirring constantly, just until the chocolate is melted and the mixture is smooth.

2. Remove from the heat. Stir in the vanilla and nuts, if desired. Spread into the lined pan. Refrigerate until firm, about 2 hours. Lift the candy from the pan. Peel off the foil lining and cut into squares. Store in an airtight container in the refrigerator.

French Fudge

1 cup	semisweet chocolate chips	250 mL
1/3 cup plus 1 tbsp	sweetened condensed milk	90 mL
Pinch	salt	Pinch
1/2 cup	sweetened flaked coconut, or pecans or walnuts, in large pieces (optional)	125 mL

> Ooh la la! For those who love the taste of rich dark chocolate, nothing could be easier.

Makes about 12 oz (375 g)

- Plate or a small baking sheet, lined with waxed paper
- Double boiler

1. In the top pan of a double boiler over hot but not boiling water, melt the chocolate chips, stirring until smooth.

2. Remove from the heat. Blend in the milk and salt, stirring until smooth. Stir in the coconut, if desired. Pour onto the waxed paper and pat to the desired thickness using the back of a spoon or a flat spatula. Refrigerate about 20 minutes or until firm. Cover and slice as needed or cut into pieces and store in an airtight container in the refrigerator.

Chocolate Velvet Fudge

1 to 1 1/4 lbs	confectioner's (icing) sugar, sifted, divided	500 to 625 g
1/4 cup	unsweetened cocoa powder	60 mL
4 oz	Velveeta pasteurized process cheese product	125 g
1/2 cup	butter or margarine (preferably butter)	125 mL
1/2 tsp	vanilla extract	2 mL
1/2 cup	pecans or walnuts, in large pieces (optional)	125 mL

> When I got the recipe for Wacky Potato Fudge (page 135), I thought I had seen it all, but then I met a woman who makes fudge with Velveeta cheese spread. Later I learned that this recipe has been floating around in my family for years and I just had not seen it. This unusually creamy fudge may not be for everyone, but many people think it is delicious. For the best flavor, let it stand overnight before serving.

Makes about 1 1/4 lbs (625 g)

- Double boiler
- 9- by 5-inch (23 by 12.5 cm) loaf pan or a plate, buttered

1. In a medium bowl, stir together 1 lb (500 g) of the confectioner's sugar and the cocoa until well blended.

2. In the top pan of a double boiler over hot but not boiling water, melt the cheese spread and the butter, stirring until smooth. Gradually add the cheese mixture to the confectioner's sugar mixture, blending well. Stir in the vanilla. Blend on low speed with an electric mixer or by hand until the candy is smooth and creamy. If the candy is too soft, gradually add more confectioner's sugar until it reaches the desired consistency.

3. Stir in the nuts, if desired. Pour into the prepared pan. Cool 1 hour or more before cutting into squares. Store in an airtight container in the refrigerator.

Wacky Potato Fudge

3 tbsp	butter or margarine	45 mL
3 tbsp	unsweetened cocoa powder	45 mL
1/3 cup	unseasoned cold mashed potatoes	75 mL
1/8 tsp	salt	0.5 mL
1 tsp	vanilla extract	5 mL
4 cups	confectioner's (icing) sugar, sifted (approx.)	1 L
1/2 cup	pecans, in large pieces (optional)	125 mL

As bizarre as it may sound, this old-time favorite is quite tasty, reminding some of thick chocolate buttercream frosting. Children love watching the potatoes turn to liquid as the sugar is added, so save some leftover potatoes and entertain your kids.

Cook's Note

If unseasoned, leftover cooked potatoes are not available, bake a large potato in the microwave. Scoop out half of the cooked potato and place it into a small bowl. Mash the potato with a fork, adding a few drops of milk and 1 1/2 tsp (7 mL) butter, then measure. One-half of a large potato will yield about 1/3 cup (75 mL) mashed potatoes.

Skill Level: Novice, Easy

Makes about 1 1/4 lbs (625 g)

- 9- by 5-inch (23 by 12.5 cm) loaf pan, lined with parchment (see Cook's Note, page 130) or buttered

1. In a medium microwave-safe bowl, heat the butter and cocoa in the microwave on High until the butter is melted, about 45 seconds. Stir to blend. Add the potatoes, salt and vanilla, mixing thoroughly. Blend in the confectioner's sugar a little at a time until the mixture is thick and reaches the desired consistency. If necessary, knead by hand until the candy is smooth. Add the nuts, if desired.

2. Press the candy into the prepared pan. Refrigerate about 20 minutes or until set. Cut into squares. Store in an airtight container.

Storing Candy

Most candies should be stored in an airtight container to keep them fresh. Unless specifically instructed in the recipe, refrigeration is often a matter of personal choice, but generally, most fudges and fudge-like candies should keep at least 1 week at room temperature and at least 1 month, sometimes much longer, if refrigerated. Excessive heat, high humidity, or added ingredients such as fruit may shorten the storage time so it is important to use common sense. If the color or texture of the candy has changed, dispose of it and make a fresh batch.

Emergency Chocolate Fudge

¼ cup	butter or margarine	60 mL
¼ cup	water	60 mL
3 cups	confectioner's (icing) sugar, sifted	750 mL
½ cup	instant dry nonfat dry milk powder	125 mL
½ cup	unsweetened cocoa powder	125 mL
⅛ tsp	salt	0.5 mL
1 tsp	vanilla extract	5 mL
½ cup	pecans, in large pieces (optional)	125 mL

- 9- by 5-inch (23 by 12.5 cm) loaf pan, lined with parchment (see below) or buttered
- 1½-quart saucepan

1. In saucepan, heat the butter and water together over medium heat until the butter melts.

2. In a medium bowl, mix the confectioner's sugar, dry milk, cocoa and salt. Gradually add the butter mixture to the dry ingredients, stirring in about ¼ cup (60 mL) of the butter mixture at a time. Beat the candy until smooth after each addition of the butter. Stir in the vanilla and nuts, if desired. Pour into the prepared pan. Cover and refrigerate until firm, about 30 minutes. Cut into squares. Store in an airtight container.

While this may seem unbelievable to anyone born after about 1970, baby boomers can remember the days when grocery stores closed for the night sometime near the dinner hour. Our mothers and grandmothers often kept a box of instant nonfat dry milk on hand for emergencies, as milk was a staple in every household. No doubt, this old recipe was probably invented by someone who found herself craving chocolate at 8:00 P.M. and was unable to quell her sweet tooth until morning.

Cutting into Perfect Squares and Special Shapes

Cutting candy becomes much easier with the use of parchment paper. Rather than buttering the pan directly, butter a piece of parchment paper larger than the pan and press it into the bottom and up the sides of the pan, tucking and creasing the paper as needed to create corners, and leaving a generous overhang over the sides of the pan. Pour the candy into the parchment-lined pan. Once the candy has cooled, use the parchment to lift the entire block of candy out of the pan. Place the block of candy on a cutting board and use a long, serrated knife to cut straight, uniform rows of the candy, and then cut the rows into squares. For a special presentation cut the block of candy into diamonds, triangles or other shapes, as desired.

The parchment paper method is optional, but over the years I have found it much easier than cutting candy in the pan, and it saves my pans from deep scratches left by sharp knives. At times I have shipped large blocks of candy to friends and family with the candy still wrapped in the parchment paper and then wrapped again in foil wrap. It simplifies shipping and allows others to cut the candy as they choose.

Peanut Butter Fudges

Traditional Peanut Butter Fudge

2 cups	granulated sugar	500 mL
1 cup	evaporated milk	250 mL
1 tsp	vanilla extract	5 mL
3 to	smooth or crunchy peanut	45 to
4 tbsp	butter, to taste	60 mL

Nothing beats the old-fashioned goodness of this peanut butter fudge.

Skill Level: Advanced

Makes about 1$\frac{1}{2}$ lbs (750 g)

- 9- by 5-inch (23 by 12.5 cm) loaf pan, lined with parchment (see page 136) or buttered
- 3-quart heavy saucepan
- Candy thermometer

1. In heavy saucepan over medium-low heat, bring the sugar and milk to a boil, stirring until the sugar dissolves and the mixture begins to boil. Cover and cook 2 to 3 minutes to dissolve the sugar crystals on the sides of the pan. Remove the lid. Cook, stirring occasionally to prevent scorching, to the soft ball stage (234°F to 240°F/112°C to 116°C, with 238°F/114°C recommended).

2. Remove from the heat. Add the vanilla and peanut butter. Beat by hand until the candy thickens and loses its gloss. Pour into the prepared pan. Cool and cut into squares. Store in an airtight container.

Variation

Old-Time Peanut Butter Fudge: Use $\frac{3}{4}$ cup (175 mL) milk and $\frac{1}{4}$ cup (60 mL) peanut butter.

Important Tip

In many recipes, it is important to be prepared for all the steps because timing can be critical. Have all ingredients available and ready to use, and have the pan, baking sheet, or surface prepared before you begin cooking.

One Sharp Peanut Butter Fudge

2 cups	granulated sugar	500 mL
1 cup	milk	250 mL
2 tbsp	light (white) corn syrup	30 mL
3 heaping tbsp	smooth peanut butter	45 heaping mL

> Without a doubt, this creamy version of old-fashioned peanut butter fudge is one sharp candy, especially since it is a favorite with my Sharp family cousins.

Variation

Pioneer Peanut Butter Fudge: Use $2/3$ cup (150 mL) milk and $1/2$ cup (125 mL) smooth peanut butter. Add $1/4$ tsp (1 mL) salt to the sugar, corn syrup and milk mixture. Cook in a heavy 2-quart saucepan to 236°F (113°C). Stir in 1 tsp (5 mL) vanilla while beating the candy.

Skill Level: Advanced
Makes about 1 lb (500 g)

- 9- by 5-inch (23 by 12.5 cm) loaf pan or plate, lined with parchment (see Cook's Note, page 141) or buttered
- 3-quart heavy saucepan
- Candy thermometer

1. In heavy saucepan over medium-low heat, bring the sugar, milk and corn syrup to a boil, stirring until the sugar dissolves and the mixture begins to boil. Cook, stirring to prevent scorching, to the soft ball stage (234°F to 240°F/112°C to 116°C, with 234°F/112°C recommended).

2. Remove from the heat. Stir in the peanut butter. Beat by hand until the candy loses its gloss and begins to hold its shape. Pour into prepared pan. Cool and cut into squares. Store in an airtight container.

Super Peanut Butter Fudge

2 cups	granulated sugar	500 mL
3 tbsp	butter or margarine	45 mL
1 cup	evaporated milk	250 mL
1 cup	miniature marshmallows	250 mL
1¼ cups	smooth peanut butter	300 mL

> Extra peanut butter gives either of these two candies a strong peanut butter flavor and a semifirm texture.

Skill Level: Average
Makes about 1½ lbs (750 g)

- 9- by 5-inch (23 by 12.5 cm) loaf pan, lined with parchment (see Cook's Note, page 141) or buttered
- 2-quart heavy saucepan
- Candy thermometer

1. In heavy saucepan over medium heat, bring the sugar, butter and milk to a boil, stirring until the sugar dissolves and the mixture begins to boil. Cook, stirring constantly, to the soft ball stage (234°F/112°C).

2. Remove from the heat. Add the marshmallows and peanut butter. Blend well. Pour into the prepared pan. Cool and cut into squares. Store in an airtight container.

Peanut Smoothies

1 cup	granulated sugar	250 mL
1/2 cup	evaporated milk	125 mL
1 tbsp	butter	15 mL
1	package (3 oz/90 g) vanilla pudding mix (not instant)	1
1/2 cup	crunchy peanut butter	125 mL
1/2 tsp	vanilla extract	2 mL

With a medium peanut butter flavor, this pudding-smooth candy is perfect every time.

Makes about 1 1/4 lbs (625 g)

- 9- by 5-inch (23 by 12.5 cm) loaf pan, lined with parchment (see Cook's Note, page 141) or buttered
- 2-quart heavy saucepan
- Candy thermometer

1. In heavy saucepan over medium heat, bring the sugar, milk, butter and pudding mix to a boil, stirring until the sugar dissolves and the mixture begins to boil. Cook, stirring constantly to prevent scorching, to the soft ball stage (234°F to 240°F/112°C to 116°C, with 234°F/112°C recommended).

2. Remove from the heat. Stir in the peanut butter until melted. Add the vanilla. Beat by hand until the candy begins to thicken slightly. Pour into the prepared pan. Cool and cut into squares. Store in an airtight container.

Variation

Peanut-Pecan Smoothies: Smooth peanut butter may be substituted for the crunchy peanut butter. Add 1/2 cup (125 mL) chopped pecans before pouring the candy into the pan.

Lindsay's Luscious Peanut Butter Fudge

3 cups	granulated sugar	750 mL
2/3 cup	evaporated milk	150 mL
3/4 cup	butter or margarine	175 mL
1 2/3 cups	peanut butter chips (10 oz/300 g)	400 mL
1	jar (7 oz/198 g) marshmallow creme	1
1 1/2 cups	pecans, in large pieces (optional)	375 mL
1 tsp	vanilla extract	5 mL

My niece Lindsay and I fell in love with this light and creamy peanut butter fudge when she was just a young child. Twenty years later, her eyes still sparkle as we share our favorite holiday tradition.

Cook's Note

Peanut butter chips are often slow to melt. If desired, place the beaters of an electric mixer directly into the kettle and beat for 1 to 2 minutes to blend the chips with the other ingredients.

Skill Level: Average

Makes about 3 1/2 lbs (1.75 kg)

- 9-inch (23 cm) square pan, lined with parchment (see Cook's Note, page 141) or buttered
- 5-quart heavy candy kettle or pot
- Candy thermometer

1. In heavy candy kettle over medium heat, bring the sugar, milk and butter to a boil, stirring until the sugar dissolves and the mixture begins to boil. Cook, stirring constantly to prevent scorching, to the soft ball stage (234°F to 240°F/112°C to 116°C, with 234°F/112°C recommended), about 5 minutes.

2. Remove from the heat. Stir in the peanut butter chips until melted. Add the marshmallow creme and stir until smooth. Stir in the pecans, if desired, and vanilla. Pour into the prepared pan. Cool and cut into squares. Store in an airtight container.

Important Tip

In many recipes, it is important to be prepared for all the steps because timing can be critical. Have all ingredients available and ready to use, and have the pan, baking sheet, or surface prepared before you begin cooking.

Peanut Cremes

2 cups	granulated sugar	500 mL
2/3 cup	evaporated milk	150 mL
1	jar (7 oz/198 g) marshmallow creme	1
1 cup	crunchy peanut butter	250 mL
1 tsp	vanilla extract (optional)	5 mL

Extra smooth and extra scrumptious, this very lightly flavored peanut butter candy is so popular that the recipe often comes with slightly different variations. For a double dose of decadence, try dipping chilled squares of this candy into luscious, melted chocolate.

Cook's Note

Cutting candy becomes much easier with the use of parchment paper. Rather than buttering the pan directly, butter a piece of parchment paper larger than the pan and press it into the bottom and up the sides of the pan, tucking and creasing the paper as needed to create corners, and leaving a generous overhang over the sides of the pan.

Skill Level: Average

Makes about 2 lbs (1 kg)

- 8-inch (20 cm) square pan, lined with parchment (see Cook's Note, left) or buttered
- 3-quart saucepan
- Candy thermometer

1. In heavy saucepan over medium heat, bring the sugar and milk to a boil, stirring until the sugar dissolves and the mixture begins to boil. Cook, stirring constantly to prevent scorching, to the soft ball stage (234°F to 240°F/112°C to 116°C, with 236°F/113°C recommended).

2. Remove from the heat. Add the marshmallow creme and peanut butter, stirring until the candy is smooth and well blended. Stir in the vanilla, if desired. Pour into the prepared pan. Cool and cut into squares. Store in an airtight container.

Variation

Double Peanut Cremes: For a stronger peanut butter flavor, use 2 cups (500 mL) crunchy peanut butter.

Storing Candy

Most candies should be stored in an airtight container to keep them fresh. Unless specifically instructed in the recipe, refrigeration is often a matter of personal choice, but generally, most fudges and fudge-like candies should keep at least 1 week at room temperature and at least 1 month, sometimes much longer, if refrigerated. Excessive heat, high humidity, or added ingredients such as fruit may shorten the storage time so it is important to use common sense. If the color or texture of the candy has changed, dispose of it and make a fresh batch.

Classic Combo Fudge

4 cups	granulated sugar	1 L
6 tbsp	unsweetened cocoa powder	90 mL
Pinch	salt	Pinch
2 cups	milk	500 mL
1 cup	smooth peanut butter	250 mL
17	large marshmallows	17
1 tsp	vanilla extract	5 mL
1 cup	chopped peanuts, pecans or walnuts (optional)	250 mL

With the same, unforgettable flavor as the enormously popular chocolate-peanut butter no-bake cookies, this candy is destined to become a family classic.

Skill Level: Average

Makes about 2½ lbs (1.25 kg)

- 9-inch (23 cm) square pan, lined with parchment (see Cook's Note, page 141) or buttered
- 5-quart heavy candy kettle or pot
- Candy thermometer

1. In heavy candy kettle, combine the sugar, cocoa and salt until well blended. Stir in the milk. Bring to a boil over medium-low heat, stirring until the sugar dissolves and the mixture begins to boil. Cover and cook 2 to 3 minutes to dissolve the sugar crystals on the sides of the pan. Remove the lid. Cook, stirring frequently to prevent scorching, to the soft ball stage (234°F to 240°F/112°C to 116°C, with 236°F/113°C recommended).

2. Remove from the heat. Add the peanut butter, marshmallows and vanilla. Stir until the candy is smooth and well blended. Stir in the nuts, if desired. Pour into the prepared pan. Cool and cut into squares. Store in an airtight container.

Fancy Chocolate Fudge

1 cup	milk	250 mL
2 oz	unsweetened chocolate, finely chopped	60 g
3 cups	granulated sugar	750 mL
3 tbsp	light (white or golden) corn syrup	45 mL
1/8 tsp	salt	0.5 mL
1 tsp	vanilla extract	5 mL
1/2 cup	smooth peanut butter	125 mL
3/4 cup	walnuts or pecans, in large pieces (optional)	175 mL

Those who prefer old-fashioned fudge to marshmallow fudge will enjoy the hint of peanut butter in this two-flavor chocolate candy.

Skill Level: Advanced

Makes about 2 lbs (1 kg)

- 8-inch (20 cm) square pan, lined with parchment (see Cook's Note, page 141) or buttered
- 3-quart heavy saucepan
- Candy thermometer

1. In heavy saucepan, combine the milk and chocolate over low heat, stirring constantly until the milk is hot and the chocolate is completely melted.

2. Remove from the heat temporarily. Stir in the sugar, corn syrup and salt. Bring to a boil over medium-low heat, stirring until the sugar dissolves and the mixture begins to boil. Cover and cook 2 to 3 minutes to dissolve the sugar crystals on the sides of the pan. Remove the lid. Cook, stirring only as needed to prevent scorching, to the soft ball stage (234°F to 240°F/112°C to 116°C, with 236°F/113°C recommended).

3. Remove from the heat. Add the vanilla without stirring. Cool to lukewarm (110°F/43°C), about 1 hour.

4. Stir in the peanut butter. Beat by hand until the candy begins to thicken and lose its gloss. Stir in the nuts, if desired. Pour into the prepared pan. Cool and cut into squares. Store in an airtight container.

Twice-as-Tempting Two-Tone Fudge

$\frac{1}{2}$ cup	butter or margarine, divided	125 mL
$\frac{1}{4}$ cup	unsweetened cocoa powder	60 mL
$1\frac{2}{3}$ cups	peanut butter chips (10 oz/300 g)	400 mL
$4\frac{1}{2}$ cups	granulated sugar	1.125 L
1	can (12 oz or 370 mL) evaporated milk	1
1	jar (7 oz/198 g) marshmallow creme	1
1 tsp	vanilla extract	5 mL

My uncle John, a renowned candy connoisseur and the official family taste tester for all recipes containing sugar, chose this layered fudge as his favorite of all the candies he sampled. Declared "absolutely delicious" by more than one taster, this recipe combines two old favorites, chocolate and peanut butter, to create a doubly tempting treat for the taste buds.

Cook's Note

Chopping the peanut butter chips in the food processor helps them melt more quickly.

Skill Level: Average

Makes about 4 lbs (2 kg)

- 13- by 9-inch (33 by 23 cm) pan, lined with parchment (see Cook's Note, page 141) or buttered
- Food processor
- 5-quart heavy candy kettle or pot
- Candy thermometer

1. In a small microwave-safe bowl, melt $\frac{1}{4}$ cup (60 mL) of the butter in the microwave. Blend in the cocoa, stirring until smooth. Set aside. Using a food processor, chop the peanut butter chips into small pieces. Set aside.

2. In heavy candy kettle over medium heat, bring the sugar, milk and remaining $\frac{1}{4}$ cup (60 mL) butter to a boil, stirring until the sugar dissolves and the mixture begins to boil. Cook, stirring constantly to prevent scorching, to the soft ball stage (234°F to 240°F/112°C to 116°C, with 234°F/112°C recommended).

3. Remove from the heat. Stir in the peanut butter chips until melted. Add the marshmallow creme and vanilla and stir until the candy is smooth and well blended.

4. Pour half of the candy mixture into the prepared pan, spreading evenly. Add the cocoa and butter mixture to the remaining candy mixture in the kettle. Stir until the candy is thoroughly blended. Pour on top of the peanut butter layer in the pan, spreading evenly. Cool and cut into squares. Store in an airtight container.

Blissful Butterscotch-Chocolate Fudge

2 cups	packed light brown sugar	500 mL
1 cup	granulated sugar	250 mL
1 cup	evaporated milk	250 mL
½ cup	butter or margarine	125 mL
1 cup	butterscotch chips	250 mL
1 cup	semisweet chocolate chips	250 mL
1	jar (7 oz/198 g) marshmallow creme	1
1 tsp	vanilla extract	5 mL
1 cup	pecans or walnuts, in large pieces (optional)	250 mL

> Delight the butterscotch lovers in your life with this ultra-smooth blend of two beloved flavors, chocolate and butterscotch.

- 13- by 9-inch (33 by 23 cm) pan, lined with parchment (see Cook's Note, page 141) or buttered
- 5-quart heavy candy kettle or pot
- Candy thermometer

1. In heavy candy kettle over medium heat, bring the brown and granulated sugars, milk and butter to a boil, stirring until the sugars dissolve and the mixture begins to boil. Cook, stirring constantly to prevent scorching, to the soft ball stage (234°F to 240°F/112°C to 116°C, with 236°F/113°C recommended).

2. Remove from the heat. Stir in the butterscotch chips and chocolate chips until melted. Add the marshmallow creme and vanilla. Stir until the candy is smooth and well blended. Stir in the nuts, if desired. Pour into the prepared pan. Cool and cut into squares. Store in an airtight container.

Important Tip

In many recipes, it is important to be prepared for all the steps because timing can be critical. Have all ingredients available and ready to use, and have the pan, baking sheet, or surface prepared before you begin cooking.

Double-Duty Fudge

5 to 6 oz	semisweet chocolate, coarsely chopped	150 to 175 g
2 cups	granulated sugar	500 mL
3/4 cup	sour cream	175 mL
1/2 cup	butter or margarine	125 mL
Pinch	salt	Pinch
4 oz	white chocolate, coarsely chopped	125 g
1	jar (7 oz/198 g) marshmallow creme, divided	1
1 tsp	vanilla extract, divided	5 mL

This gorgeous "snowcapped" candy pulls double duty, pleasing both the white chocolate lovers and the dark chocolate lovers with one simple recipe. For a truly dazzling treat, try adding chopped nuts to the dark chocolate layer and chopped candied cherries to the white chocolate layer (see the Variation, below).

Cook's Note

This fudge can be cut into neat squares if slightly chilled first.

- 8-inch (20 cm) square pan, lined with parchment (see Cook's Note, page 141) or buttered
- 2-quart heavy saucepan
- Candy thermometer

1. Place the chopped semisweet chocolate into a medium mixing bowl.

2. In heavy saucepan over medium heat, bring the sugar, sour cream, butter and salt to a boil, stirring until the sugar dissolves and the mixture begins to boil. Cook, stirring occasionally to prevent scorching, to the soft ball stage (234°F to 240°F/112°C to 116°C, with 238°F/114°C recommended).

3. Remove from the heat. Pour half of the hot mixture over the semisweet chocolate in the bowl. Add the white chocolate to the remaining hot mixture to melt. Add half of the marshmallow creme and 1/2 tsp (2 mL) of the vanilla to the semisweet chocolate mixture and stir until the chocolate is melted and the mixture is smooth and well blended. Pour into the prepared pan, spreading evenly.

4. Add the remaining marshmallow creme and 1/2 tsp (2 mL) vanilla to the white chocolate mixture and stir until the white chocolate is melted and the mixture is smooth and well blended. Pour the white chocolate mixture on top of the semisweet chocolate layer in the pan, spreading evenly. Cool and cut into squares. Store in an airtight container.

Variation

Evenly divide 3/4 to 1 cup (175 to 250 mL) chopped candied cherries, walnuts or pecans between the two mixtures just before they are poured into the pan. If preferred, one layer can contain 1/2 cup (125 mL) chopped cherries, with the other layer containing 1/2 cup (125 mL) chopped walnuts or pecans. As another option, crushed peppermint candies may be sprinkled on top of the white layer, or be creative and use your own combinations.

Tuxedo Fudge

Coconut Layer

2 cups	granulated sugar	500 mL
Pinch	salt	Pinch
1/2 cup	butter or margarine	125 mL
1/4 cup	light (white) corn syrup	60 mL
1/2 cup	milk	125 mL
1 tsp	vanilla extract	5 mL
1/2 cup	sweetened flaked coconut	125 mL

Chocolate Layer

2 cups	granulated sugar	500 mL
2 tbsp	unsweetened cocoa powder	30 mL
Pinch	salt	Pinch
1/2 cup	butter or margarine	125 mL
1/4 cup	light (white) corn syrup	60 mL
1/2 cup	milk	125 mL
1 tsp	vanilla extract	5 mL
1/2 cup	pecans, in large pieces (optional)	125 mL

Make a date with this black and white old-fashioned fudge, combining coconut, pecans and chocolate into one layered candy.

Skill Level: Advanced
Makes about 3 1/2 lbs (1.75 kg)

- 8- or 9-inch (20 or 23 cm) square pan, lined with parchment (see Cook's Note, page 141) or buttered
- 2-quart heavy saucepan
- Candy thermometer

1. *To make the coconut layer:* In heavy saucepan over low to medium-low heat, bring the sugar, salt, butter, corn syrup and milk to a boil, stirring until the sugar dissolves and the mixture begins to boil. Cover and cook 2 to 3 minutes to dissolve the sugar crystals on the sides of the pan. Remove the lid. Cook, stirring only as needed to prevent scorching, to the soft ball stage (234°F to 240°F/112°C to 116°C, with 236°F/113°C recommended).

2. Remove from the heat. Cool slightly, about 10 minutes. Add the vanilla. Beat by hand until the candy begins to thicken and lose its gloss. Stir in the coconut. Spread the candy into the prepared pan. Cool at room temperature while making the chocolate layer.

3. *To make the chocolate layer:* In a clean saucepan, combine the sugar and cocoa until well blended. Add the salt, butter, corn syrup and milk. Bring to a boil over low to medium-low heat, stirring until the sugar dissolves and the mixture begins to boil. Cover and cook 2 to 3 minutes to dissolve the sugar crystals on the sides of the pan. Remove the lid. Cook, stirring only as needed to prevent scorching, to the soft ball stage (234°F to 240°F/112°C to 116°C, with 236°F/113°C recommended).

4. Remove from the heat. Cool slightly, about 10 minutes. Add the vanilla. Beat by hand until the candy begins to thicken and lose its gloss. Stir in the pecans, if desired. Spread the chocolate layer over the coconut layer in the pan. Cool and cut into squares. Store in an airtight container.

Brown Sugar Panocha

2½ cups	packed light brown sugar	625 mL
¾ cup	milk	175 mL
1 tbsp	butter or margarine	15 mL
1 tbsp	light (white or golden) corn syrup	15 mL
Pinch	salt	Pinch
1 tsp	vanilla extract	5 mL
½ cup	walnuts or pecans, in large pieces (optional)	125 mL

> Made with all brown sugar rather than a mixture of brown and white sugars, this version of panocha has a robust flavor.

Cook's Note

This recipe can be made without the corn syrup, if desired, though corn syrup does help make candies creamier.

Skill Level: Advanced

Makes about 1½ lbs (750 g)

- 9- by 5-inch (23 by 12.5 cm) loaf pan, lined with parchment (see Cook's Note, page 141) or buttered
- 2-quart heavy saucepan
- Candy thermometer

1. In heavy saucepan over low to medium-low heat, bring the sugar, milk, butter, corn syrup and salt to a boil, stirring until the sugar dissolves and the mixture begins to boil. Cook, stirring very gently (never vigorously) a few times to prevent scorching, to the soft ball stage (234°F to 240°F/112°C to 116°C, with 238°F/114°C recommended).

2. Remove from the heat. Cool to lukewarm (110°F/43°C), about 1 hour.

3. Add the vanilla. Beat by hand until the candy begins to hold its shape. Stir in the nuts, if desired. Quickly spread in the prepared pan. Cool and cut into squares. Store in an airtight container.

Variation

Brown Sugar Penuche: Omit the corn syrup and the salt. Substitute half-and-half (10%) cream for the milk. Cook as directed to 236°F (113°C).

What's in a Name

Amaze your friends with a bit of candy trivia by citing the different spellings for penuche, a fudge-like candy usually made with brown sugar, cream or milk, butter and nuts. The various spellings are penuche, penuchi, panocha, panoche, pinoche or pinochi.

Panache Penuche

1½ cups	granulated sugar	375 mL
1 cup	packed light brown sugar	250 mL
¾ cup	half-and-half (10%) cream	175 mL
¼ tsp	salt	1 mL
2 tbsp	butter or margarine	30 mL
1 tsp	vanilla extract	5 mL
1 tsp	freshly grated lemon zest	5 mL
⅓ cup	raisins or pecans, in large pieces	75 mL

Personalize this creamy, fudge-like candy by adding your choice of lemon peel, cherries, orange zest, raisins or nuts. This versatile 1950s-style recipe will accommodate a range of tastes.

Makes about 1½ lbs (750 g)

- 8-inch (20 cm) square pan, lined with parchment (see Cook's Note, page 141) or buttered
- 2-quart heavy saucepan
- Candy thermometer

1. In heavy saucepan over low to medium-low heat, bring the granulated and brown sugars, half-and-half and salt to a boil, stirring until the sugars dissolve and the mixture begins to boil. Cover and cook 2 to 3 minutes to dissolve the sugar crystals on the sides of the pan. Remove the lid. Cook, without stirring, to the soft ball stage (234°F to 240°F/112°C to 116°C with 238°F/114°C recommended).

2. Add the butter without stirring. Cool to lukewarm (110°F/43°C), about 1 hour.

3. Add the vanilla. Beat by hand until the candy becomes creamy. Stir in the zest and raisins. Continue beating until the candy begins to lose its gloss. Quickly spread into the prepared pan. Cool and cut into squares. Store in an airtight container.

Variations

This recipe can also be made using ⅓ cup (75 mL) half-and-half (10%) cream and ⅓ cup (75 mL) milk.

Cherry-Nut Penuche: Omit the lemon zest. Use ⅓ cup (75 mL) nuts instead of the raisins. Add ⅓ cup (75 mL) well-drained, finely cut maraschino cherries when adding the nuts.

Orange Penuche: Substitute 2 tsp (10 mL) freshly grated orange zest for the lemon zest.

Raisin-Nut Penuche: Omit the lemon zest. Use ⅓ cup (75 mL) raisins and ⅓ cup (75 mL) pecans.

Panache Panocha Fudge: Omit the salt and lemon zest. Use ⅓ cup (75 mL) half-and-half (10%) cream and ⅓ cup (75 mL) milk. Cook to 236°F (113°C). Substitute 1 cup (250 mL) coarsely chopped pecans for the ⅓ cup (75 mL) raisins or nuts.

Quick Walnut Penuche

½ cup	butter or margarine	125 mL
1 cup	packed light brown sugar	250 mL
¼ cup	milk	60 mL
1¾ to 2 cups	confectioner's (icing) sugar, sifted	425 to 500 mL
1 cup	walnuts, in large pieces (optional)	250 mL

For the flavor of penuche without the hand beating, this quick recipe is an excellent choice.

Skill Level: Novice, Easy

Makes about ½ lb (250 g)

- Plate, buttered
- 1-quart heavy saucepan

1. In heavy saucepan over medium-low heat, melt the butter. Stir in the brown sugar. Cook, stirring constantly, 2 minutes. Add the milk and bring to a boil, stirring constantly.

2. Remove from the heat. Cool to room temperature, 30 to 45 minutes. Gradually add the confectioner's sugar, stirring until well blended and the mixture has the consistency of fudge. Stir in the walnuts, if desired. Pour onto the prepared plate. Cool and cut into squares. Store in an airtight container in the refrigerator.

Storing Candy

Most candies should be stored in an airtight container to keep them fresh. Unless specifically instructed in the recipe, refrigeration is often a matter of personal choice, but generally, most fudges and fudge-like candies should keep at least 1 week at room temperature and at least 1 month, sometimes much longer, if refrigerated. Excessive heat, high humidity, or added ingredients such as fruit may shorten the storage time so it is important to use common sense. If the color or texture of the candy has changed, dispose of it and make a fresh batch.

Extra-Buttery Buttermilk Fudge

2 cups	granulated sugar	500 mL
1 cup	buttermilk	250 mL
Pinch	salt	Pinch
$\frac{1}{2}$ cup	butter or margarine	125 mL
$\frac{1}{2}$ cup	pecans, in large pieces (optional)	125 mL
1 tbsp	vanilla extract	15 mL

Adding the butter and the pecans before cooking gives this blonde creamy candy a rich, nutty flavor.

Cook's Note
For a very soft fudge, cook to 236°F (113°C).

Skill Level: Advanced

Makes about 1$\frac{1}{2}$ lbs (750 g)

- 9- by 5-inch (23 by 12.5 cm) loaf pan, lined with parchment (see Cook's Note, page 141) or buttered
- 3-quart heavy saucepan
- Candy thermometer

1. In heavy saucepan over medium heat, bring the sugar, buttermilk and salt to a boil, stirring until the sugar dissolves and the mixture begins to boil. Reduce the heat to low. Stir in the butter. Cook slowly over low heat, stirring only if needed to prevent scorching, 5 minutes. Stir in the pecans, if desired. Cook, gently stirring a few times to prevent scorching, to the soft ball stage (234°F to 240°F/112°C to 116°C, with 238°F/114°C recommended).

2. Remove from the heat. Cool 20 minutes. Add the vanilla. Beat by hand until the candy thickens and loses its gloss. Pour into the prepared pan. Cool and cut into squares. Store in an airtight container.

Sinfully Rich Buttermilk Fudge

1 tsp	baking soda	5 mL
1 cup	buttermilk	250 mL
2 cups	granulated sugar	500 mL
2 tbsp	light (white) corn syrup	30 mL
2 tbsp	butter or margarine	30 mL
1 tsp	vanilla extract	5 mL
¾ to	pecans, in large pieces	175 to
1 cup	(optional)	250 mL

Caramel colored, pecan packed and absolutely yummy, this ultra-rich candy is sometimes slightly grainy but is so delicious no one will care.

Cook's Notes

Slow cooking will make this candy creamier.

For a candy similar to Sinfully Rich Buttermilk Fudge, see Fresh Buttermilk Candy (page 30).

For a candy with a flavor similar to the variation Sweet and Creamy Buttermilk Fudge (right), see Sweet Buttermilk Candy (page 31).

Skill Level: Advanced

Makes about 1½ lbs (750 g)

- 9- by 5-inch (23 by 12.5 cm) loaf pan, lined with parchment (see Cook's Note, page 141) or buttered
- 5-quart heavy candy kettle or pot
- Candy thermometer

1. In heavy candy kettle, dissolve the baking soda in the buttermilk, stirring until well blended. Stir in the sugar and corn syrup. Bring to a boil over low heat, stirring until the sugar dissolves and the mixture begins to boil. Cover and cook 2 to 3 minutes to dissolve the sugar crystals on the sides of the pan, lifting the lid a few times so the candy will not boil over. Remove the lid. Cook slowly over low heat, stirring occasionally to prevent scorching, to the soft ball stage (234°F to 240°F/112°C to 116°C, with 238°F/114°C recommended).

2. Remove from the heat. Add the butter without stirring. Cool 15 to 20 minutes.

3. Add the vanilla. Beat by hand until the candy thickens and loses its gloss. Quickly stir in the pecans, if desired. Pour into the prepared pan. Cool and cut into squares. Store in an airtight container.

Variation

Sweet and Creamy Buttermilk Fudge: For a creamy, buttery-yellow fudge that retains the mild flavor of buttermilk, omit the baking soda. Cook in a heavy 2-quart saucepan as described above. Add 1 additional tbsp (15 mL) butter or margarine after removing the candy from the heat.

Coffee Fudge

3 cups	granulated sugar	750 mL
1 cup	milk	250 mL
$\frac{1}{2}$ cup	half-and-half (10%) cream	125 mL
$\frac{1}{3}$ cup	light (white or golden) corn syrup	75 mL
2 tbsp	instant coffee granules	30 mL
3 tbsp	butter	45 mL
$\frac{1}{2}$ cup	semisweet chocolate chips	125 mL
1 tsp	vanilla extract	5 mL
$\frac{1}{2}$ cup	coarsely chopped pecans, walnuts or hazelnuts (optional)	125 mL

Even those who do not like coffee-flavored desserts will be impressed with the sophisticated blend of chocolate and coffee in this candy. Give your dinner guests a few pieces to take home with them.

Cook's Note

The amount of coffee used is a matter of personal preference. This candy has a distinct coffee flavoring that is loved by some, but not by all. The coffee may be reduced or omitted entirely.

Skill Level: Advanced

Makes about 2$\frac{1}{2}$ lbs (1.25 kg)

- 8-inch (20 cm) square pan, lined with parchment (see Cook's Note, page 141) or buttered
- 3-quart heavy saucepan
- Candy thermometer

1. In heavy saucepan over medium heat, bring the sugar, milk, half-and-half, corn syrup and coffee to a boil, stirring until the sugar dissolves and the mixture begins to boil. Cover and cook 2 to 3 minutes to remove the sugar crystals from the sides of the pan. Remove the lid. Cook, stirring occasionally to prevent scorching, to the soft ball stage (234°F to 240°F/112°C to 116°C, with 236°F/113°C recommended).

2. Remove from the heat. Add the butter and chocolate chips without stirring. Cool slightly, about 10 minutes or until the chocolate is partially melted.

3. Add the vanilla. Beat by hand until the candy begins to thicken, hold its shape and lose its gloss. Stir in the nuts, if desired. Pour into the prepared pan. Cool and cut into squares. Store in an airtight container.

Important Tip

In many recipes, it is important to be prepared for all the steps because timing can be critical. Have all ingredients available and ready to use, and have the pan, baking sheet, or surface prepared before you begin cooking.

Mocha Fudge

2 cups	granulated sugar	500 mL
2/3 cup	evaporated milk	150 mL
1/2 cup	butter or margarine	125 mL
1 1/2 tsp	instant coffee granules	7 mL
6 oz	white chocolate, coarsely chopped	175 g
16	large marshmallows	16
1 tsp	vanilla extract	5 mL
1 cup	pecans or walnuts, in large pieces (optional)	250 mL

With just a hint of coffee flavoring, this white chocolate–marshmallow fudge will entice the coffee lovers in your family.

Cook's Notes

The amount of coffee used is a matter of personal preference. This candy has a light coffee flavor. The coffee can be doubled or omitted entirely if preferred.

This recipe produces semifirm fudge. To soften it a bit, add a few more marshmallows.

Skill Level: Average

Makes about 2 lbs (1 kg)

- 8-inch (20 cm) square pan, lined with parchment (see Cook's Notes, page 155) or buttered
- 3-quart heavy saucepan
- Candy thermometer

1. In heavy saucepan over medium heat, bring the sugar, milk, butter and coffee to a boil, stirring until the sugar dissolves and the mixture begins to boil. Cook, stirring frequently to prevent scorching, to the soft ball stage (234°F to 240°F/112°C to 116°C, with 234°F/112°C recommended).

2. Remove from the heat. Add the white chocolate, stirring until melted. Add the marshmallows. Let the marshmallows stand 1 to 2 minutes to soften. Stir the candy until it is smooth and well blended. Stir in the vanilla and nuts, if desired. Pour into the prepared pan. Cool and cut into squares. Store in an airtight container.

Variation

Dark Mocha Fudge: Substitute 6 oz (175 g) chopped semisweet chocolate for the white chocolate.

Storing Candy

Most candies should be stored in an airtight container to keep them fresh. Unless specifically instructed in the recipe, refrigeration is often a matter of personal choice, but generally, most fudges and fudge-like candies should keep at least 1 week at room temperature and at least 1 month, sometimes much longer, if refrigerated. Excessive heat, high humidity, or added ingredients such as fruit may shorten the storage time so it is important to use common sense. If the color or texture of the candy has changed, dispose of it and make a fresh batch.

Out-of-This-World Maple Fudge

3 cups	granulated sugar	750 mL
1 cup	sour cream	250 mL
1 tbsp	light (white) corn syrup	15 mL
1/2 cup	butter or margarine	125 mL
1/4 tsp	butter flavoring	1 mL
1/4 tsp	cream of tartar	1 mL
1/4 tsp	salt	1 mL
1/2 to 1 tsp	maple extract	2 to 5 mL
1 cup	coarsely chopped walnuts (optional)	250 mL

Deserving of its name, this exceptionally smooth and creamy fudge will definitely be a hit with maple lovers of all ages. Our family did not discover this recipe until after my mother had retired from candy making and turned the job over to me, but once she tasted this special fudge I could count on her to ask for it every Christmas. I often use 1/2 teaspoon (2 mL) maple extract instead of a full teaspoon (5 mL) because I prefer the lighter flavor. Note that reducing the maple extract can make the sour cream flavor a bit more prominent, but if you love sour cream then you won't mind a bit!

Skill Level: Advanced

Makes about 2 1/2 lbs (1.25 kg)

- 8-inch (20 cm) square pan, lined with parchment (see Cook's Notes, below) or buttered
- 3-quart heavy saucepan
- Candy thermometer

1. In heavy saucepan over medium-low heat, bring the sugar, sour cream, corn syrup, butter, butter flavoring, cream of tartar and salt to a boil, stirring until the sugar dissolves and the mixture begins to boil. Cover and cook 2 to 3 minutes to dissolve the sugar crystals on the sides of the pan. Remove the lid. Cook very slowly over low to medium-low heat, without stirring, to the soft ball stage (234°F to 240°F/112°C to 116°C, with 238°F/114°C recommended for soft fudge or 240°F/116°C for firmer fudge.)

2. Remove from the heat. Cool to lukewarm (110°F/43°C), 45 minutes to 1 hour.

3. Beat by hand until the candy begins to hold its shape. Stir in the maple extract and walnuts, if desired. Pour into the prepared pan. Cool and cut into squares. Store in an airtight container.

Cook's Notes

Cutting candy becomes much easier with the use of parchment paper. Rather than buttering the pan directly, butter a piece of parchment paper larger than the pan and press it into the bottom and up the sides of the pan, tucking and creasing the paper as needed to create corners, and leaving a generous overhang over the sides of the pan.

This recipe is an excellent example of how candy ingredients interact to produce smooth and creamy candies. For further explanation, see The Science of Candy Making (page 13).

Maple Sugar Fudge

1 cup	granulated sugar	250 mL
1 cup	granulated maple sugar	250 mL
1 cup	milk (or $3/4$ cup/175 mL evaporated milk and $1/2$ cup/125 mL water)	250 mL
2 tbsp	light (white or golden) corn syrup	30 mL
Pinch	salt	Pinch
2 tbsp	butter or margarine	30 mL
1 tsp	vanilla extract	5 mL

> This candy is smooth, creamy and rich in maple flavor.

Cook's Note

Granulated maple sugar can be purchased via the Internet from companies and farms that produce high-quality maple syrups, and is also available in specialty stores and many farmers' markets.

Skill Level: Advanced

Makes about $1\frac{1}{2}$ lbs (750 g)

- 9- by 5-inch (23 by 12.5 cm) loaf pan, lined with parchment (see Cook's Notes, page 155) or buttered
- 3-quart heavy saucepan
- Candy thermometer

1. In heavy saucepan over low to medium-low heat, bring the granulated and maple sugars, milk, corn syrup and salt to a boil, stirring until the sugars dissolve and the mixture begins to boil. Cover and cook 2 to 3 minutes to dissolve the sugar crystals on the sides of the pan. Remove the lid. Cook, without stirring, to the soft ball stage (234°F to 240°F/112°C to 116°C, with 236°F/113°C recommended for soft fudge or 238°F/114°C for firm fudge).

2. Remove from the heat. Add the butter without stirring. Cool to lukewarm (110°F/43°C), 45 minutes to 1 hour.

3. Add the vanilla. Beat by hand until the candy is thick and creamy. (The candy may retain some of its gloss.) Pour into the prepared pan. Cool and cut into squares. Store in an airtight container.

Variation

Wildcat Brown Sugar Fudge: Substitute 1 cup (250 mL) packed light brown sugar for the maple sugar.

Norway Black Walnut Fudge

3 cups	granulated sugar	750 mL
3 cups	packed light brown sugar	750 mL
2 cups	half-and-half (10%) cream	500 mL
2 tbsp	light (white) corn syrup	30 mL
	Butter the size of an egg ($\frac{1}{4}$ cup/60 mL butter)	
1 cup	coarsely chopped black walnuts (optional)	250 mL
1 cup	chopped dates with no sugar additives (optional)	250 mL
1 tsp	vanilla extract	5 mL

This interesting old recipe is surprisingly delicious with black walnuts and dates giving the candy a unique flavor and charm. The original recipe called for a piece of butter the size of an egg.

Cook's Notes

Before starting this recipe, read the package label to be certain the dates contain no sugar additives such as dextrose. These additives will spark a chain reaction, causing sugar crystals to form and the candy to sugar in the pan.

This recipe may be reduced by half, cooked in a heavy 3-quart saucepan and poured into a buttered 8-inch (20 cm) square pan.

Makes about 4 lbs (2 kg)

- 13- by 9-inch (33 by 23 cm) pan, lined with parchment (see Cook's Notes, page 155) or buttered
- 5-quart heavy candy kettle or pot
- Candy thermometer

1. In heavy candy kettle over medium heat, bring the granulated and brown sugars, half-and-half and corn syrup to a boil, stirring until the sugars dissolve and the mixture begins to boil. Reduce the heat to medium low. Cover and cook 2 to 3 minutes to dissolve the sugar crystals on the sides of the pan. Remove the lid. Cook slowly, stirring only as needed to prevent scorching, to the soft ball stage (234°F to 240°F/112°C to 116°C, with 234°F/112°C recommended).

2. Remove from the heat. Add the butter and walnuts and dates, if desired, without stirring or shaking the pan. Cool to lukewarm (110°F/43°C), about 1 hour.

3. Add the vanilla. Beat by hand until the candy begins to thicken and lose its gloss. Pour into the prepared pan. Cool and cut into squares. Store in an airtight container.

Important Tip

In many recipes, it is important to be prepared for all the steps because timing can be critical. Have all ingredients available and ready to use, and have the pan, baking sheet, or surface prepared before you begin cooking.

Creamy Orange Fudge

2¼ cups	granulated sugar	550 mL
¾ cup	half-and-half (10%) cream	175 mL
1 tbsp	butter	15 mL
2 tbsp	freshly grated orange zest	30 mL
6 tbsp	orange juice	90 mL
1 tsp	lemon juice	5 mL
¼ tsp	cream of tartar	1 mL
1 cup	pecans or walnuts, in large pieces (optional)	250 mL

Perfect for a springtime luncheon or Mother's Day celebration, this enchanting orange delicacy is a nice change of pace from the usual chocolate fudges.

Skill Level: Advanced

Makes about 1½ lbs (750 g)

- 9- by 5-inch (23 by 12.5 cm) loaf pan, lined with parchment (see Cook's Notes, page 155) or buttered
- 2-quart heavy saucepan
- Candy thermometer

1. In heavy saucepan over low to medium-low heat, bring the sugar, half-and-half, butter, orange zest, orange juice, lemon juice and cream of tartar to a boil, stirring until the sugar dissolves and the mixture begins to boil. Cover and cook 2 to 3 minutes to dissolve the sugar crystals on the sides of the pan. Remove the lid. Cook over low heat, stirring only as needed to prevent scorching, to the soft ball stage (234°F to 240°F/112°C to 116°C, with 238°F/114°C recommended).

2. Remove from the heat. Cool to lukewarm (110°F/43°C), 45 minutes to 1 hour.

3. Beat by hand until the candy begins to thicken and lose its gloss. Quickly stir in the nuts, if desired. Pour into the prepared pan. Cool and cut into squares. Store in an airtight container.

Storing Candy

Most candies should be stored in an airtight container to keep them fresh. Unless specifically instructed in the recipe, refrigeration is often a matter of personal choice, but generally, most fudges and fudge-like candies should keep at least 1 week at room temperature and at least 1 month, sometimes much longer, if refrigerated. Excessive heat, high humidity, or added ingredients such as fruit may shorten the storage time so it is important to use common sense. If the color or texture of the candy has changed, dispose of it and make a fresh batch.

Banana Fudge

2 cups	granulated sugar	500 mL
2 tbsp	light (white) corn syrup	30 mL
2/3 cup	milk	150 mL
2	ripe bananas, mashed	2
2 tbsp	butter or margarine	30 mL
1/2 tsp	vanilla extract	2 mL
3/4 cup	pecans, in large pieces (optional)	175 mL

This recipe may not be for everyone, but those who love banana-flavored sweets will find this an interesting and unusual treat.

Cook's Note

This candy is more likely to need stirring during the last few minutes of cooking.

Makes about 1 1/4 lbs (625 g)

- 9-by 5-inch (23 by 12.5 cm) loaf pan, lined with parchment (see Cook's Notes, page 155) or buttered
- 2-quart heavy saucepan
- Candy thermometer

1. In heavy saucepan over medium-low heat, bring the sugar, corn syrup, milk and bananas to a boil, stirring until the sugar dissolves and the mixture begins to boil. Cook, stirring occasionally to prevent scorching, to the soft ball stage (234°F to 240°F/112°C to 116°C, with 236°F/113°C recommended).

2. Remove from heat. Stir in butter, vanilla and pecans, if desired. Set saucepan in a pan of cool water about 20 minutes to allow candy to cool.

3. Beat by hand until the candy changes texture, lightens in color and becomes smooth. Pour into the prepared pan. Cool and cut into squares. Store in an airtight container.

Hawaiian Fudge

2 cups	granulated sugar	500 mL
1 cup	packed light brown sugar	250 mL
1 cup	canned crushed pineapple, drained	250 mL
1/2 cup	half-and-half (10%) cream or evaporated milk	125 mL
1 tsp	ground ginger	5 mL
2 tbsp	butter or margarine	30 mL
2 tsp	vanilla extract	10 mL
1 cup	pecans, in large pieces (optional)	250 mL

A hint of ginger adds interest to this unusual pineapple-flavored candy.

Makes about 2 lbs (1 kg)

- 9- by 5-inch (23 by 12.5 cm) loaf pan, lined with parchment (see Cook's Notes, page 155) or buttered
- 3-quart saucepan
- Candy thermometer

1. In heavy saucepan over medium-low heat, bring the sugars, pineapple, half-and- half and ginger to a boil, stirring until the sugars dissolve and the mixture begins to boil. Cover and cook 2 to 3 minutes to remove the sugar crystals from the sides of the pan. Remove the lid. Cook, stirring occasionally to prevent scorching, to the soft ball stage (234°F to 240°F/112°C to 116°C, with 234°F/112°C recommended).

2. Remove from the heat. Add the butter without stirring. Cool to lukewarm (110°F/43°C), 45 minutes to 1 hour.

3. Add the vanilla and pecans, if desired. Beat by hand until the candy is thick and creamy. Pour into the prepared pan. Cool and cut into squares.

Coconut Fudge

3 cups	granulated sugar	750 mL
1 cup	half-and-half (10%) cream	250 mL
1 cup	light (white) corn syrup	250 mL
1 tbsp	vanilla extract	15 mL
1/2 cup	sweetened flaked coconut	125 mL
1 cup	coarsely chopped pecans (optional)	250 mL
1/2 to 1 cup	chopped candied cherries (optional)	125 to 250 mL
1/2 cup	chopped candied pineapple (optional)	125 mL

> Bright red candied cherries make this light brown coconut fudge particularly fun and festive.

Cook's Note

Adjust the coconut, cherries and pineapple to taste.

Skill Level: Advanced

Makes about 2 1/2 lbs (1.25 kg)

- 8-inch (20 cm) square pan, lined with parchment (see Cook's Notes, page 155) or buttered
- 5-quart heavy candy kettle or pot
- Candy thermometer

1. In heavy candy kettle over medium-low heat, bring the sugar, half-and-half and corn syrup to a boil, stirring until the sugar dissolves and the mixture begins to boil. Reduce the heat to low. Cook slowly, gently stirring only a few times to prevent scorching, to the soft ball stage (234°F to 240°F/112°C to 116°C, with 240°F/116°C recommended).

2. Remove from the heat. Cool 20 minutes.

3. Add the vanilla. Beat by hand until the candy thickens and begins to hold its shape. (The candy will retain some of its gloss.) Stir in the coconut and the pecans, cherries and pineapple, if desired. Pour into the prepared pan. Cool and cut into squares. Store in an airtight container.

Pineapple Sherbet Fudge

3 cups	granulated sugar	750 mL
1 cup	half-and-half (10%) cream	250 mL
3 tbsp	light (white) corn syrup	45 mL
1	can (8 oz/227 mL) crushed pineapple, drained	1
2 tsp	lemon juice	10 mL
1/4 tsp	cream of tartar	1 mL
1/4 cup	butter	60 mL
1/4 tsp	pure lemon extract	1 mL
3/4 cup	coarsely chopped walnuts (optional)	175 mL

> With just a hint of lemon, this creamy white, pineapple-speckled fudge will help you welcome friends with style.

Skill Level: Advanced

Makes about 2 1/4 lbs (1.125 kg)

- 8-inch (20) square pan, lined with parchment or buttered
- 3-quart heavy saucepan
- Candy thermometer

1. In heavy saucepan over medium heat, bring sugar, half-and-half, syrup, pineapple, lemon juice and cream of tartar to a boil, stirring until sugar dissolves and mixture begins to boil. Reduce heat to low or medium low. Cover and cook 2 to 3 minutes to dissolve sugar crystals on sides of pan. Remove lid. Cook, without stirring, to the soft ball stage (234°F to 240°F/112°C to 116°C, with 236°F/113°C recommended).

2. Remove from heat. Add butter and extract. Beat by hand until it begins to thicken and hold its shape. (Although most candies are cooled before beating, this candy must be beaten while still hot.) Stir in walnuts. Pour into pan. Cool and cut into squares. Store in an airtight container.

The Preacher's Pineapple Fudge

3 cups	granulated sugar	750 mL
1 cup	evaporated milk	250 mL
2 tbsp	butter or margarine	30 mL
1 cup	canned crushed pineapple, drained	250 mL
2 tsp	lemon juice	10 mL

A retired minister friend chose this dense, light brown fudge as his favorite of all the candies he tasted.

Skill Level: Advanced

Makes about 2 lbs (1 kg)

- 8-inch (20 cm) square pan, lined with parchment (see Cook's Notes, page 155) or buttered
- 2-quart heavy saucepan
- Candy thermometer

1. In heavy saucepan over medium-low heat, bring the sugar, milk and butter to a boil, stirring until the sugar dissolves and the mixture begins to boil. Stir in the pineapple. Cover and cook 2 to 3 minutes to dissolve the sugar crystals on the sides of the pan. Remove the lid. Cook over low heat to medium-low heat, stirring occasionally to prevent scorching, to the soft ball stage (234°F to 240°F/112°C to 116°C, with 236°F/113°C recommended).

2. Remove from the heat. Cool to lukewarm (110°F/43°C), 45 minutes to 1 hour.

3. Add the lemon juice. Beat by hand until the candy loses its gloss and begins to thicken and hold its shape. Pour into the prepared pan. Cool and cut into squares. Store in an airtight container.

Pumpkin Fudge

3 cups	granulated sugar	750 mL
$1/2$ cup	butter or margarine	125 mL
1 cup	half-and-half (10%) cream	250 mL
$1/2$ cup	unsweetened canned pumpkin purée (not pie filling)	125 mL
$1/2$ tsp	ground cinnamon	2 mL
$1/4$ tsp	ground nutmeg	1 mL
Pinch	ground cloves	Pinch
2 cups	butterscotch chips (12 oz/375 g)	500 mL
1	jar (7 oz/198 g) jar marshmallow creme	1
1 tsp	vanilla extract	5 mL
$1^1/_2$ cups	coarsely chopped pecans or walnuts (optional)	375 mL

> Do not be surprised if pumpkin-loving friends say that this is the best pumpkin-flavored food they have ever tasted.

Cook's Note

Though this is a popular combination of spices, the particular spices used and the amount used may be adjusted for personal tastes. For example, ground ginger can be substituted for the nutmeg. Look at your favorite pumpkin pie recipe for ideas.

Skill Level: Average

Makes about 2½ to 3 lbs (1.25 to 1.5 kg)

- 8- or 9-inch (20 or 23 cm) square pan, lined with parchment (see Cook's Notes, page 155) or buttered
- 5-quart heavy candy kettle or pot
- Candy thermometer

1. In heavy candy kettle over medium-low to medium heat, bring the sugar, butter, half-and-half, pumpkin, cinnamon, nutmeg and cloves to a boil, stirring until the sugar dissolves and the mixture begins to boil. Cook, stirring constantly to prevent scorching, to the soft ball stage (234°F to 240°F/112°C to 116°C, with 234°F/112°C recommended). Remove from the heat.

2. Stir in the butterscotch chips until melted. Stir in the marshmallow creme until blended. Add the vanilla and walnuts, if desired. Pour into the prepared pan. Cool and cut into squares. Store in an airtight container.

Variation

Light Pumpkin Fudge: For a lighter flavor, substitute vanilla-flavored baking chips for the butterscotch chips.

Creamy Blonde Fudge

3 cups	granulated sugar	750 mL
1 cup	half-and-half (10%) cream	250 mL
1/2 cup	milk	125 mL
1/4 cup	light (white) corn syrup	60 mL
2 tbsp	butter or margarine	30 mL
1 1/2 tsp	vanilla extract	7 mL
1 cup	pecans or walnuts, in large pieces (optional)	250 mL

Additional cream and butter make this candy richer than its cousin, Creamy White Fudge (below). Both candies have a creamy, but slightly sticky texture due to the ingredients.

Skill Level: Advanced

Makes about 2 1/2 lbs (1.25 kg)

- 8-inch (20 cm) square pan, lined with parchment (see Cook's Notes, page 155) or buttered
- 5-quart heavy candy kettle or pot
- Candy thermometer

1. In heavy candy kettle over medium heat, bring the sugar, half-and-half, milk, corn syrup and butter to a boil, stirring until the sugar dissolves and the mixture begins to boil. Cook, stirring occasionally to prevent scorching, to the soft ball stage (234°F to 240°F/112°C to 116°C, with 238°F/114°C recommended).

2. Remove from the heat. Cool to lukewarm (110°F/43°C), 45 minutes to 1 hour.

3. Add the vanilla. Beat by hand until the mixture begins to thicken and lose its gloss. Stir in the nuts, if desired. Quickly spread the candy into the prepared pan. Cool and cut into squares. Store in an airtight container.

Creamy White Fudge

3 cups	granulated sugar	750 mL
1/2 cup	half-and-half (10%) cream or milk	125 mL
1 cup	light (white) corn syrup	250 mL
1 tsp	vanilla extract	5 mL
1 cup	coarsely chopped pecans or walnuts (optional)	250 mL

With less cream and no butter, this candy is not quite as rich as its cousin, Creamy Blonde Fudge (above). Both candies have a creamy, but slightly sticky texture due to the ingredients.

Skill Level: Advanced

Makes about 2 1/2 lbs (1.25 kg)

- 8-inch (20 cm) square pan, lined with parchment (see Cook's Notes, page 155) or buttered
- 5-quart heavy candy kettle or pot
- Candy thermometer

1. In heavy candy kettle over medium heat, bring the sugar, half-and-half and corn syrup to a boil, stirring until the sugar dissolves and the mixture begins to boil. Reduce the heat to medium low. Cover and cook 2 to 3 minutes to dissolve the sugar crystals on the sides of the pan. Remove the lid. Cook, stirring occasionally, to the soft ball stage (234°F to 240°F/112°C to 116°C, with 238°F/114°C recommended).

2. Remove from the heat. Cool 20 minutes without stirring.

3. Add the vanilla. Beat by hand until the candy thickens and loses its gloss. Stir in the nuts, if desired. Pour into the prepared pan. Cool and cut into squares. Store in an airtight container.

White Cherry Fudge

2¼ cups	granulated sugar	550 mL
½ cup	sour cream	125 mL
¼ cup	milk	60 mL
2 tbsp	butter or margarine	30 mL
1 tbsp	light (white) corn syrup	15 mL
¼ tsp	salt	1 mL
2 tsp	vanilla extract	10 mL
1 cup	walnuts, in large pieces (optional)	250 mL
⅓ cup	chopped candied cherries	75 mL

A bite of this colorful, ultra-sweet and creamy fudge is just the thing to put me into a festive holiday mood. I often include a few pieces in gift tins to add a bit of color and cheer.

Cook's Notes

For step-by-step photographs of making fudge, see color pages A and B.

Cutting candy becomes much easier with the use of parchment paper. Rather than buttering the pan directly, butter a piece of parchment paper larger than the pan and press it into the bottom and up the sides of the pan, tucking and creasing the paper as needed to create corners, and leaving a generous overhang over the sides of the pan.

This fudge is not very thick when poured into an 8-inch (20 cm) square pan. If preferred, pour the candy into a smaller pan or double the recipe, cooking the candy in a heavy 3- to 4-quart saucepan.

Makes about 1½ lbs (750 g)

- 8-inch (20 cm) square pan, lined with parchment (see Cook's Notes, left) or buttered
- 2-quart heavy saucepan
- Candy thermometer

1. In heavy saucepan over medium-low to medium heat, bring the sugar, sour cream, milk, butter, corn syrup and salt to a boil, stirring until the sugar dissolves and the mixture begins to boil. Cook, stirring constantly to prevent scorching, to the soft ball stage (234°F to 240°F/112°C to 116°C, with 238°F/114°C recommended).

2. Remove from the heat. Cool to lukewarm (110°F/43°C), about 1 hour.

3. Add the vanilla. Beat by hand just until the candy begins to lose its gloss and hold its shape. Quickly stir in the walnuts, if desired, and cherries. Immediately turn into the prepared pan. (Note: The candy can set up very rapidly once it begins to cool, so it is important to work quickly. It may be necessary to pat or press the candy into the pan using the back of a large spoon.) Cool and cut into squares. Store in an airtight container.

Important Tip

In many recipes, it is important to be prepared for all the steps because timing can be critical. Have all ingredients available and ready to use, and have the pan, baking sheet, or surface prepared before you begin cooking.

Royal Eggnog Fudge

2 cups	granulated sugar	500 mL
1/4 tsp	ground cinnamon	1 mL
1/8 tsp	ground nutmeg	0.5 mL
1/8 tsp	ground cloves	0.5 mL
1 cup	commercially prepared eggnog (no alcohol added)	250 mL
1/4 cup	butter or margarine	60 mL
8 oz	white chocolate, coarsely chopped	250 g
1	jar (7 oz/198 g) marshmallow creme	1
1 tsp	vanilla extract	5 mL
1 cup	pecans or walnuts, in large pieces (optional)	250 mL

Spice up your holidays with this unusual combination of white chocolate, cinnamon, nutmeg and cloves.

Cook's Note

The amount of spices needed may depend upon both personal taste and the brand of eggnog used in the candy. If highly spiced eggnog is used, additional nutmeg may not be necessary. Taste the eggnog before making the candy and then adjust the spices, as desired. The cinnamon, nutmeg and cloves may be omitted entirely if preferred.

Makes about 2 1/2 lbs (1.25 kg)

- 8- or 9-inch (20 or 23 cm) square pan, lined with parchment (see Cook's Notes, page 164) or buttered
- 2- to 3-quart heavy saucepan
- Candy thermometer

1. In heavy saucepan, combine the sugar, cinnamon, nutmeg and cloves, stirring until well blended. Add the eggnog and butter. Bring to a boil over medium heat, stirring constantly. Cook, stirring constantly to prevent scorching, to the soft ball stage (234°F to 240°F/112°C to 116°C, with 238°F/114°C recommended).

2. Remove from the heat. Stir in the chocolate until melted. Add the marshmallow creme and vanilla and stir until smooth and well blended. Add the nuts, if desired. Pour into the prepared pan. Cool and cut into squares. Store in an airtight container.

Variation

Cherry Eggnog Fudge: Omit the cinnamon, nutmeg and cloves. Stir in 1/2 to 3/4 cup (125 to 175 mL) chopped candied cherries when adding the nuts.

Storing Candy

Most candies should be stored in an airtight container to keep them fresh. Unless specifically instructed in the recipe, refrigeration is often a matter of personal choice, but generally, most fudges and fudge-like candies should keep at least 1 week at room temperature and at least 1 month, sometimes much longer, if refrigerated. Excessive heat, high humidity, or added ingredients such as fruit may shorten the storage time so it is important to use common sense. If the color or texture of the candy has changed, dispose of it and make a fresh batch.

Lemon–White Chocolate Fudge

2 cups	granulated sugar	500 mL
3/4 cup	sour cream	175 mL
1/2 cup	butter or margarine	125 mL
Pinch	salt	Pinch
	Freshly grated zest of 2 lemons	
8 oz	white chocolate, coarsely chopped	250 g
1	jar (7 oz/198 g) marshmallow creme	1
1 to 1 1/2 tsp	pure lemon extract	5 to 7 mL
1 to 2	drops yellow food coloring (optional)	1 to 2

> This versatile recipe has enough white chocolate to capture attention, but not enough to overwhelm. For deeper flavor, use up to 12 oz (375 g) white chocolate.

Skill Level: Average

Makes about 2 1/4 lbs (1.125 kg)

- 8-inch (20 cm) square pan, lined with parchment (see Cook's Notes, page 164) or buttered
- 2-quart heavy saucepan
- Candy thermometer

1. In heavy saucepan over medium heat, bring the sugar, sour cream, butter, salt and lemon zest to a boil, stirring until the sugar dissolves and the mixture begins to boil. Cook, stirring occasionally to prevent scorching, to the soft ball stage (234°F to 240°F/112°C to 116°C, with 238°F/114°C recommended).

2. Remove from the heat. Stir in the chocolate until melted. Add the marshmallow creme and lemon extract. Stir until the candy is smooth and well blended. Stir in the food coloring, if using. Pour into the prepared pan. Cool to room temperature, chill and cut into squares. Store in an airtight container.

Variations

Orange–White Chocolate Fudge: Substitute orange zest for the lemon zest. Substitute 1 tsp (5 mL) orange extract for the lemon extract. Omit the food coloring.

Rum Raisin– or Rum Nut–White Chocolate Fudge: Omit the lemon zest and the food coloring. Substitute 1 tsp (5 mL) rum extract for the lemon extract. Add 3/4 cup (175 mL) raisins before pouring the candy into the pan. Coarsely chopped nuts can be used in place of the raisins.

Apricot–White Chocolate Fudge: Omit the lemon zest and the food coloring. Substitute 1 tsp (5 mL) vanilla or almond extract for the lemon extract. Add 3/4 cup (175 mL) chopped dried apricots. If desired, add 3/4 cup (175 mL) coarsely chopped nuts before pouring the candy into the pan.

Cherry–White Chocolate Fudge: Omit the lemon zest and the food coloring. Substitute 1 tsp (5 mL) cherry extract for the lemon extract. Add 3/4 cup (175 mL) chopped dried, candied or maraschino cherries. If desired, add 3/4 cup (175 mL) coarsely chopped nuts before pouring the candy into the pan.

Cranberry–White Chocolate Fudge: Omit the lemon zest and the food coloring. Substitute 1 tsp (5 mL) vanilla extract for the lemon extract. Add 3/4 cup (175 mL) chopped dried cranberries. If desired, add 3/4 cup (175 mL) coarsely chopped nuts before pouring the candy into the pan.

White Chocolate Fudge: Omit the lemon zest and the food coloring. Substitute 1 tsp (5 mL) vanilla extract for the lemon extract. If desired, add 3/4 cup (175 mL) coarsely chopped nuts before pouring the candy into the pan.

Chocolate Fudge: Omit the lemon zest and the food coloring. Substitute 10 oz (300 g) semisweet chocolate for the white chocolate. If desired, add 3/4 cup (175 mL) coarsely chopped nuts, candied cherries or maraschino cherries.

Dreamy White Christmas Fudge

2½ cups	confectioner's (icing) sugar	625 mL
⅔ cup	milk	150 mL
¼ cup	butter or margarine	60 mL
12 oz	white chocolate, coarsely chopped	375 g
½ tsp	almond extract	2 mL
¾ cup	coarsely chopped dried apricots, cherries or cranberries	175 mL
¾ cup	sliced almonds, toasted	175 mL

> You will be dreaming of a different kind of white Christmas once you taste my cousin Margaret's special recipe. The incredible blend of white chocolate, toasted almonds and fruit all in one luscious fudge, what could possibly be better?

Cook's Note

This fudge is very soft and best served cold. Do not try cooking this candy to a soft ball stage (234°F to 240°F/112°C to 116°C). For a slightly firmer fudge, boil the candy mixture about 1 minute longer.

Skill Level: Average

Makes about 1½ lbs (750 g)

- 8-inch (20 cm) square pan, lined with foil, buttered
- 3-quart heavy saucepan
- Candy thermometer

1. In heavy saucepan over medium heat, bring the sugar, milk and butter to a boil, stirring until the sugar dissolves and the mixture begins to boil. Reduce the heat slightly. Cook at a steady boil, without stirring, for 5 minutes. (If using a candy thermometer, the mixture will reach approximately 222°F/106°C.)

2. Remove from the heat. Add the white chocolate and stir until melted and smooth. Add the almond extract, fruit and almonds. Pour into the prepared pan. Refrigerate 2 hours. Invert the pan and remove the foil lining. Cut into squares. Store in an airtight container in the refrigerator.

Important Tip

In many recipes, it is important to be prepared for all the steps because timing can be critical. Have all ingredients available and ready to use, and have the pan, baking sheet, or surface prepared before you begin cooking.

Designer Delights

● ●

One of the great pleasures of being a candy maker is adding our own personal signature to the candies we make. Many of the recipes in Designer Delights inspire this creativity, letting us shape, mold and decorate a candy just to our liking.

Those of us who love chocolate-coated candies know that a minor change in the type of chocolate we choose allows us to customize a coating to our personal tastes. A simple white chocolate drizzle often adds a touch of elegance to a favorite dark chocolate–coated candy, signaling to others that this special creation deserves to be noticed. Nut-loving candy makers may prefer to sprinkle freshly dipped candies with toasted pecans, walnuts, hazelnuts or almonds, while others may add a bit of artistry by topping their candies with white or dark chocolate shavings or decorator sprinkles.

One of the great pleasures of being a candy maker is adding our own personal signature to the candies we make.

Fondants are the most versatile confections on earth, with fondant recipes providing us with basic instructions and then letting us choose the flavorings, colorings, shapes and ingredients that will create the candies that we crave. A fondant can become the maple cream center in a box of Forrest Gump's chocolates or the delicate pastel wafer we serve with a cup of hot tea. Though we often think of fondants as the filling for bonbons, nothing says that our fondant-based candies must always be round. When candy makers dream of oval pink Easter eggs coated in fluffy white coconut, they simply turn to their fondant recipes and let their imaginations soar.

Nothing gives us that pampered feeling quite like the taste of a silky smooth, light and fluffy truffle. Considered the ultimate luxury candy, truffles are much easier to make than most people think, usually requiring more time than talent. Once again, many basic truffle recipes can be flavored, coated and decorated any way a budding gourmet desires. And remember, truffles do not have to be perfectly shaped to taste good. Sometimes handmade imperfections only add charm to this divine and thoughtful hand-fashioned gift.

Chocolate-Cherry Creams

1 cup	semisweet chocolate chips (6 oz/175 g)	250 mL
1/3 cup	evaporated milk	75 mL
1 1/2 cups	confectioner's (icing) sugar, sifted	375 mL
1/3 cup	finely chopped pecans or walnuts	75 mL
1/3 cup	well-drained maraschino cherries, chopped	75 mL
1/2 tsp	cherry extract (optional)	2 mL
1 1/4 cups	sweetened flaked coconut	300 mL

Anyone who loves chocolate-covered cherries will adore these pretty little chocolate snowballs, especially when cherry extract is added.

Cook's Note

If the mixture is too soft to hold its shape, stir in additional confectioner's sugar, a spoonful at a time, until it reaches the desired consistency. If the mixture is too thick, stir in additional milk, a few drops at a time, until it is the desired consistency.

Skill Level: Novice, Easy

Makes about 30

- 2-quart heavy saucepan

1. In heavy saucepan over low heat, heat the chocolate chips and milk together until the chocolate melts, stirring until smooth.
2. Remove from the heat. Stir in the confectioner's sugar, nuts, cherries, and cherry extract, if using, blending well. Cover and refrigerate until the mixture is cool enough to handle, about 1 hour.
3. Shape the mixture into balls 1 inch (2.5 cm) in diameter. Roll the balls in the coconut. Store in an airtight container in the refrigerator.

Variation

Almond Cherry Creams: Substitute 1/4 to 1/2 tsp (1 to 2 mL) pure almond extract for the cherry extract. Substitute finely chopped toasted almonds for the pecans or walnuts.

Forming Balls and Centers

The easiest way to form balls and centers of candies is to invest in a very small (about 0.5 oz/15 mL) metal scoop, which is somewhat like an ice cream or cookie dough scoop but much smaller in size. If you purchase a good quality tool with a spring handle it should last many years. Restaurant supply stores carry these scoops, or they can be ordered from Internet sources.

If a small scoop is not available, most candies can be shaped into a ball by placing a small amount of mixture into your hand and then using both hands to roll the candy into a ball. For soft fillings, such as truffles, it may be easier to drop a rounded teaspoon (5 mL) of filling directly onto the lined baking sheet. Soft fillings can also be placed into a pastry bag and piped onto the lined baking sheet using a plain decorator's tip.

Chocolate Angel Sweets

1 cup	semisweet chocolate chips	250 mL
2 tbsp	butter or margarine	30 mL
1 cup	sifted confectioner's (icing) sugar	250 mL
1 to 2 tbsp	evaporated milk	15 to 30 mL
1 cup	chopped walnuts or pecans	250 mL
2 cups	miniature marshmallows	500 mL
1	can (3.5 oz/105 g) sweetened flaked coconut or 1 1/3 cups (325 mL)	1

> In just a few minutes, you can be eating these yummy little fudge candies.

Cook's Note

For coconut: 1 1/3 cups (325 mL) coconut = 3.5 ounces (105 g) and 2 2/3 cups (650 mL) = 7 ounces (210 g).

Skill Level: Novice, Easy

Makes about 36

- 2 large baking sheets, lined with waxed paper
- 1-quart heavy saucepan

1. In heavy saucepan, heat the chocolate chips and butter together over low heat until melted, stirring to prevent scorching. Remove from the heat. Blend in the confectioner's sugar and 1 tbsp (15 mL) milk. Stir in the nuts and marshmallows, blending well. (The marshmallows will only partially melt.) If the mixture is too thick to handle, stir in additional milk, a few drops at a time, until the mixture reaches the desired consistency. Cool slightly, about 5 minutes.

2. Shape the mixture into balls 1 inch (2.5 cm) in diameter. Roll the balls in the coconut. Place on the prepared baking sheet(s). Refrigerate until firm, about 30 minutes. Store in an airtight container in the refrigerator.

Variation

Butterscotch Angel Sweets: Substitute 1 cup (250 mL) butterscotch chips for the semisweet chocolate chips.

Storing Candy

Most candies should be stored in an airtight container to keep them fresh. Unless specifically instructed in the recipe, refrigeration is often a matter of personal choice, but generally, most fudges and fudge-like candies should keep at least 1 week at room temperature and at least 1 month, sometimes much longer, if refrigerated. Excessive heat, high humidity, or added ingredients such as fruit may shorten the storage time so it is important to use common sense. If the color or texture of the candy has changed, dispose of it and make a fresh batch.

Festive Chocolate Nut Balls

1 cup	very fine vanilla wafer crumbs	250 mL
1 cup	confectioner's (icing) sugar	250 mL
2 tbsp	unsweetened cocoa powder	30 mL
2 tbsp	light (white or golden) corn syrup	30 mL
2 tbsp	half-and-half (10%) cream	30 mL
1 tsp	vanilla, almond or rum extract	5 mL
¾ cup	finely chopped pecans or walnuts	175 mL
¾ cup	sweetened flaked coconut	175 mL
1½ cups	ground pecans or walnuts, or flaked coconut, for rolling (approx.)	375 mL

Skill Level: Novice, Super Simple

Makes about 30

1. Cover a large countertop area or a large baking sheet with waxed paper.

2. Pour the crumbs into a medium mixing bowl. Add the confectioner's sugar and cocoa, mixing well. Blend in the corn syrup, half-and-half and vanilla. Stir in the finely chopped nuts and ¾ cup (175 mL) coconut.

3. Shape the mixture into balls 1 inch (2.5 cm) in diameter. Roll the balls in the ground nuts, coconut or a combination of both as desired. Place on the waxed paper to dry, about 15 minutes. Store in an airtight container in the refrigerator.

> Just change the extract in this good and simple recipe and you have a new candy flavor.

Creamy Apricot Balls

1½ cups	finely chopped dried apricots	375 mL
2 cups	sweetened flaked coconut	500 mL
⅔ cup	sweetened condensed milk	150 mL
¾ cup	confectioner's (icing) sugar, for rolling (approx.)	175 mL

Skill Level: Novice, Super Simple

Makes about 35

1. Cover a large countertop area or a large baking sheet with waxed paper.

2. In a large mixing bowl, mix together the apricots and coconut. Stir in the milk, blending well.

3. Shape the mixture into balls 1 inch (2.5 cm) in diameter. Roll in confectioner's sugar. Place on the waxed paper. Let stand, uncovered, until firm. Store in an airtight container in the refrigerator.

> A few of these creamy apricot candies make a wonderful addition to a holiday gift tin.

Zesty Apricot Nut Balls

³/₄ cup	dried apricots	175 mL
¹/₂ cup	pecans or walnut halves or pieces	125 mL
1 cup	sweetened flaked coconut	250 mL
2 tbsp	confectioner's (icing) sugar	30 mL
1 tsp	freshly grated lemon zest	5 mL
1 tsp	lemon juice	5 mL
1 tsp	freshly grated orange zest	5 mL
1 tbsp	orange juice	15 mL
¹/₂ cup	confectioner's (icing) sugar, for rolling (approx.)	125 mL

Flavored with coconut, lemon and orange, Zesty Apricot Nut Balls are a delightful combination, especially for a spring or summer event.

Makes about 18

1. Cover a large countertop area or a large baking sheet with waxed paper.

2. Steam the apricots over boiling water for 10 minutes. Finely chop the apricots and the nuts by hand or in a food processor. Transfer the apricots and nuts to a medium mixing bowl. Add the coconut, 2 tbsp (30 mL) confectioner's sugar, lemon zest, lemon juice, orange zest and orange juice and stir until well blended.

3. Shape the mixture into balls ³/₄ inch (2 cm) in diameter. Roll in the confectioner's sugar. Place on the waxed paper until dry. Store in an airtight container in the refrigerator.

Apricot Nuggets

1 lb	confectioner's (icing) sugar	500 g
6 tbsp	butter or margarine, softened	90 mL
2 tbsp	orange juice	30 mL
1 tsp	vanilla extract	5 mL
1¹/₂ cups	finely chopped dried apricots	375 mL
1¹/₂ cups	finely chopped pecans, for rolling	375 mL

With a flavor somewhat like apricot buttercream frosting, these nut-coated candies only get better with age.

Skill Level: Novice, Super Simple

Makes about 70

1. In a large mixing bowl, combine the confectioner's sugar, butter, orange juice and vanilla until thoroughly blended. Stir in the apricots. Knead the mixture by hand until well mixed.

2. Shape the mixture into balls 1 inch (2.5 cm) in diameter. Roll in the chopped pecans. Store in an airtight container in the refrigerator. These candies taste best after 1 to 2 days in the refrigerator.

Apricot Tea Balls

1¼ lbs	dried apricots, finely ground	625 g
1	peeled, finely chopped orange, seeds removed	1
2 cups	granulated sugar	500 mL
½ cup	finely chopped pecans	125 mL
¾ cup	granulated sugar, for rolling	175 mL

In the 1950s, candies made of apricots and oranges were extremely popular, with fruit-flavored balls such as these often appearing at ladies' teas. A food grinder was used to grind the apricots and orange in the '50s, but today's cook can use a food processor.

Makes about 40

1. In a medium mixing bowl, combine the apricots, orange and 2 cups (500 mL) sugar. Cover and let stand at room temperature 2 to 3 hours. Stir in the pecans.

2. Shape the mixture into balls 1 inch (2.5 cm) in diameter. Roll the balls in granulated sugar. Store in an airtight container in the refrigerator.

Cook's Note

To grind apricots, place dried apricots in a food processor, in batches as necessary to avoid crowding, and pulse until apricots are finely ground.

Orange-Nut Tea Balls

12 oz	vanilla wafers	375 g
1 lb	confectioner's (icing) sugar	500 g
1	can (6 oz/175 mL) frozen orange juice concentrate, thawed	1
½ cup	butter or margarine, melted	125 mL
3 cups	finely chopped walnuts or pecans, divided	750 mL

Served in small fluted paper cups, these moist and delicious orange balls make a wonderful addition to any dessert table.

Variations

The balls may be rolled in sweetened flaked coconut if preferred. The walnuts or pecans may also be lightly toasted. The butter may be reduced by up to half, though the balls will not be quite as moist.

Makes about 50

- Food processor

1. Using a food processor, chop the vanilla wafers until they are very fine crumbs. Transfer the wafer crumbs to a large mixing bowl. Add the confectioner's sugar, orange juice concentrate and butter, stirring until blended. Stir in 1 cup (250 mL) of the nuts. Cover and refrigerate until firm enough to handle, 30 minutes to 1 hour.

2. Working with half the mixture at a time to prevent drying, shape the mixture into balls 1 inch (2.5 cm) in diameter. Roll each ball in the remaining chopped nuts. Place in an airtight container, separating each layer with waxed paper. Store in the refrigerator up to 1 week or in the freezer up to 1 month. These candies taste best when served cold.

Elegant Sparkling Strawberries

1	can (14 oz or 300 mL) sweetened condensed milk	1
1	package (3 oz/86 g) strawberry-flavored gelatin	1
2 cups	sweetened flaked coconut	500 mL
1½ to 2 cups	finely chopped walnuts or pecans	375 to 500 mL
40	blanched slivered almonds (about 3.5 oz/100 g)	40
2 to 3	drops green food coloring	2 to 3
½ cup	red decorator sugar, for rolling (approx.)	125 mL
¼ cup	green decorator sugar, for rolling (approx.)	60 mL

Let your creativity flow with these elegant, sparkling red strawberries. Perfect as a garnish or as a special event candy, these beauties are guaranteed to brighten up any tray.

Cook's Notes

Other versions of this recipe contain varying amounts of coconut and nuts, with most recipes using two to three times as much strawberry gelatin. A few versions also add about 2 tbsp (30 mL) granulated sugar to the mixture. While I prefer the lighter strawberry flavor that this recipe offers, the ingredients may be adjusted as desired as long as the mixture is thick enough to hold its shape when formed into a strawberry. If needed, a small amount of confectioner's (icing) sugar can be added to the mixture to help it hold its shape.

It is often easier to work with a few strawberries at a time. Dip about 12 shaped strawberries into the red decorator sugar and place them on the waxed paper. When all 12 are coated in red, dip the ends in the green sugar, insert the stems and place them on the waxed paper again. Repeat until all the mixture is used.

Skill Level: Novice, Easy

Makes about 40 strawberries

- Large baking sheet, lined with waxed paper

1. In a large mixing bowl, combine the milk and strawberry gelatin, stirring until well blended. Stir in the coconut and chopped nuts, blending well. Cover and refrigerate 30 minutes to make the mixture easier to handle.

2. Place the almonds into a small plastic bag. Add the green food coloring to the bag. Seal tightly and shake until the almonds are tinted to resemble green stems. Remove the almonds from the bag and place them on paper towels to dry.

3. Pour the red decorator sugar into a small custard cup. Pour the green decorator sugar into another small custard cup.

4. Shape the milk mixture into small balls about ¾ to 1 inch (2 to 2.5 cm) in diameter. Pinch one end of the ball between the thumb and index finger until it resembles a strawberry. Roll the bottom two-thirds of the strawberry in red decorator sugar. Dip the top end of the strawberry in green decorator sugar. Place a green almond into the green end of the strawberry to resemble a stem. Place on waxed paper. Repeat until all strawberries are shaped. Store in an airtight container in the refrigerator, separating each layer with a sheet of waxed paper. These candies may be refrigerated for up to 1 week or frozen for up to 1 month.

Important Tip

In many recipes, it is important to be prepared for all the steps because timing can be critical. Have all ingredients available and ready to use, and have the pan, baking sheet, or surface prepared before you begin cooking.

Marzipan Potatoes

1¼ cups	finely ground almonds or hazelnuts	300 mL
1 cup	confectioner's (icing) sugar	250 mL
1	egg yolk, pasteurized, or equivalent egg substitute (see Cook's Notes, below)	1
1 tbsp	butter, melted	15 mL
1 tbsp	rum or cognac	15 mL
	Unsweetened cocoa powder, for dusting	

Shaped like miniature potatoes, these rum-flavored, nut-filled candies will be the talk of your next cocktail party.

Cook's Notes

Since this recipe contains an uncooked egg yolk or egg substitute, these candies should be eaten within 2 days.

Uncooked eggs should not be eaten by young children, the elderly or anyone with a compromised immune system because they may contain salmonella bacteria that can cause serious illness.

Pasteurized eggs are available in many markets and are safe to eat raw in dishes that are not cooked.

Skill Level: Novice, Super Simple

Makes 18 to 20

1. In a medium mixing bowl, combine the nuts, confectioner's sugar, egg yolk, butter and rum, stirring to blend. Knead by hand until well blended. Form into a ball.

2. Pinch off small pieces about the size of a walnut and shape into oval-shaped balls that resemble small potatoes. Using a toothpick, poke a few holes into the marzipan potatoes to resemble the eyes on potatoes. Dust generously with cocoa. Place in an airtight container and refrigerate until ready to serve.

Storing Candy

Most candies should be stored in an airtight container to keep them fresh. Unless specifically instructed in the recipe, refrigeration is often a matter of personal choice, but generally, most fudges and fudge-like candies should keep at least 1 week at room temperature and at least 1 month, sometimes much longer, if refrigerated. Excessive heat, high humidity, or added ingredients such as fruit may shorten the storage time so it is important to use common sense. If the color or texture of the candy has changed, dispose of it and make a fresh batch.

Cream Cheese Bonbons

3 oz	cream cheese, softened	90 g
2½ cups	confectioner's (icing) sugar, sifted	625 mL
¼ tsp	vanilla extract	1 mL
Pinch	salt	Pinch
	Few drops food coloring	
½ to 1 cup	sweetened flaked coconut, for rolling	125 to 250 mL

Perfect for a bridal shower or a springtime luncheon, these attractive cream cheese candies can be tinted to match any party theme.

Cook's Note

If preferred, the coconut used for rolling can also be tinted as desired. To tint the coconut, place the coconut in a small plastic bag and sprinkle lightly with water. Add a few drops of food coloring to the bag. Seal the bag and shake well.

Skill Level: Novice, Super Simple

Makes about 24

• Large baking sheet, lined with waxed paper

1. In a medium bowl, beat the cream cheese by hand or with an electric mixer until smooth. Gradually add the confectioner's sugar, blending thoroughly. Add the vanilla, salt and food coloring as desired. Cover and refrigerate 1 hour.

2. Shape the mixture into balls ¾ inch (2 cm) in diameter. Roll the balls in the coconut, flattening the tops of the balls slightly if desired. Place on the prepared baking sheet. Cover and refrigerate 1 hour or until firm. Store in an airtight container in the refrigerator.

Caramel-Raisin Balls

½ cup	packed light brown sugar	125 mL
2 tbsp	butter or margarine	30 mL
2 tbsp	water	30 mL
½ tsp	vanilla extract	2 mL
¼ cup	raisins, chopped	60 mL
¾ to 1 cup	nonfat dry milk	175 to 250 mL
¼ cup	sweetened flaked coconut, for rolling	60 mL

Filled with chewy raisins and covered in coconut, these little candies are a fruit lover's delight.

Skill Level: Novice, Easy

Makes about 24

1. Cover a large countertop area or a large baking sheet with waxed paper.

2. In a very small saucepan over medium heat, bring the brown sugar, butter and water to a boil, stirring until the sugar dissolves and the mixture begins to boil. Boil 1 minute.

3. Remove from the heat. Add the vanilla and raisins. Gradually stir in the milk, mixing well after each addition. Add enough milk that the candy has the consistency of mashed potatoes.

4. Shape the mixture into balls 1 inch (2.5 cm) in diameter. Roll each ball in the coconut. Place the balls on waxed paper until firm. Store in an airtight container in the refrigerator.

Cinnamon Walnut Balls

2 cups	very fine vanilla wafer crumbs	500 mL
1/2 cup	finely chopped drained maraschino cherries	125 mL
1 cup	finely chopped walnuts	250 mL
1/3 cup	granulated sugar	75 mL
1/2 tsp	ground cinnamon	2 mL
1 tsp	lemon juice	5 mL
2/3 cup	sweetened condensed milk	150 mL
1/2 cup	confectioner's (icing) sugar, for rolling (approx.) (optional)	125 mL

Skill Level: Novice, Super Simple

Makes about 36

1. Place the crumbs in a large mixing bowl. Add the cherries and walnuts to the crumbs. Stir in the granulated sugar, cinnamon, lemon juice and milk, blending well.
2. Shape the mixture into balls 1 inch (2.5 cm) in diameter. If desired, roll the balls in confectioner's (icing) sugar to decorate. Store in an airtight container in the refrigerator or freezer. Serve slightly chilled or at room temperature.

Busy hosts and hostesses will love these moist little cinnamon cakelike balls almost as much as their guests do. With the option to coat the balls in confectioner's sugar or to leave the cherries peeking out from the walnut-cinnamon mixture, these candies make a grand statement at any gathering.

Date-Nut Balls

2	eggs, lightly beaten	2
1 cup	granulated sugar	250 mL
1 1/2 cups	chopped pitted dates	375 mL
1 tsp	vanilla extract	5 mL
1 tbsp	butter or margarine	15 mL
1 cup	crisp rice cereal	250 mL
1 cup	finely chopped pecans	250 mL
1 1/2 cups	sweetened flaked coconut, for rolling (approx.)	375 mL

Skill Level: Novice, Easy

Makes about 50

- 2-quart heavy saucepan

1. Cover a large countertop area or 2 large baking sheets with waxed paper.
2. In heavy saucepan over medium-low to medium heat, combine the eggs, sugar and dates. Cook until thick, about 10 minutes, stirring constantly.
3. Remove from the heat. Stir in the vanilla and butter. Cool. Stir in the cereal and pecans.
4. Shape the mixture into balls 1 inch (2.5 cm) in diameter. Roll the balls in the coconut. Place on the waxed paper. Let stand until firm. Store in an airtight container in the refrigerator.

Coated in delicious coconut, these crunchy date balls are an old-time favorite.

Humdinger Date Balls

½ cup	butter or margarine	125 mL
1 cup	granulated sugar	250 mL
8 oz	pitted dates, chopped	250 g
1 cup	finely chopped pecans	250 mL
1 tsp	vanilla extract	5 mL
1½ cups	crisp rice cereal	375 mL
1½ cups	confectioner's (icing) sugar, for rolling (approx.)	375 mL

> Someone should write a self-help book about how to overcome an addiction to these crunchy little candies.

Cook's Notes

For similar recipes, see Date-Nut Balls (page 178).

Skill Level: Novice, Easy

Makes about 50

- 2-quart heavy saucepan

1. Cover a large countertop area or 2 large baking sheets with waxed paper.

2. In heavy saucepan over medium-low to medium heat, melt the butter. Stir in the sugar, dates and pecans. Cook, stirring until the sugar melts and the ingredients are thoroughly mixed, thick and well blended, 8 to 10 minutes.

3. Remove from the heat. Stir in the vanilla and cereal. Cool slightly, about 3 minutes.

4. Shape the mixture into balls 1 inch (2.5 cm) in diameter. Roll the balls in the confectioner's sugar. Place on the waxed paper to cool. Store in an airtight container in the refrigerator.

Variation

Snowballs: Add 1 beaten egg to the butter, sugar and date mixture. Bring to a boil, stirring. Boil, stirring constantly, 4 minutes. Remove from the heat. Stir in the vanilla and 2 cups (500 mL) cereal. Complete as described above, rolling the balls in about 1½ cups (375 mL) sweetened flaked coconut instead of confectioner's sugar. Store in the refrigerator.

Important Tip

In many recipes, it is important to be prepared for all the steps because timing can be critical. Have all ingredients available and ready to use, and have the pan, baking sheet, or surface prepared before you begin cooking.

Bourbon Balls

2½ cups	very fine vanilla wafer or graham cracker crumbs	625 mL
1 cup	confectioner's (icing) sugar	250 mL
1 cup	finely chopped pecans or walnuts	250 mL
1 tbsp	chocolate syrup, such as Hershey's	15 mL
3 tbsp	light (white or golden) corn syrup	45 mL
¼ cup	bourbon	60 mL
¾ cup	confectioner's (icing) sugar, for rolling (approx.)	175 mL

Anything made with chocolate syrup cannot possibly be bad for you.

Makes about 48

1. Pour the crumbs into a medium mixing bowl. Add the 1 cup (250 mL) confectioner's sugar and nuts, stirring until well blended. Stir in the chocolate syrup, corn syrup and bourbon, mixing thoroughly.

2. Shape the mixture into balls 1 inch (2.5 cm) in diameter. Roll the balls in the confectioner's sugar. Refrigerate in an airtight container until ready to serve.

Risky Whiskey Rumba Balls

1 lb	vanilla wafers	500 g
2 cups	pecan halves	500 mL
2 cups	confectioner's (icing) sugar	500 mL
3 tbsp	light (white) corn syrup	45 mL
3	jiggers bourbon or rum (slightly more than ½ cup/125 mL)	3
¾ cup	confectioner's (icing) sugar, for rolling (approx.)	175 mL

This two-timing recipe has two times the flavor.

Makes about 48

• Food processor

1. Using a food processor, chop the vanilla wafers until they are very fine crumbs. Transfer the crumbs to a medium mixing bowl. Using a food processor, chop the pecans until they are finely ground.

2. Add the pecans to the crumbs. Stir in the 2 cups (500 mL) confectioner's sugar, blending thoroughly.

3. In a small bowl, combine the corn syrup and bourbon, mixing well. Pour the liquor mixture over the crumb mixture. Blend together thoroughly.

4. Shape the mixture into balls 1 inch (2.5 cm) in diameter. Roll the balls in the confectioner's sugar. Refrigerate in an airtight container for 1 week before serving.

Chocolate Cocktails

3½ cups	very fine vanilla wafer crumbs	875 mL
1 cup	finely chopped pecans or walnuts	250 mL
1 cup	confectioner's (icing) sugar	250 mL
3 tbsp	unsweetened cocoa powder	45 mL
⅓ cup	light or dark rum	75 mL
⅓ cup	light (white or golden) corn syrup	75 mL
¾ cup	confectioner's (icing) sugar, for rolling (approx.)	175 mL

These chocolate rum balls give new meaning to the term "happy hour."

Makes about 48

1. Pour the crumbs into a medium mixing bowl. Stir in the nuts, 1 cup (250 mL) confectioner's sugar and cocoa until well blended. Stir in the rum and corn syrup, mixing well.

2. Shape the mixture into balls 1 inch (2.5 cm) in diameter. Roll the balls in the confectioner's sugar. Store in an airtight container in the refrigerator.

Variation

Chocolate Bourbon Balls: Substitute ⅓ cup (75 mL) bourbon for the rum.

Dipsy Doodles

1 lb	chocolate wafers	500 g
1 cup	confectioner's (icing) sugar	250 mL
2½ cups	finely chopped pecans, divided	625 mL
⅓ cup	coffee-flavored liqueur, such as Kahlúa	75 mL
⅓ cup	light (white or golden) corn syrup	75 mL
2 tsp	vanilla extract	10 mL

Chocolate and Kahlúa make an intoxicating combination.

Makes about 48

- Food processor

1. Using a food processor, chop the chocolate wafers until they are very fine crumbs. Transfer to a medium mixing bowl. Add the confectioner's sugar and 1½ cups (375 mL) of the pecans, stirring until well blended. Stir in the Kahlúa and corn syrup, a little at a time, until the mixture is the consistency of cookie dough. Do not let the mixture become too soft. Stir in the vanilla, mixing well.

2. Using the food processor, chop the remaining 1 cup (250 mL) pecans until they are almost a fine powder.

3. Shape the chocolate mixture into balls 1 inch (2.5 cm) in diameter. Roll the balls in the ground pecans. Store in an airtight container in the refrigerator.

Coconut Bonbons

1/2 cup	butter or margarine, softened	125 mL
1	can (14 oz or 300 mL) sweetened condensed milk	1
1 1/2 lbs	confectioner's (icing) sugar, sifted	750 g
1	package (7 oz/210 g) sweetened flaked coconut or 2 2/3 cups (650 mL)	1
1 to 2 cups	finely chopped pecans	250 to 500 mL
18 oz	dark chocolate candy coating	540 g

One of my favorite childhood memories is of standing on my tiptoes watching my mother dip her delicious Coconut Bonbons in mouthwatering melted chocolate. This recipe is as popular today as it was decades ago, finding new fans in generation after generation of family and friends.

Cook's Notes

For helpful tips, see Dipping Candies in Chocolate (page 22). For alternate chocolate coating recipes, see Chocolate Coatings (page 185).

Skill Level: Novice, Easy

Makes 100 to 110 pieces

- 2 large baking sheets, lined with waxed paper
- Double boiler

1. In a large mixing bowl, combine the butter and milk by hand or with an electric mixer. Gradually add the confectioner's sugar, blending until smooth. Stir in the coconut and pecans. Cover and chill 2 hours or until firm.

2. Shape the coconut mixture into balls 3/4 inch (2 cm) in diameter. Place the balls on the prepared baking sheet(s). Cover and chill 1 hour or more.

3. Cover a large countertop area or two large baking sheets with waxed paper.

4. In the top pan of a double boiler over hot but not boiling water, melt the candy coating, stirring until smooth. Using a toothpick, fork or specially designed dipping tool, dip the balls into the melted chocolate until coated. Drop the balls onto waxed paper. Let stand until the chocolate is firm. Store in an airtight container in the refrigerator.

Variation

Margaret's Coconut Bonbons: Use 2 lbs (1 kg) confectioner's (icing) sugar and 4 cups (1 L) finely chopped pecans, adding 1/4 tsp (1 mL) salt and 1 tsp (5 mL) vanilla to the bonbon mixture. Have an additional 6 oz (175 g) chocolate candy coating on hand in case additional coating is needed. My cousin, Margaret, prefers to make this candy approximately 1 week in advance of serving to allow the flavors to blend.

Martha Washingtons

1 cup	butter or margarine, softened	250 mL
1	can (14 oz or 300 mL) sweetened condensed milk	1
2 lbs	confectioner's (icing) sugar	1 kg
1	can (3.5 oz/105 g) sweetened flaked coconut or 1⅓ cups (325 mL)	1
4 cups	finely chopped pecans	1 L
1	jar (6 oz/175 g) maraschino cherries, well drained and finely chopped	1
1½ lbs	dark chocolate candy coating	750 g

George Washington probably regretted cutting down the cherry tree once he tasted Martha's cherry-filled candy.

Cook's Notes

For helpful tips, see Dipping Candies in Chocolate (page 22). For alternate chocolate coating recipes, see Chocolate Coatings (page 185).

See Dipping Candies in Chocolate (page 22). For alternate chocolate coating recipes, see Chocolate Coatings (page 185).

Skill Level: Novice, Easy

Makes about 150 pieces

- 2 large baking sheets, lined with waxed paper
- Double boiler

1. In a large mixing bowl, combine the butter and milk by hand or with an electric mixer. Gradually add the confectioner's sugar, blending until smooth. Stir in the coconut, pecans and cherries. Cover and chill 2 hours or until firm.

2. Shape the mixture into balls ¾ inch (2 cm) in diameter. Place the balls on the prepared baking sheet(s). Cover and chill 1 hour or more.

3. Cover a large countertop area or 2 large baking sheets with waxed paper.

4. In the top pan of a double boiler over hot but not boiling water, melt the candy coating, stirring until smooth. Using a toothpick, fork or specially designed dipping tool, dip each ball into the melted chocolate until coated. Drop onto the waxed paper. Let stand until the chocolate is firm. Store in an airtight container in the refrigerator.

Giving Chocolate-Coated Candies a Professional Gloss

Chocolate candy coating products are convenient to use but many leave the candy with a dull appearance after the chocolate dries. A few years ago I discovered that specialty stores carry edible lacquer sprays that give chocolate-coated candies the gloss and sheen we might expect from high-quality or tempered chocolates. This lacquer can also be used to protect candies such as pralines from humidity, or to preserve sugar art. Edible lacquer can be expensive but a single can of this spray will cover many batches of candy. One such product is Lacquer Spray by Confectionery Arts International. Similar products may be found in specialty stores and from Internet sources.

Chocolate-Cherry Coconut Drops

¹/₂ cup	butter or margarine, softened	125 mL
1 cup	sweetened condensed milk	250 mL
1 lb	confectioner's (icing) sugar	500 g
2	cans (each 7 oz/210 g) sweetened flaked coconut or 5¹/₂ cups (1.375 L)	2
2 cups	finely chopped pecans	500 mL
1 cup	well-drained maraschino cherries, finely chopped	250 mL
1¹/₂ lbs	dark chocolate candy coating	750 g

Martha Washingtons (page 183) are a very similar candy. This one has less sugar and pecans but more coconut. With two versions to try, surely one of these candies will find its way to your next holiday celebration.

Cook's Notes

For helpful tips, see Dipping Candies in Chocolate (page 22). For alternate chocolate coating recipes, see Chocolate Coatings (page 185).

Skill Level: Novice, Easy

Makes about 150 pieces

- 2 large baking sheets, lined with waxed paper
- Double boiler

1. In a large mixing bowl, combine the butter and milk by hand or with an electric mixer. Gradually add the confectioner's sugar, blending until smooth. Stir in the coconut, pecans and cherries. Cover and chill 2 hours or until firm.

2. Shape the mixture into balls ³/₄ inch (2 cm) in diameter. Place the balls on the prepared baking sheet(s). Cover and chill 1 hour or more.

3. Cover a large countertop area or 2 large baking sheets with waxed paper.

4. In the top pan of a double boiler over hot but not boiling water, melt the candy coating, stirring until smooth. Using a toothpick, fork or specially designed dipping tool, dip each ball into the melted chocolate until coated. Drop onto the waxed paper. Let stand until the chocolate is firm. Store in an airtight container in the refrigerator.

Important Tip

In many recipes, it is important to be prepared for all the steps because timing can be critical. Have all ingredients available and ready to use, and have the pan, baking sheet, or surface prepared before you begin cooking.

Chocolate Coatings

The combination of products used for chocolate candy coatings is often a matter of personal preference and product availability. Many of our grandmothers never heard of premixed chocolate candy coating products so they created their own blend by combining 12 oz (375 g) melted semisweet chocolate chips with 2 oz (60 g) melted paraffin wax. The wax served as a firming agent and gave the candies a glossy finish. Some countries, including the United States, no longer approve the use of paraffin wax in food products so recipes for homemade chocolate coatings containing paraffin wax are far less common today than 20 or 30 years ago.

Another older method is to use melted chocolate-flavored almond bark (see Candy Glossary, page 18) for dipping candies. A few people mix chocolate almond bark with semisweet chips, letting the almond bark substitute for the paraffin wax. I have only seen this combination used in a few recipes and prefer other options.

Most new or updated candy recipes rely on premixed candy coating products that include both chocolate and a firming agent. Candy coating is available in dark chocolate, milk chocolate and white chocolate, with some brands offering various colors. These products require no decision-making whatsoever. Just melt the chocolate and dip. Most products dry in a matter of minutes, making them very convenient to use.

The price, quality, taste and firmness of chocolate coating products vary by brand. Some candy coating is made from chocolate and contains cocoa butter, others are imitation chocolate-flavored. I recommend using the highest quality chocolate coating products you can find. If possible, visit specialty stores in your area that sell confectionery or baking supplies to see what chocolate coating products they offer. You may want to buy small amounts of several brands to determine which product gives the taste and crispness you prefer. If you do not have a specialty store nearby then look in high-end grocery stores and at Internet sources. Brand names include Bakels, Baker's, Felchlin,

Ghirardelli, Merckens, Nestlé and Wilton, though other brands may be available in your area or via the Internet. My personal favorites are Bakels, Nestlé and Ghirardelli.

Those who cannot buy chocolate candy coating can create their own coating using the combinations below. Except for the White Chocolate Drizzle, I am not a huge fan of chocolate coatings that use butter or shortening because they usually create a soft shell that melts very easily. Generally, 12 oz (375 g) chocolate will cover approximately 60 candies, with some variation depending on the size of the candies. It is always a good idea to have a little extra chocolate on hand in case your candies need more coating than a recipe indicates.

Semisweet Chocolate Coating
- Produces a soft shell that requires refrigeration
- 12 oz (375 g) chopped semisweet chocolate or chocolate chips
- 1 tbsp (15 mL) solid vegetable shortening

Bittersweet Chocolate Coating
- Produces a soft shell that requires refrigeration
- 12 oz (375 g) chopped bittersweet chocolate
- 1 tbsp (15 mL) butter

Sweet Chocolate Coating
- Produces a semisoft shell that usually requires refrigeration
- 12 oz (375 g) chopped sweet chocolate, preferably German's sweet chocolate

Almond Bark Coating
- Produces a firm to semifirm shell that does not require refrigeration
- 12 oz (375 g) imitation-flavored chocolate almond bark (see Candy Glossary, page 18)

White Chocolate Drizzle
- For decorating the tops of chocolate-coated candies (see Luscious Raspberry-Fudge Truffles, page 220)
- 3 oz (90 g) white chocolate
- 1 tbsp (15 mL) solid vegetable shortening
- or 3 oz (90 g) white chocolate candy coating

Avoiding Chocolate Pools and Cracks

One of the most common mistakes we make is to dip candy into very hot chocolate. We know when this happens because the chocolate coating is thin, runny and pools underneath the candy when dropped onto waxed paper. To avoid these pools, remove the melted chocolate from the heat and allow it to cool and thicken a bit before dipping the candy. I often test the chocolate's consistency by dipping just one candy at a time. If the shell is thin and the chocolate pools, I wait about 2 minutes and try again. When the chocolate reaches the right consistency I dip all of the candies. If the chocolate becomes too thick I reheat it until it softens again.

Chocolate shells can also crack if they are too thin. To avoid cracks allow the chocolate to cool slightly before dipping the candy.

Melting Chocolate

All chocolate should be melted slowly over low heat, preferably in the top pan of a double boiler over hot, but not boiling water. Careful candy makers remove the double boiler from the stove as soon as the water is hot to ensure the chocolate does not seize from too much heat. In addition to protecting the chocolate, this method helps prevent the chocolate from becoming too thin to give a good coating (see Avoiding Chocolate Pools and Cracks, above). If using a microwave to melt chocolate, watch the chocolate very carefully because chocolate can scorch.

White chocolate lovers should be aware that white chocolate chips are nearly impossible to melt into a smooth liquid form. If a white chocolate coating is desired, use white chocolate candy coating.

Creating Custom Chocolate Coating Blends

I often create custom blends of chocolate coating because I want a particular firmness or taste. For example, one of my favorite coating products produces a very crisp shell. If I want a softer shell I add a handful of semisweet chocolate chips to thin the coating just a bit, or if I want a slightly lighter flavor I might add a 1.55 oz (44 g) milk chocolate bar. I have also combined dark chocolate candy coating with milk chocolate candy coating, added a small amount of bittersweet chocolate to dark or milk chocolate candy coating, and combined various brands of coating. When creating a custom blend, test a few candies before dipping the entire batch. If needed, add more candy coating to make the chocolate firmer, or more chocolate to make the coating softer.

Cheery Cherry Date Balls

1 cup	butter or margarine, softened	250 mL
1	can (14 oz or 300 mL) sweetened condensed milk	1
2 lbs	confectioner's (icing) sugar	1 kg
1 tsp	vanilla extract	5 mL
2 cups	finely chopped pecans	500 mL
1 lb	pitted dates, finely chopped	500 g
6 oz	candied cherries, finely chopped	175 g
1½ lbs	dark chocolate candy coating	750 g

This recipe puts a new twist on Martha Washingtons (page 183) by adding dates and candied cherries rather than coconut and maraschino cherries.

Cook's Notes

For helpful tips, see Dipping Candies in Chocolate (page 22). For alternate chocolate coating recipes, see Chocolate Coatings (page 185).

Skill Level: Novice, Easy

Makes about 150 pieces

- 2 large baking sheets, lined with waxed paper
- Double boiler

1. In a large mixing bowl, combine the butter and milk by hand or with an electric mixer. Gradually add the confectioner's sugar, blending until smooth. Stir in the vanilla, pecans, dates and cherries. Cover and chill 2 hours or until firm.

2. Shape the mixture into balls ¾ inch (2 cm) in diameter. Place the balls on the prepared baking sheet(s). Cover and chill 1 hour or more.

3. Cover a large countertop area or 2 large baking sheets with waxed paper.

4. In the top pan of a double boiler over hot but not boiling water, melt the candy coating, stirring until smooth. Using a toothpick, fork or specially designed dipping tool, dip the balls into the melted chocolate until coated. Drop onto the waxed paper. Let stand until the chocolate is firm. Store in an airtight container in the refrigerator.

Disposable Gloves

Disposable food preparation gloves are great for handling candy because the gloves keep your hands clean and help prevent the spread of germs. Gloves are especially helpful when forming balls and centers of chocolate-coated candies, but I also wear them to break brittles and toffees into pieces and when storing candy or packaging it as a gift. As delicious as my candy may be, no one really wants to eat toffee that has my thumbprint.

Many sources carry disposable gloves, including restaurant supply companies and specialty stores that carry baking or candy supplies.

Chocolate Fudge Drops

1 lb	confectioner's (icing) sugar	500 g
1/4 cup	unsweetened cocoa powder	60 mL
1/2 cup	butter or margarine, softened	125 mL
1	can (14 oz or 300 mL) sweetened condensed milk	1
1 tsp	vanilla extract	5 mL
1 1/2 cups	finely chopped pecans or walnuts	375 mL
12 oz	dark chocolate candy coating	375 g

> The only thing better than chocolate coated in chocolate is chocolate and nuts coated in chocolate.

Cook's Notes

For a slightly firmer filling, add an additional 1/2 to 3/4 cup (125 to 175 mL) confectioner's (icing) sugar to the filling mixture or use only 1 cup (250 mL) sweetened condensed milk.

If desired, an additional 1 tbsp (15 mL) unsweetened cocoa powder may be added to give the candy a deeper chocolate flavor.

For helpful tips, see Dipping Candies in Chocolate (page 22). For alternate chocolate coating recipes, see Chocolate Coatings (page 185).

Skill Level: Novice, Easy

Makes about 50 pieces

- 2 large baking sheets, lined with waxed paper
- Double boiler

1. In a medium bowl, combine the confectioner's sugar and cocoa, stirring to blend.

2. In a large mixing bowl, combine the butter and milk by hand or with an electric mixer. Gradually add the confectioner's sugar mixture, blending until smooth. Stir in the vanilla and nuts. Cover and chill 2 hours or until firm.

3. Shape the mixture into balls 3/4 to 1 inch (2 to 2.5 cm) in diameter. Place the balls on the prepared baking sheets. Cover and chill 1 hour or more.

4. Cover a large countertop area or 2 large baking sheets with waxed paper.

5. In the top pan of a double boiler over hot but not boiling water, melt the candy coating, stirring until smooth. Using a toothpick, fork or specially designed dipping tool, dip each ball into the melted chocolate. Drop onto the waxed paper. Let stand until the chocolate is firm. Store in an airtight container in the refrigerator.

Variation

Chocolate-Nut Drops: Omit the unsweetened cocoa powder. Use only 1 cup (250 mL) sweetened condensed milk.

Crispy Peanut Butter Balls

2 cups	creamy or crunchy peanut butter	500 mL
½ cup	butter or margarine, softened	125 mL
1 lb	confectioner's (icing) sugar	500 g
1 tsp	vanilla extract	5 mL
2 cups	crisp rice cereal	500 mL
12 oz	dark chocolate candy coating	375 g

Something about these crunchy little nuggets is just too good to resist. Make an extra-large batch, because these old favorites have a way of disappearing quickly.

Cook's Notes

For helpful tips, see Dipping Candies in Chocolate (page 22). For alternate chocolate coating recipes, see Chocolate Coatings (page 185).

For helpful tips, see Dipping Candies in Chocolate (page 22). For alternate chocolate coating recipes, see Chocolate Coatings (page 185).

Skill Level: Novice, Easy

Makes about 70 pieces

- 2 large baking sheet, lined with waxed paper
- Double boiler

1. In a large mixing bowl, combine the peanut butter and butter by hand or with an electric mixer. Gradually add the confectioner's sugar and vanilla, blending until smooth. If the mixture appears dry and crumbly, knead by hand until smooth. Stir in the cereal.

2. Shape into balls 1 inch (2.5 cm) in diameter. Place the balls on the prepared baking sheet. Freeze 10 to 20 minutes or while preparing the chocolate coating.

3. Cover a large area of the countertop or 2 large baking sheets with waxed paper.

4. In the top pan of a double boiler over hot but not boiling water, melt the candy coating, stirring until smooth. Using a toothpick, fork or specially designed dipping tool, dip the chilled balls in the melted chocolate until coated. Drop onto the waxed paper. Let stand until the chocolate is firm. Store in an airtight container in the refrigerator.

Variation

Crispy Hazelnut Balls: Substitute chocolate hazelnut spread, such as Nutella, for the peanut butter. Omit the vanilla extract.

Buckeyes

1 cup	creamy peanut butter	250 mL
1/4 cup	butter or margarine, softened	60 mL
1 tsp	vanilla extract	5 mL
2 1/2 to 3 cups	confectioner's (icing) sugar	625 to 750 mL
6 oz	dark chocolate candy coating	175 g

> A much-loved favorite, these deliciously smooth "peanut butter eyeballs" are the perfect treat for little ghosts and goblins.

Cook's Notes

The peanut butter filling is very soft. For a firmer filling, add more confectioner's sugar.

For helpful tips, see Dipping Candies in Chocolate (page 22). For alternate chocolate coating recipes, see Chocolate Coatings (page 185).

For helpful tips, see Dipping Candies in Chocolate (page 22). For alternate chocolate coating recipes, see Chocolate Coatings (page 185).

Skill Level: Novice, Easy

Makes about 38 pieces

- Large baking sheet, lined with waxed paper
- Double boiler

1. In a large mixing bowl, combine the peanut butter, butter and vanilla by hand or with an electric mixer. Gradually add the confectioner's sugar, blending until smooth and mixture can be shaped into balls. Shape into balls 3/4 to 1 inch (2 to 2.5 cm) in diameter. Place the balls on the prepared baking sheet. Cover and chill or freeze 20 minutes or longer.

2. Cover a large countertop area or a large baking sheet with waxed paper.

3. In the top pan of a double boiler over hot but not boiling water, melt the candy coating, stirring until smooth. Insert a toothpick into the top of each ball and dip the bottom two-thirds of each ball into the melted chocolate, leaving the top one-third uncoated. (If preferred, the entire ball may be coated in chocolate.) Carefully slide the balls onto waxed paper so the undipped portion is pointed upwards. Remove the toothpick. Using a knife or metal spatula, smooth over the hole left by the toothpick. Let stand until the chocolate is firm. Store in an airtight container in the refrigerator.

Important Tip

In many recipes, it is important to be prepared for all the steps because timing can be critical. Have all ingredients available and ready to use, and have the pan, baking sheet, or surface prepared before you begin cooking.

Golf Balls

1 cup	creamy peanut butter	250 mL
1 cup	butter or margarine, softened	250 mL
2⅓ cups	graham cracker crumbs	575 mL
1 lb	confectioner's (icing) sugar	500 g
1½ cups	chopped salted roasted peanuts	375 mL
12 oz	dark chocolate candy coating	375 g

These nutty peanut butter candies may remind you of one of your favorite candy bars.

Cook's Notes

For helpful tips, see Dipping Candies in Chocolate (page 22). For alternate chocolate coating recipes, see Chocolate Coatings (page 185).

Skill Level: Novice, Easy

Makes about 60 pieces

- Large baking sheet, lined with waxed paper
- Double boiler

1. In a large mixing bowl, combine the peanut butter and butter by hand or with an electric mixer. Gradually add the crumbs and confectioner's sugar, blending until smooth. Stir in the peanuts.

2. Shape into balls 1 inch (2.5 cm) in diameter. Place the balls on the prepared baking sheet. Cover and freeze 1 hour or more.

3. Cover a large countertop area or a large baking sheet with waxed paper.

4. In the top pan of a double boiler over hot but not boiling water, melt the candy coating, stirring until smooth. Using a toothpick, fork or specially designed dipping tool, dip the frozen balls into the melted chocolate until coated. Drop onto the waxed paper. Let stand until the chocolate is firm. Store in an airtight container in the refrigerator.

Storing Candy

Most candies should be stored in an airtight container to keep them fresh. Unless specifically instructed in the recipe, refrigeration is often a matter of personal choice, but generally, most fudges and fudge-like candies should keep at least 1 week at room temperature and at least 1 month, sometimes much longer, if refrigerated. Excessive heat, high humidity, or added ingredients such as fruit may shorten the storage time so it is important to use common sense. If the color or texture of the candy has changed, dispose of it and make a fresh batch.

Peanut Butter–Date Balls

1 cup	creamy peanut butter	250 mL
1 tbsp	butter or margarine, softened	15 mL
1 cup	confectioner's (icing) sugar	250 mL
2 tsp	vanilla extract	10 mL
1½ cups	chopped pitted dates	375 mL
½ cup	finely chopped pecans	125 mL
10 oz	dark chocolate candy coating	300 g

The unusual combination of peanut butter, dates and pecans is a real treat for date lovers.

Cook's Note

For helpful tips, see Dipping Candies in Chocolate (page 22). For alternate chocolate coating recipes, see Chocolate Coatings (page 185).

Skill Level: Novice, Easy

Makes about 36 pieces

- Large baking sheet, lined with waxed paper
- Double boiler

1. In a large mixing bowl, combine the peanut butter and butter by hand or with an electric mixer. Gradually add the confectioner's sugar, blending until smooth. Stir in the vanilla, dates and pecans.

2. Shape into balls ¾ to 1 inch (2 to 2.5 cm) in diameter. Place the balls on the prepared baking sheet. Cover and chill 30 minutes or more.

3. Cover a large countertop area or a large baking sheet with waxed paper.

4. In the top pan of a double boiler over hot but not boiling water, melt the candy coating, stirring until smooth. Using a toothpick, fork or specially designed dipping tool, dip each ball into the melted chocolate until coated. Drop onto the waxed paper. Let stand until the chocolate is firm. Store in an airtight container in the refrigerator.

From top down and left to right: Bullet Fudge (page 119), Lemon-White Chocolate Fudge, variation (page 166), White Cherry Fudge (page 164), Out-of-This-World Maple Fudge (page 155), Microwave Rocky Road Fudge (page 131) and Pumpkin Fudge (page 162)

Tuxedo Fudge (page 147)

Chocolate-Cherry Creams (page 170) and
Elegant Sparkling Strawberries (page 175)

Marzipan Potatoes (page 176)

Blue Ribbon Turtles (page 200)

Luscious Raspberry-Fudge Truffles (page 220)

Old-Fashioned Pastel Butter Mints (page 207)

Carnival Candied Apples (page 251) and
Old-Fashioned Caramel Apples (page 253)

Pineapple Date Roll (page 260)

Gourmet Layered Peppermint Bark (page 258)

Chocolate Birds' Nests (page 272)

Honey Do Candy (page 270) and
Chocolate Peanut Clusters (page 264)

Toasted Coconut Chocolate Drops

1	can (3.5 oz/105 g) sweetened flaked coconut or 1⅓ cups (325 mL)	1
1 cup	marshmallow creme (about half 7 oz/198 g jar)	250 mL
½ tsp	vanilla extract	2 mL
Pinch	salt	Pinch
12 oz	dark chocolate candy coating	375 g

> The combination of soft, fluffy marshmallow filling mixed with crispy, toasted coconut gives this candy an interesting contrast in textures.

Cook's Notes

The marshmallow creme mixture remains very soft and can be difficult to shape into balls. As an alternative, drop small amounts of the mixture onto the lined baking sheet from the tip of a buttered spoon. Cover and freeze about 30 minutes. The frozen mixture can then be rolled into a ball more easily.

For helpful tips, see Dipping Candies in Chocolate (page 22). For alternate chocolate coating recipes, see Chocolate Coatings (page 185).

Skill Level: Novice, Easy

Makes about 45 pieces

- Preheat oven to 350°F (180°C)
- Large baking sheet, lined with waxed paper
- Double boiler

1. Spread the coconut across the bottom of a shallow pan. Toast the coconut in the preheated oven about 8 minutes or until golden brown, watching carefully and stirring halfway through cooking. Cool.

2. In a large mixing bowl, combine the marshmallow creme, vanilla, salt and coconut, stirring until well blended. Cover and chill 30 minutes or more (see Cook's Notes, left).

3. With lightly buttered hands, shape the marshmallow mixture into balls ¾ inch (2 cm) in diameter. Cover and chill or freeze 30 minutes or more.

4. Cover a large countertop area or a large baking sheet with waxed paper.

5. In the top pan of a double boiler over hot but not boiling water, melt the candy coating, stirring until smooth. Using a toothpick, fork or specially designed dipping tool, dip the chilled balls into the melted chocolate until coated. Drop onto the waxed paper. Let stand until the chocolate is firm. Store in an airtight container.

Chocolate-Covered Haystacks

$2/3$ cup	granulated sugar	150 mL
3 tbsp	water	45 mL
1 cup plus 1 tbsp	light (white) corn syrup	265 mL
4 cups	sweetened flaked coconut	1 L
12 oz	chocolate candy coating	375 g

With extra coconut and granulated sugar instead of brown these chocolate-covered haystacks have a different taste and texture than Coconut Haystacks (page 77).

- 1-quart heavy saucepan
- Candy thermometer

1. Cover a large countertop area or a large baking sheet with waxed paper.

2. In a heavy saucepan over medium heat, bring the sugar, water and corn syrup to a boil, stirring until the sugar dissolves and the mixture begins to boil. Cook, without stirring, to the soft ball stage (234°F to 240°F/112°C to 116°C, with 236°F/113°C recommended).

3. Remove from the heat. Stir in the coconut until well blended. Quickly drop by spoonfuls onto the waxed paper. To create the haystacks, dip your fingers into cold water and shape the candy into cones $1\frac{1}{2}$ inches (4 cm) high while the candy is still warm.

4. In the top pan of a double boiler over hot but not boiling water, melt the candy coating, stirring until smooth.

5. Spoon the melted chocolate over the top of candies. Let stand until the chocolate is firm. Cool. Store in an airtight container.

Kentucky Bourbon Balls

1 cup	finely chopped pecans or walnuts	250 mL
1/2 cup	bourbon	125 mL
1/2 cup	butter, softened	125 mL
1 lb	confectioner's (icing) sugar	500 g
1/2 tsp	vanilla extract	2 mL
12 oz	dark chocolate candy coating	375 g

Perfect for a New Year's Eve or Derby Day celebration, these chocolate-coated, nut-filled candies have just the right amount of bourbon flavor.

Cook's Notes

For helpful tips, see Dipping Candies in Chocolate (page 22). For alternate chocolate coating recipes, see Chocolate Coatings (page 185).

For helpful tips, see Dipping Candies in Chocolate (page 22). For alternate chocolate coating recipes, see Chocolate Coatings (page 185).

Skill Level: Novice, Easy

Makes about 50 pieces

- Large baking sheet, lined with waxed paper
- Double boiler

1. In a small bowl, combine the nuts and bourbon. Cover and let stand at room temperature at least 2 hours, preferably 8 hours, so the nuts can absorb the bourbon.

2. In a large mixing bowl, combine the butter, confectioner's sugar and vanilla by hand or with an electric mixer. Stir in the pecans and bourbon. Cover and freeze 1 hour or more.

3. Shape the mixture into balls $3/4$ inch (2 cm) in diameter. Place the balls on the prepared baking sheet. Cover and freeze 1 hour or until firm.

4. Cover a large countertop area or a baking sheet with waxed paper.

5. In the top pan of a double boiler over hot but not boiling water, melt the candy coating, stirring until smooth. Using a toothpick, fork or specially designed dipping tool, dip the frozen balls into the melted chocolate until coated. Drop onto the waxed paper. Let stand until the chocolate is firm. Store in an airtight container in the refrigerator.

Almond Coffee Walnuts

²/₃ cup	almond paste	150 mL
2 tbsp	coffee liqueur	30 mL
1 tbsp	instant espresso powder	15 mL
72	walnut halves, toasted	72
9 oz	semisweet chocolate, coarsely chopped	270 g

> Perfect for entertaining, these elegant dipped walnuts are a favorite dessert with Aunt Shirley, a legendary hostess and seasoned gourmet.

Skill Level: Novice, Easy

Makes 36

• Double boiler

1. In a small bowl, combine the almond paste, liqueur and espresso, blending until smooth. Spread about ½ tsp (2 mL) of the mixture onto the flat side of one walnut half. Place another walnut half on top of the filling, pressing lightly so that the filling holds the two halves together. Repeat until all the walnut halves are used.

2. Cover a large countertop area or a large baking sheet with waxed paper.

3. In the top pan of a double boiler over hot but not boiling water, melt the chocolate, stirring until smooth. Dip one half of the filled walnuts into the melted chocolate. Place on the waxed paper. Let stand until the chocolate is firm. Store in an airtight container in the refrigerator up to 1 week.

Storing Candy

Most candies should be stored in an airtight container to keep them fresh. Unless specifically instructed in the recipe, refrigeration is often a matter of personal choice, but generally, most fudges and fudge-like candies should keep at least 1 week at room temperature and at least 1 month, sometimes much longer, if refrigerated. Excessive heat, high humidity, or added ingredients such as fruit may shorten the storage time so it is important to use common sense. If the color or texture of the candy has changed, dispose of it and make a fresh batch.

Chocolate-Dipped Strawberries

8 to 10	medium fresh strawberries	8 to 10
1 oz	semisweet chocolate square	30 g
1 tbsp	evaporated milk	15 mL
1 tsp	orange or almond liqueur (or $1/8$ tsp/0.5 mL vanilla extract)	5 mL

Makes 8 to 10 strawberries

- Small or medium baking sheet, lined with waxed paper
- Double boiler

> So easy, so romantic and so delectable, this recipe is too good not to share. These delightful strawberries are the perfect ending to a candlelit dinner for two. This recipe is especially delicious when made with Triple Sec or Grand Marnier.

1. Leaving the green stems intact, wash, drain and completely dry the strawberries by patting with a paper towel.

2. In the top pan of a double boiler over hot but not boiling water, melt the chocolate, milk and liqueur together, stirring until smooth. Insert a toothpick into the stem end of the strawberries and dip the lower two-thirds of the berries into the chocolate. Drop the berries onto the prepared baking sheet. Let stand until the chocolate is firm. Serve immediately or lightly cover and refrigerate until ready to serve, storing for up to 8 hours for optimal freshness and visual appeal. However, the berries can be refrigerated for up to 2 days but may lose their eye appeal when stored more than a few hours.

Variation

White Chocolate-Dipped Strawberries: Substitute white chocolate or white chocolate coating for the semisweet chocolate.

Cook's Notes

Work very quickly if doubling the recipe. The chocolate will become grainy if it is heated too long or held at too high a temperature.

Instead of using a large double boiler to melt the chocolate, create a small double boiler by placing a small glass dish into a pan of hot water. This method often makes dipping easier when working with small amounts of chocolate. Do not allow the water to seep into the chocolate mixture.

To keep the berries from having a flat side, turn a plastic colander upside down and place the toothpicks holding the dipped berries into the holes of the colander. Place the colander filled with berries into the refrigerator until ready to serve.

Chocolate-Covered Cherries

1	jar (16 oz/500 mL) maraschino cherries with stems	1
3 tbsp	butter, softened	45 mL
3 tbsp	light (white) corn syrup	45 mL
1/4 tsp	salt	1 mL
2 cups	confectioner's (icing) sugar	500 mL
12 oz	dark chocolate candy coating	375 g

> Just a few of these fondant-coated cherries will brighten up anyone's day.

Cook's Notes

This recipe can be reduced to make just a few cherries at a time using the melted chocolate left over from another chocolate-dipped candy recipe.

For helpful tips, see Dipping Candies in Chocolate (page 22). For alternate chocolate coating recipes, see Chocolate Coatings (page 185).

(page 22)

(page 185)

Skill Level: Novice, Easy

Makes about 40 cherries

- Large baking sheet, lined with waxed paper
- Double boiler

1. Leaving the stems intact, wash, drain and completely dry the cherries by patting with a paper towel.

2. In a medium bowl, combine the butter, corn syrup and salt. Gradually add the confectioner's sugar, stirring until smooth. Knead by hand until the fondant is smooth and creamy. Pinch off a small amount and shape around each cherry. Place on the prepared baking sheet. Cover and chill 1 hour or until firm.

3. Cover a large countertop area or a large baking sheet with waxed paper.

4. In the top pan of a double boiler over hot but not boiling water, melt the candy coating, stirring until smooth. Hold each cherry by the stem and dip into the melted chocolate until coated. Place on the waxed paper. Let stand until the chocolate is firm. Store in an airtight container in the refrigerator 2 to 3 days before serving to allow the fondant to soften and liquefy. The more time allowed, the more liquid the center will become. The cherries will keep up to 1 week in the refrigerator.

Variation

Stuffed Cherries: Rinse and dry the cherries as directed, removing the stems. Using the tip of a sharp knife or kitchen shears, carefully cut a small X in the top of each cherry. Pinch off a small amount of the fondant and stuff it into the center cavity of each cherry. Roll the cherries in granulated sugar or red decorator's sugar if desired. Store in an airtight container in the refrigerator 2 to 3 days before serving to allow the fondant to soften and liquefy. The cherries will keep up to 1 week in the refrigerator.

Aunt Mary's Turtles

14 oz	soft caramels, unwrapped	400 g
3 tbsp	evaporated milk	45 mL
2 cups	pecans, in large pieces	500 mL
18 oz	dark chocolate candy coating	540 g

Hardly a Father's Day passed without one of us kids buying my father a box of his favorite chocolate-covered turtles, but only because we did not have my aunt Mary's recipe. If my father were here today, he would undoubtedly prefer to have this homemade version.

Cook's Notes

Use a large metal spatula to remove the chilled caramel centers from the baking sheet.

For helpful tips, see Dipping Candies in Chocolate (page 22). For alternate chocolate coating recipes, see Chocolate Coatings (page 185).

Dipping Candies in Chocolate (page 22). For alternate chocolate coating recipes, see Chocolate Coatings (page 185).

Skill Level: Novice, Easy

Makes about 30 pieces

- Large baking sheet, generously buttered
- 2-quart heavy saucepan
- Double boiler

1. Unwrap the caramels. In heavy saucepan, melt the caramels and milk together over low heat, stirring until smooth. Stir in the pecans until well coated. Drop the caramel-nut mixture by spoonfuls onto the prepared baking sheet. Do not drop the uncoated caramel centers onto waxed paper. The waxed paper will adhere to the caramel and be very difficult to remove. Chill until set, about 30 minutes to 1 hour.

2. Cover a large countertop area or a large baking sheet with waxed paper.

3. In the top pan of a double boiler over hot but not boiling water, melt the candy coating, stirring until smooth. Using a toothpick, fork or specially designed dipping tool, dip the chilled caramel-nut centers into the melted chocolate until coated. Drop onto the waxed paper. Let stand until the chocolate is firm. Store in an airtight container.

Variation

Margaret's Turtles: Substitute 4 tsp (20 mL) milk for the evaporated milk.

Blue Ribbon Turtles

72	pecan halves	72
36	soft caramels, unwrapped	36
2 to	semisweet chocolate,	60 to
4 oz	chopped	125 g

> Simply delicious.

Cook's Note

The chocolate may be melted in the microwave if preferred.

Skill Level: Novice, Easy

Makes 18 pieces

- Preheat oven to 325°F (160°C)
- Large baking sheet, lined with aluminum foil, foil buttered
- Double boiler

1. Place the pecans on the prepared baking sheet, arranging the pecan halves in X-shaped groups of four. Press the caramels by hand until slightly flattened. Place 2 caramels on top of each cluster, lightly pressing the caramels into the pecans. Heat the clusters in the oven 5 to 8 minutes or until the caramels soften. Remove from the oven and place the baking sheet on a wire rack. If needed, use a buttered spatula to spread the softened caramels over the pecans. Cool.

2. Cover a large countertop area with waxed paper. Remove the clusters from the baking sheet and place on the waxed paper.

3. In the top pan of a double boiler over hot but not boiling water, melt the chocolate, stirring until smooth. Brush the tops of the clusters with the melted chocolate. Let stand until the chocolate is firm. Store in an airtight container in the refrigerator.

Variation

Caramel-Pecan Clusters: Use 24 caramels in place of 36 caramels. Arrange the pecan halves in clusters of three. Lightly press one caramel into the center of each pecan cluster. Complete the recipe as described above. *Makes 24 candies.*

Gordon's Christmas Caramels

14 oz	soft caramels	400 g
12 oz	dark chocolate candy coating	375 g
	Multicolored decorator sprinkles, chocolate decorator sprinkles or colored decorator's sugar	

This fun recipe was invented when a family member casually dropped a few leftover caramels in some leftover melted chocolate and then tossed a few decorator sprinkles on top to add a little pizzazz. Gordon's invention was so popular that these caramels became a holiday tradition to be shared with family and friends throughout Louisiana. Let the kids have a turn and see how creative they can be.

Cook's Note

For helpful tips, see Dipping Candies in Chocolate (page 22). For alternate chocolate coating recipes, see Chocolate Coatings (page 185).

Skill Level: Novice, Easy

Makes about 52 pieces

- Double boiler

1. Unwrap the caramels and set aside. Line a large countertop area or a large baking sheet with waxed paper.
2. In the top pan of a double boiler over hot but not boiling water, melt the candy coating, stirring until smooth. Using a fork or a specially designed dipping tool, dip the caramels in the melted chocolate until coated. Drop onto the waxed paper. Sprinkle the top of the caramels with decorative sprinkles while the chocolate is still warm. Let stand until the chocolate is firm. Store in an airtight container.

Important Tip

In many recipes, it is important to be prepared for all the steps because timing can be critical. Have all ingredients available and ready to use, and have the pan, baking sheet, or surface prepared before you begin cooking.

Old-Fashioned Cooked Fondant

1 cup	granulated sugar	250 mL
½ cup	water	125 mL
Pinch	cream of tartar (or 1 tbsp/ 15 mL light (white) corn syrup)	Pinch
¼ to ½ tsp	flavoring of choice (see Intro, below)	1 to 2 mL
	Few drops of food coloring as desired	
2 to 4 tbsp	chopped nuts, chopped candied fruits or sweetened flaked coconut (optional)	30 to 60 mL

Adventurous candy makers will love this recipe for its many variations. Read all instructions before beginning and choose any combination of options that sound best to you. Some suggested flavorings include vanilla extract, almond extract, strawberry extract, rum extract, maple extract or butter flavoring.

Skill Level: Advanced

Makes about 1 cup (250 mL)

• Candy thermometer
• Heatproof platter

1. In a small saucepan, combine the sugar, water and cream of tartar, stirring until the sugar dissolves. Bring to a boil over medium heat, stirring until the sugar dissolves and the mixture begins to boil. Cover and cook 2 to 3 minutes to dissolve the sugar crystals on the sides of the pan. Remove the lid. Cook, without stirring, to the soft ball stage (234°F to 240°F/112°C to 116°C, with 238°F/114°C recommended). Just before the candy reaches the desired temperature, rinse a heatproof platter with cold water; dry thoroughly.

2. Remove the boiling mixture from the heat. Pour onto the cool platter. Cool to 110°F (43°C), about 30 minutes. Work the mixture back and forth on the platter by hand until it is white and creamy and then knead the candy by hand until it is perfectly smooth. Working the candy mixture can take 30 minutes or more. Professionals often use a special flat tool that looks somewhat like a scraper, scraping the candy on one side, lifting it up and folding it over and then scraping it on the other side, lifting it up and folding it over.

3. Place the smooth, kneaded fondant into a bowl or an airtight container. Cover tightly. Let the fondant stand to ripen at room temperature at least 24 hours before using. The fondant may be stored several days if tightly covered. If the fondant becomes dry, place a damp cloth over it until it softens again. If the fondant sugars, add ⅞ cup (220 mL) water and cook it again.

4. When the fondant has ripened 24 hours, knead it by hand until it is soft and pliable, flavoring it as desired. Tint the fondant with a few drops of food coloring, if desired.

5. At this point, other ingredients, such as nuts, may be worked into the candy by hand, kneading the fondant only enough to mix the ingredients. The candy is now ready to shape or mold as desired.

Finished Fondant Variation

To Shape Bonbons: Shape the ripened fondant into small balls. Place the balls on waxed paper and let stand until firm but not dry. If desired, dip the bonbons into melted chocolate. See Chocolate Coatings (page 185) for options. For useful tips, see Dipping Candies in Chocolate (page 22). Recipes found in Chocolate-Coated Candies (pages 182 to 201) can be used as examples. If desired, decorate the plain or chocolate-coated bonbons with chopped nuts or other candies. Store in an airtight container.

To Mold a Cream Loaf: Mold the ripened fondant into a small buttered loaf pan. Let the fondant stand, uncovered, until firm. Cover and slice as needed.

To Mold a Marbled Cream Loaf: Divide the ripened fondant into 2 or 3 portions and tint each a different color. (For example, tint 1 portion pink, 1 portion yellow and leave 1 portion white.) Press the different colors together, twisting slightly to create a marbled effect and place in a small buttered loaf pan. If preferred, layer the different colors of fondant when pressing into the buttered pan. Let the fondant stand, uncovered, until firm. Cover and slice as needed.

To Make Cream Mints: In the top pan of a double boiler over hot but not boiling water, heat about 1 cup (250 mL) of the ripened fondant at a time until the fondant is melted. Stir the fondant as little as possible. If the fondant does not melt rapidly, add a very small amount of water. Flavor the fondant with peppermint, wintergreen, clove, cinnamon, orange oil or as desired. Tint the fondant using a few drops of food coloring if desired. Stir the fondant as little as possible when adding flavoring and coloring. Drop from the tip of a spoon onto waxed paper. Cool completely. If desired, dip the cream mints into melted chocolate. See Chocolate Coatings (page 185) for options. For useful tips, see Dipping Candies in Chocolate (page 22). Store in an airtight container.

Fondant Cooking Variations

To Make Easy Fondant: Make the recipe and cool as directed. Spread 1 stiffly beaten egg white, preferably pasteurized, over the cooled fondant. Work the fondant back and forth in the saucepan used for cooking. Add the flavoring and form the fondant into the desired candy as soon as it is smooth and creamy, allowing the fondant to ripen in its finished form. (See Cook's Note about eating uncooked eggs on page 176.)

To Make Bonbons: Add $\frac{1}{8}$ tsp (0.5 mL) glycerin as the fondant mixture comes to a boil. (Glycerin can be purchased in the pharmacy section of most large grocery stores.) Glycerin produces a very soft, fluffy fondant that is wonderful but sometimes difficult to handle. If adding glycerin to this recipe, do not allow the fondant to ripen 24 hours. Fondants that contain glycerin must be immediately worked back and forth after being poured onto the rinsed platter. If allowed to stand, they will soften and become difficult to handle.

Fondant Flavor Variations

Maple Fondant: Decrease the water to $\frac{1}{3}$ cup (75 mL). Add $\frac{1}{3}$ cup (75 mL) maple syrup.

Caramel Fondant: Decrease the water to $\frac{1}{3}$ cup (75 mL). Add $\frac{1}{3}$ cup (75 mL) caramel syrup.

Coffee Fondant: Substitute clear, strong coffee for water.

Brown Sugar Fondant: Use $\frac{1}{2}$ cup (125 mL) granulated sugar and $\frac{1}{2}$ cup (125 mL) packed light brown sugar.

Opera Cream Fondant: Substitute heavy or whipping (35%) cream for the water. Cook this option in a heavy aluminum saucepan to prevent scorching.

Chocolate Fondant: Add 1 to 2 oz (30 to 60 g) melted semisweet baking chocolate to finished fondant. Knead the candy by hand until well blended.

Ultra-Creamy Fondant

$\frac{1}{3}$ cup	butter or margarine, softened	75 mL
$\frac{1}{3}$ cup	light (white) corn syrup	75 mL
1 tsp	flavoring of choice (see Variation, page 205)	5 mL
$\frac{1}{2}$ tsp	salt	2 mL
	Few drops of food coloring (optional)	
1 lb	confectioner's (icing) sugar	500 g

Coating options

Sweetened flaked coconut, chopped nuts, multicolored decorator sprinkles, or Chocolate Coatings (page 185)

> Though similar to Buttercream Fondant (page 206), corn syrup makes this fondant creamy and slightly soft.

Cook's Notes

For step-by-step photographs, see color page K.

If desired, this fondant may be prepared 1 to 2 days in advance and stored tightly wrapped in foil. It may also be stored in an airtight container in the freezer 1 to 2 months.

This fondant is the same filling recipe used for Chocolate-Covered Mint Patties (page 210).

Skill Level: Novice, Super Simple
Makes 50 to 80 candies

- 2 large baking sheets, lined with waxed paper, optional

1. In a medium mixing bowl, blend the butter, corn syrup, flavoring, salt, and food coloring, if using, with a wooden spoon. Gradually add the confectioner's sugar, first mixing with the wooden spoon and then kneading by hand until the mixture is smooth and well blended and no longer sticks to the hands. Shape the mixture into a ball or a mound.

2. *To make bonbons or patties:* Pinch off small pieces of the fondant and shape into balls $\frac{3}{4}$ inch (2 cm) in diameter. Place the balls on the prepared baking sheets. If making patties, flatten the balls with the palm of the hand or with a flat spatula. Roll or dip in the coating of choice.

3. *To make rolls:* Cover the countertop with a large sheet of waxed paper. Shape the fondant into a roll about $1\frac{1}{4}$ inches (3 cm) in diameter. Secure the rolls in the waxed paper, sealing the ends tightly. Refrigerate 1 hour or until firm. Slice into $\frac{1}{4}$-inch (0.5 cm) rounds. Serve plain or cover with the coating of choice.

4. *To make wafers:* Place the ball or mound on a sheet of waxed paper. Cover with another sheet of waxed paper. Roll out like pie crust or cookie dough. Cut into shapes using cookie cutters. Decorate as desired.

Creamy Bonbon Fondant

2 cups	granulated sugar	500 mL
1 cup	water	250 mL
1 tbsp	light (white) corn syrup	15 mL
1/4 tsp	glycerin	1 mL
1	egg white, pasteurized, stiffly beaten (see Cook's Notes, below)	1
1 tsp	vanilla extract	5 mL
	Chocolate Coatings (page 185)	

This soft, luscious fondant combines several options found under Old-Fashioned Cooked Fondant (page 202) to create the perfect centers for bonbons or chocolate creams or other candies.

Cook's Notes

Pasteurized eggs are available in many markets and are safe to eat raw in dishes that are not cooked.

For helpful tips, see Dipping Candies in Chocolate (page 22). For alternate chocolate coating recipes, see Chocolate Coatings (page 185). If desired, decorate the chocolate-coated bonbons with chopped nuts.

Glycerin used for bonbons can be purchased in the pharmacy section of most large grocery stores or craft stores.

Skill Level: Advanced

Makes about 2 cups (500 mL) fondant

- 2-quart heavy saucepan
- Candy thermometer
- Heatproof platter

1. In saucepan over medium heat, bring the sugar, water and corn syrup to a boil, stirring until the sugar dissolves and the mixture begins to boil. Add the glycerin just when the boiling begins. Cook, without stirring, to the soft ball stage (234°F to 240°F/112°C to 116°C, with 238° F/114°C recommended). Just before the candy reaches the desired temperature, rinse a heatproof platter with cold water; dry thoroughly.

2. Remove the boiling mixture from the heat. Pour onto the cool platter. Cool to 110°F (43°C), about 30 minutes.

3. Spread the egg white over the cooled fondant. Work the mixture back and forth on the platter by hand until it is white and creamy. Working the candy mixture can take 30 minutes or more. Professionals often use a special flat tool that looks somewhat like a scraper, scraping the candy on one side, lifting it up and folding it over and then scraping it on the other side, lifting it up and folding it over.

4. Cover a countertop area with waxed paper. Flavor the candy with the vanilla, working the flavoring into the candy. Immediately shape the fondant into small balls. Place the balls on waxed paper. Dip the centers in melted chocolate as soon as the centers are firm. This candy will soften if allowed to stand too long. Store in an airtight container.

Variation

Other extracts may be substituted for the vanilla. Suggested flavorings are maple extract, orange extract, cherry extract, coconut extract, strawberry extract or peppermint extract.

Buttercream Fondant

1 lb	confectioner's (icing) sugar	500 g
¼ cup	butter, softened	60 mL
Pinch	salt	Pinch
3 tbsp	boiling water (or ¼ cup/60 mL fruit juice)	45 mL
1 tsp	flavoring of choice (see Cook's Notes, below)	5 mL
	Few drops food coloring (optional)	
	Chocolate Coatings (page 185) (optional)	

This easy fondant recipe creates a creamy filling for candies similar to those found in a box of assorted chocolates.

Cook's Notes

Suggested flavorings are vanilla extract, maple extract, orange extract, cherry extract, coconut extract, strawberry extract or peppermint extract.

If preferred, fruit juices such as orange juice may be used in place of the boiling water, giving the candy additional flavor. If fruit juice is used, flavor the candy with vanilla extract or with an extract that complements the flavor of the fruit juice.

Makes about 55

1. Make a mound of confectioner's sugar on a marble slab, a large cutting board or a clean countertop. Put the softened butter and salt in the center of the mound. Knead the mixture by hand, adding the water to the mixture a few drops at a time. Add the flavoring and coloring, if using. Knead by hand until the fondant is very smooth and does not stick to the hands or fingers.

2. Pat the fondant into a ball or mound. Pinch off small amounts and shape as desired into small balls, squares or wafers.

3. If desired, dip the fondant centers into melted chocolate using the techniques and recipes found in Dipping Candies in Chocolate (page 22) or Chocolate Coatings (page 185). Store in an airtight container.

Storing Candy

Most candies should be stored in an airtight container to keep them fresh. Unless specifically instructed in the recipe, refrigeration is often a matter of personal choice, but generally, most fudges and fudge-like candies should keep at least 1 week at room temperature and at least 1 month, sometimes much longer, if refrigerated. Excessive heat, high humidity, or added ingredients such as fruit may shorten the storage time so it is important to use common sense. If the color or texture of the candy has changed, dispose of it and make a fresh batch.

Old-Fashioned Pastel Butter Mints

2 cups	confectioner's (icing) sugar	500 mL
1 cup	cornstarch	250 mL
2 cups	granulated sugar	500 mL
3/4 cup	water	175 mL
1/4 cup	butter (do not use margarine)	60 mL
1/4 tsp	cream of tartar (or 2 tbsp/30 mL cider vinegar)	1 mL
	Food coloring as desired	
10	drops peppermint oil (or 1/2 tsp/2 mL peppermint extract)	10

At one time, these creamy pastel butter mints were just as essential to a proper Southern wedding as having a bride and groom. Traditionally served in a crystal bowl or silver compote, the mints were placed between the white wedding cake and the equally essential bowl of roasted cocktail nuts. We Southerners have loosened up a bit the past few decades, but not enough to stop loving this old-fashioned candy.

Cook's Note

When pulling and stretching the candy, dip your fingers into a little cornstarch to prevent the candy from sticking.

Skill Level: Advanced

Makes about 50

- Large rimmed baking sheet, buttered
- 2-quart heavy saucepan
- Candy thermometer

1. In a flat container that can be sealed, combine the confectioner's sugar and cornstarch, mixing well.

2. In heavy saucepan, bring the granulated sugar, water, butter and cream of tartar to a boil, stirring until the sugar dissolves and the mixture begins to boil. Cover and cook 2 to 3 minutes to dissolve the sugar crystals on the sides of the pan. Remove the lid. Cook at a rapid boil, without stirring, to 265°F (129°C). When the temperature is nearly 265°F (129°C), drop in a few drops of food coloring, tinting the mixture to a light pastel color.

3. Remove from the heat. Quickly add the peppermint oil and turn onto the prepared baking sheet to cool. As soon as the candy can be handled, knead by hand until it can be picked up and pulled. Pull or stretch the candy until it is firm. Stretch the candy into a rope about 1/2 inch (1 cm) in diameter. Using kitchen shears, snip the rope into 1/2- to 1-inch (1 to 2.5 cm) pieces, letting the pieces fall into the confectioner's sugar and cornstarch mixture. Store the mints with the sugar mixture in the airtight container until the mints soften and become creamy, 2 to 3 days. When the mints have softened, turn the mints and the sugar mixture into a sieve, shaking the sieve to remove the excess sugar. Store the softened mints in an airtight container at room temperature.

Marvelous Marbled Mints

½ cup	butter, softened	125 mL
1 lb	confectioner's (icing) sugar, divided	500 g
2 tbsp	half-and-half (10%) cream or evaporated milk	30 mL
1 tsp	peppermint or mint extract	5 mL
	Food coloring as desired	
	Confectioner's (icing) sugar, for rolling, optional	

Pretty as a picture and delicious to boot, this recipe is as much fun as opening your first can of Play-Doh. Whether you serve these mints for a special event or just as a special treat, everyone will want to know how you came up with such a marvelous creation.

Cook's Notes

The mint fondant may be tinted a single color or any combination of colors desired. Though the three-color mints are beautiful, two-color mints can be equally as impressive.

If preferred, roll the mixture out like cookie dough and use small cookie cutters to give the mints unusual or festive shapes. For example, tint half of the mixture red, leaving the other half white. Roll the two colors together like cookie dough and cut into heart-shaped mints. Tiny amounts of contrasting colors may be shaped into small balls and pressed lightly into the mints as decorations.

Makes about 100 small mints

1. In a small mixing bowl, cream the butter with an electric mixer until fluffy. Gradually add half of the confectioner's sugar, mixing until smooth. Add the half-and-half and peppermint extract. Gradually add the remaining confectioner's sugar, blending thoroughly.

2. Divide the mixture into 3 parts. Tint 2 of the 3 parts as desired, leaving 1 part white. (For example, tint 1 portion pink, tint 1 portion yellow and leave one portion white.)

3. Cover a countertop area with waxed paper. Lightly dust the waxed paper with a small amount of confectioner's sugar, if desired. Place equal amounts of all 3 colors of the mixture on the waxed paper. Roll the 3 colors together into a long rope about ¾ to 1 inch (2 to 2.5 cm) in diameter, creating a marbled effect. Repeat until all the mixture is used. Secure the rolls in waxed paper, tightly sealing the ends. Transfer to a baking sheet and refrigerate until firm, about 1 hour.

4. Remove the rolls from the refrigerator. Slice into ¼-inch (0.5 cm) rounds. Cover an area of the countertop with waxed paper. Place the sliced mints on the waxed paper and cover lightly with another sheet of waxed paper. Let stand at room temperature until dry, 6 to 8 hours. Transfer the mints to an airtight container, separating each layer with waxed paper and store in the refrigerator if keeping more than 1 week.

Luscious Cream Cheese Mints

8 oz	cream cheese, softened	250 g
1/4 cup	butter or margarine, softened	60 mL
2 lbs	confectioner's (icing) sugar	1 kg
1 tsp	peppermint or mint extract	5 mL
	Food coloring as desired	
	Confectioner's (icing) sugar, for dipping	

> Rich and creamy, these scrumptious little mints are always a popular choice.

Makes about 100 mints

• 2 to 3 large baking sheets, lined with waxed paper

1. In a large mixing bowl, mix the cream cheese and butter with an electric mixer until smooth. Gradually add the confectioner's sugar, blending thoroughly. Add the peppermint extract, adjusting to taste if desired. Tint the mixture with food coloring, as desired. Cover and refrigerate 1 hour or until firm enough to handle.

2. Shape the mixture into balls 1 inch (2.5 cm) in diameter. Place the balls on the prepared baking sheets. Dip the bottom of a glass into confectioner's sugar and press the bottom of the glass into each ball to flatten. Let stand, uncovered, 4 hours or until firm. Store in an airtight container, separating each layer with waxed paper and refrigerate. These mints may also be frozen, if desired.

Important Tip

In many recipes, it is important to be prepared for all the steps because timing can be critical. Have all ingredients available and ready to use, and have the pan, baking sheet, or surface prepared before you begin cooking.

Chocolate-Covered Mint Patties

⅓ cup	butter or margarine, softened	75 mL
⅓ cup	light (white) corn syrup	75 mL
1 tsp	peppermint extract	5 mL
½ tsp	salt	2 mL
1 lb	confectioner's (icing) sugar	500 g
12 oz	dark chocolate candy coatings	375 g

These are just as delicious as they sound, perfect for an after-dinner treat.

Cook's Notes

This basic fondant recipe can be used to create a variety of candies. Substitute the peppermint extract with an extract of choice, shape the mixture into balls or patties and dip the candies into melted chocolate.

A Wilton hollow dipping spoon is a wonderful tool for dipping these mints, often leaving an attractive swirl pattern on the top.

For helpful tips, see Dipping Candies in Chocolate (page 22). For alternate chocolate coating recipes, see Chocolate Coatings (page 185).

Skill Level: Novice, Easy
Makes about 80 mints

- 2 large baking sheets, lined with waxed paper
- Double boiler

1. In a medium mixing bowl, blend the butter, corn syrup, peppermint extract and salt with a wooden spoon. Gradually add the confectioner's sugar, first mixing with the wooden spoon and then kneading by hand until the mixture is smooth and well blended and no longer sticks to the hands. Shape the mixture into a ball or a mound.

2. Pinch off small pieces of the mint fondant and shape into balls ¾ inch (2 cm) in diameter. Place the balls on the prepared baking sheets. Flatten the balls with the palm of the hand or with a flat spatula. Cover and refrigerate until firm, about 1 hour.

3. Cover a large countertop area with waxed paper. In the top pan of a double boiler over hot but not boiling water, melt the candy coating, stirring until smooth. Using a fork or a specially designed dipping tool, dip the mints into the melted chocolate until coated. Drop the mints onto the waxed paper. Let stand until the chocolate is firm. Store in an airtight container, separating each layer with waxed paper. These mints may be refrigerated or frozen if desired.

Sensational Orange Mint Patties

¹/₂ cup	butter, softened	125 mL
1	can (14 oz or 300 mL) sweetened condensed milk	1
1¹/₂ tsp	pure orange extract	7 mL
¹/₂ tsp	peppermint extract	2 mL
7 cups	confectioner's (icing) sugar (just under 2 lbs/1 kg)	1.75 L
1 lb 12 oz	dark chocolate candy coating	875 g

- 2 to 3 large baking sheets, covered with waxed paper
- Double boiler

1. In a large mixing bowl, combine the butter, milk, orange extract and peppermint extract with an electric mixer or by hand until smooth. Gradually add the confectioner's sugar, blending thoroughly after each addition. Cover and refrigerate 4 hours or until firm.

2. Shape the mixture into balls 1 inch (2.5 cm) in diameter. Place the balls on the prepared baking sheets and flatten with the palms of the hand or the back of a spatula. Cover and freeze 1 hour or until firm.

3. Cover a large countertop area with waxed paper.

4. In the top pan of a double boiler over hot but not boiling water, melt the chocolate candy coating, stirring until smooth. Using a fork or a specially designed dipping tool, dip the mints into the melted chocolate until coated. Drop the mints onto the waxed paper. Let stand until the chocolate is firm. Store in an airtight container, separating each layer with waxed paper. These mints may be refrigerated or frozen if desired.

While I would love to claim these creamy, chocolate-covered orange mint patties as my own invention, this recipe comes from another candy maker named Jane, this one from Louisiana. Perfect for parties, gifts, or an after-dinner treat, these melt-in-your mouth mints are truly sensational.

Cook's Notes

Not all mints must be shaped and dipped at once. If preferred, part or all of the mint filling may be sealed in an airtight container and stored in the freezer for at least 1 month.

Instead of shaping each individual mint by hand, shape the chilled fondant into several long, round rolls about 1¹/₄ inches (3 cm) in diameter. Secure the rolls in waxed paper, tightly sealing the ends. Freeze for 1 hour or more. Remove the rolls from the freezer and slice into ¹/₄-inch (0.5 cm) slices, using each slice as the center for an individual mint. If desired, these slices may be placed on a waxed paper–lined baking sheet, covered and frozen again until ready to dip in melted chocolate. Shaping the fondant into rolls not only saves time but also gives the mints a uniform size.

A Wilton hollow dipping spoon is a wonderful tool for dipping these mints, often leaving an attractive swirl pattern on the top.

Plain Jane Truffles

1/2 cup	heavy or whipping (35%) cream	125 mL
2 tbsp	butter (preferably unsalted)	30 mL
1 tbsp	granulated sugar	15 mL
1 cup	semisweet chocolate chips	250 mL
1 tbsp	pure almond extract, or to taste	15 mL
3/4 cup	finely chopped toasted almonds	175 mL

With all the gourmet recipes now available, it is nice to know that we can still make something quite delicious using ingredients we have on hand.

Cook's Notes

If preferred, the truffles may be coated in unsweetened cocoa powder, chocolate decorator sprinkles, confectioner's (icing) sugar or other coatings as desired. Finely chopped walnuts or pecans may be substituted for the toasted almonds.

The truffles may also be dipped in melted chocolate if desired. For helpful tips, see Dipping Candies in Chocolate (page 22). For chocolate coating recipes, see Chocolate Coatings (page 185).

Skill Level: Novice, Easy

Makes about 18 truffles

- Baking sheet, lined with waxed paper

1. In a small heavy saucepan over low heat, warm the cream, butter and sugar until it comes to a low, simmering boil. Remove from the heat. Add the chocolate chips, gently stirring until the chocolate is completely melted and the mixture is smooth and well blended. Gently stir in the almond extract. Cover and refrigerate 1 hour or until firm enough to handle.

2. Shape the chilled mixture into balls 3/4 inch (2 cm) in diameter. Place the balls on the prepared baking sheet. Cover and chill or freeze 1 hour or until firm.

3. Cover a large countertop area with waxed paper.

4. Place the chopped almonds into a small bowl or dish. Roll the chilled or frozen truffles in the chopped almonds until well coated. Place onto the waxed paper while rolling the remaining truffles. Store in an airtight container in the refrigerator. Let stand at room temperature 10 to 15 minutes before serving.

Variation

Other flavored extracts, such as mint, cherry, rum or vanilla, may be substituted for the almond extract. Since the strength of extracts may vary, adjust flavorings to taste.

Lynda's Gourmet Chocolate Truffles

2 cups	good-quality milk chocolate chips, such as Ghirardelli (12 oz/375 g)	500 mL
6 oz	good-quality semisweet chocolate, such as Ghirardelli, finely chopped	175 g
¾ cup	heavy or whipping (35%) cream	175 mL
1 tbsp	liqueur of choice such as Frangelico, Grand Marnier, amaretto or coffee liqueur, or 1 tbsp (15 mL) almond extract	15 mL

Coating Options

1½ cups	finely chopped hazelnuts or toasted almonds	375 mL
¾ cup	unsweetened cocoa powder, such as Williams-Sonoma Pernigotti	175 mL
¾ cup	Ghirardelli Sweet Ground Chocolate	175 mL
12 oz	good-quality chocolate candy coating	375 g

After spending a day covered in chocolate, my cousin Lynda finally hit upon this delicious combination of milk chocolate, semisweet chocolate, cream and liqueur as one of her favorites. It is one of my favorites, too.

Cook's Notes

The chocolate-coated truffles may be rolled in chopped hazelnuts or toasted almonds while the chocolate coating is still warm.

For helpful tips, see Dipping Candies in Chocolate (page 22). For alternate chocolate coating recipes, see Chocolate Coatings (page 185).

Skill Level: Novice, Easy

Makes about 48 truffles

- Large baking sheet, lined with waxed paper

1. In a medium heatproof bowl, combine the milk chocolate chips and semisweet chocolate. Set aside.

2. In a small heavy saucepan over low heat, warm the cream until it comes to a low, simmering boil. Pour the hot cream over the chocolate in the bowl. Using a wire whisk, gently stir until the chocolate is completely melted and the mixture is smooth and well blended. Gently stir in the liqueur. Cover and let stand at room temperature 20 to 30 minutes or until firm enough to handle. If desired, the mixture can be tightly covered and refrigerated for up to 1 week or until ready to shape into centers. If refrigerated, the mixture will become quite firm and may need to sit at room temperature for 20 to 30 minutes before being soft enough to shape into balls.

3. Shape the chilled mixture into balls ¾ inch (2 cm) in diameter. Place the balls on the prepared baking sheet. Refrigerate 20 minutes or until firm.

4. If a nut or dry coating is desired, cover a large countertop area or a large baking sheet with waxed paper. Roll the balls in the coating of choice. Place the coated truffles onto the waxed paper while rolling the remaining truffles.

5. If a chocolate coating is desired, cover a large countertop area or a large baking sheet with waxed paper. In the top pan of a double boiler over hot but not boiling water, melt the chocolate candy coating, stirring until smooth. Using a fork or specially designed dipping tool, dip the truffles into the melted chocolate until coated. Drop the truffles onto the waxed paper. Let stand until the chocolate is firm.

6. Store in an airtight container in the refrigerator. Let stand at room temperature 5 to 10 minutes before serving.

Bittersweet Chocolate Truffles

8 oz	good-quality bittersweet chocolate, such as Valrhona, finely chopped	250 g
1 cup	heavy or whipping (35%) cream	250 mL
	Few grains sea salt, preferably fleur de sel	
2 tbsp	unsalted butter, thinly sliced	30 mL
½ to ¾ cup	chopped toasted hazelnuts (optional)	125 to 175 mL
8 oz	good-quality chocolate candy coating	250 mL

When made with gourmet chocolate, these candies can be just as exquisite as the gourmet truffles found in exclusive specialty stores. Toasted hazelnuts may be added to the truffle centers, sprinkled on top of the chocolate coating, or omitted entirely.

Cook's Notes

I prefer to use Valrhona bittersweet chocolate, a gourmet chocolate usually sold by the pound in large grocery stores and specialty stores in some large cities. If gourmet bittersweet chocolate is not available, more common brands of bittersweet chocolate may be substituted, though the candy may not be as rich.

Fleur de sel is a gourmet French sea salt. Other types of sea salt may be substituted. Though sea salt is best, a few grains of table salt may be substituted if sea salt is not available.

For helpful tips, see Dipping Candies in Chocolate (page 22). For alternate chocolate coating recipes, see Chocolate Coatings (page 185).

Skill Level: Novice, Easy

Makes about 30 truffles

- Large baking sheet, lined with waxed paper
- Double boiler

1. Place the finely chopped chocolate into a large heatproof bowl. Set aside.

2. In a small heavy saucepan over low heat, warm the cream until it reaches a low, simmering boil. Pour the hot cream over the chocolate in the bowl. Using a wire whisk, gently stir until the chocolate is completely melted. Add the salt and butter, a few small pieces at a time and stir gently until the butter is completely melted and the mixture is smooth and well blended. Set aside at room temperature to cool 15 minutes.

3. Whip the truffle mixture briskly with a wire whisk until the chocolate lightens in color, 1 to 2 minutes. Stir in the hazelnuts to taste, if desired. Set aside at room temperature until the truffle mixture becomes firm enough to handle, 30 to 35 minutes.

4. Drop the truffle mixture by rounded teaspoons (5 mL) onto the prepared baking sheet. Refrigerate until the centers are firm enough to dip in melted chocolate, 30 minutes to 1 hour.

5. Cover a large countertop area or a large baking sheet with waxed paper.

6. In the top pan of a double boiler over hot but not boiling water, melt the chocolate candy coating, stirring until smooth. Using a fork or specially designed dipping tool, dip the truffles into the melted chocolate until coated. Drop the truffles onto the waxed paper. If the hazelnuts were not added to the filling mixture, sprinkle the coated truffles with the hazelnuts, if desired, while the chocolate coating is still warm. Let stand until the chocolate is firm. Store in an airtight container in the refrigerator. Let stand at room temperature about 10 minutes before serving.

Lemon Curd Truffles

9 oz	good-quality white chocolate, such as Ghirardelli chocolate	270 g
3 tbsp	unsalted butter, thinly sliced	45 mL
6 tbsp	heavy or whipping (35%) cream	90 mL
	Few grains sea salt	
2 to 3 tsp	freshly squeezed lemon juice	10 to 15 mL
1/3 cup	prepared lemon curd	75 mL
8 oz	good-quality white chocolate candy coating	250 g

This recipe requires slightly less effort than Lynda's Luscious Lemon Truffles (page 216), yet still has a rich lemon flavor.

Cook's Notes

Lemon curd is available in most grocery stores near the jellies and jams.

The amount of butter may be reduced by up to half if desired.

For helpful tips, see Dipping Candies in Chocolate (page 22).

Skill Level: Novice, Easy

Makes about 30 truffles

- Large baking sheet, lined with waxed paper or parchment
- Food processor
- Double boiler

1. Coarsely chop the white chocolate by hand. Place the white chocolate into a food processor and chop again until it is very finely ground. (If a food processor is not available, chop the white chocolate by hand until very finely chopped.) Place the white chocolate and butter into a medium heatproof bowl.

2. In a small heavy saucepan over low heat, warm the cream until it comes to a low, simmering boil. Remove from the heat. Stir in the salt and lemon juice. Pour the hot cream mixture over the white chocolate mixture. Using a small wire whisk, gently stir until the chocolate is completely melted and the mixture is smooth and well blended. Add the lemon curd, gently stirring until blended and smooth. Cover and refrigerate until firm, about 1 hour.

3. Shape the chilled truffle mixture into balls 3/4 inch (2 cm) in diameter. Place the balls on the prepared baking sheet. Refrigerate or freeze until firm, about 20 minutes.

4. Cover a large countertop area or a baking sheet with waxed paper or parchment.

5. In the top pan of a double boiler over hot but not boiling water, melt the white chocolate candy coating, stirring until smooth. Using a fork or specially designed dipping tool, dip each chilled truffle into the melted chocolate until coated. Drop the truffles onto the waxed paper. Let stand until the chocolate is firm. Store in an airtight container in the refrigerator. Let stand at room temperature about 10 minutes before serving.

Variation

Roll the white chocolate–coated truffles in finely chopped pecans while the chocolate coating is still warm.

Lynda's Luscious Lemon Truffles

6 tbsp	heavy or whipping (35%) cream	90 mL
	Finely grated zest of 2 small lemons	
9 oz	good-quality white chocolate	270 g
4 tbsp	unsalted butter, thinly sliced	60 mL
	Few grains of sea salt, preferably fleur de sel (see Cook's Notes, page 214)	
4 tsp	freshly squeezed lemon juice	20 mL

Toasted Pecan Coating (optional)

1 1/2 cups	pecans	375 mL
1 tsp	unsalted butter	5 mL
1/8 tsp	sea salt, preferably fleur de sel	0.5 mL
8 oz	good-quality white chocolate candy coating	250 g

> Add a touch of elegance to any event with these heavenly lemon truffles from my cousin Lynda.

- Large baking sheet, lined with waxed paper or parchment
- Food processor
- Double boiler

1. In a small heavy saucepan over low heat, warm the cream and lemon zest until it comes to a low, simmering boil. Remove from the heat, cover and let stand at room temperature 15 to 20 minutes.

2. Coarsely chop the white chocolate by hand. Place the white chocolate into a food processor and chop again until it is very finely ground. (If a food processor is not available, chop the white chocolate by hand until very finely chopped.) Rinse a medium heatproof bowl in hot water and dry thoroughly. Place the white chocolate into the warmed bowl. Add the butter and sea salt. Set aside.

3. Place the saucepan containing the cream and lemon zest over low heat and bring to a low simmer a second time. Remove from the heat. Add the lemon juice, gently stirring to blend. Pour the hot cream mixture through a fine sieve placed over the white chocolate mixture. Discard the lemon zest trapped in the sieve. Using a small wire whisk, gently stir the cream and white chocolate mixture until the chocolate is completely melted and the mixture is smooth and well blended. Cover and refrigerate 4 hours or more.

4. *To prepare the Toasted Pecan Coating, if desired:* Preheat the oven to 350°F (180°C). Place the pecans in a shallow pan and toast in the oven, about 8 minutes or until light golden, stirring halfway through cooking. Remove from the oven and stir in the butter and sea salt. Cool. Finely chop the pecans by hand. Place in a small dish. Set aside.

For a special presentation, coat half the truffles in melted white chocolate and half in both melted white chocolate and the Toasted Pecan Coating. Place in fluted candy cups and serve on a beautiful china dish.

A Microplane grater is a kitchen tool designed to create very fine, fluffy zest. If a Microplane grater or a similar tool has been used to remove the lemon zest and the zest is very, very fine, the cream may be poured directly over the white chocolate without the use of a sieve.

For helpful tips, see Dipping Candies in Chocolate (page 22).

5. Shape the chilled truffle mixture into balls $\frac{3}{4}$ inch (2 cm) in diameter. Place the balls on the prepared baking sheet. Refrigerate or freeze until firm, about 20 minutes.

6. Cover a large countertop area or a baking sheet with waxed paper.

7. In the top pan of a double boiler over hot but not boiling water, melt the white chocolate candy coating, stirring until smooth. Using a fork or specially designed dipping tool, dip each chilled truffle into the melted chocolate until coated. If desired, immediately drop the chocolate-coated truffle into the dish containing the pecan coating and roll in the nuts until coated. Place the coated truffles onto the waxed paper. Let stand until the chocolate is firm. Store in an airtight container in the refrigerator. Let stand at room temperature about 10 minutes before serving.

Creating Smooth Truffle Centers

Many truffle recipes involve pouring hot cream over finely chopped chocolate and whisking the two together until the chocolate melts. Often most of the chocolate will melt but a few stubborn pieces may put up a fight. If this occurs, microwave the mixture 30 seconds, stir, and then repeat until the chocolate begins to melt. Do not microwave truffle mixtures more than 45 seconds without stirring because the chocolate can scorch very easily.

Another approach is to soften the chocolate before adding the cream by microwaving the chopped chocolate in 30-second increments just until the chocolate begins to soften. When the hot cream is added the chocolate will melt more easily.

Marzipan Truffles

9 oz	good-quality white chocolate	270 g
6 tbsp	heavy or whipping (35%) cream	90 mL
1 tbsp	amaretto liqueur (or 1 tsp/5 mL almond extract)	15 mL
1	package (7 oz/210 g) marzipan	1
¼ cup	unsalted butter, softened	60 mL
10 oz	dark or white chocolate candy coating	300 g
¼ cup	ground or finely chopped almonds or white chocolate or dark chocolate shavings (optional)	60 mL

This magnificent combination of scrumptious white chocolate and rich, almond flavoring is an unexpected surprise.

Cook's Notes

For a special presentation, dip half the batch of the truffles into melted white chocolate and half into melted dark chocolate. Decorate the tops of the truffles by sprinkling the white chocolate truffles with dark chocolate shavings and the dark chocolate truffles with white chocolate shavings.

For helpful tips, see Dipping Candies in Chocolate (page 22).

Skill Level: Average

Makes about 36 truffles

- Large baking sheet, lined with waxed or parchment paper
- Food processor
- Double boiler

1. Coarsely chop the white chocolate by hand. Place the white chocolate into a food processor and chop again until it is very finely ground. (If a food processor is not available, chop the white chocolate by hand until very finely chopped.) Place the white chocolate in the top pan of a double boiler away from the heat. Set aside.

2. In a small heavy saucepan over low heat, warm the cream until it comes to a low, simmering boil. Gently stir in the liqueur. Pour the heated cream over the white chocolate, gently stirring until the white chocolate is fully melted. Add the marzipan and butter, stirring gently to blend.

3. Heat water in the bottom pan of the double boiler until hot but not boiling. Remove from the heat. Place the top double boiler pan containing the white chocolate and marzipan mixture over the hot water, stirring until the mixture is completely melted and smooth. Remove from the heat. Cover and refrigerate 3 to 4 hours or until firm enough to handle.

4. Shape the truffle mixture into balls ¾ inch (2 cm) in diameter. Place the balls on the prepared baking sheet. Freeze until firm, about 15 minutes.

5. Cover a large countertop area or a large baking sheet with waxed paper.

6. In the top pan of a double boiler over hot but not boiling water, melt the chocolate candy coating, stirring until smooth. Using a fork or specially designed dipping tool, dip the truffles into the melted chocolate until coated. Drop the truffles onto the waxed paper. Immediately sprinkle with the almonds or chocolate shavings, if desired. Let stand until the chocolate is firm. Store in an airtight container in the refrigerator. Let stand at room temperature 10 to 15 minutes before serving.

Magic Truffles

1 cup	semisweet chocolate chips	250 mL
1/2 cup plus 1 tbsp	sweetened condensed milk	140 mL
Pinch	salt	Pinch
1/2 tsp	vanilla extract	2 mL
1/4 cup	finely chopped pecans or walnuts (optional)	60 mL

Put a little magic into your life with these creamy fudge nuggets.

Makes about 64 truffles

- 8-inch (20 cm) square pan
- Double boiler

1. Line the square pan with waxed paper or foil, leaving a 1-inch (2.5 cm) overhang on the sides of the pan.

2. In the top pan of a double boiler over hot but not boiling water, melt the chocolate chips, stirring until smooth. Remove from the heat. Add the milk, salt and vanilla, stirring only until blended. Gently stir in the nuts, if using.

3. Pour the mixture into the lined pan, spreading evenly. Cover and refrigerate until firm, about 2 hours. Remove the block of candy from the pan by gently lifting the edges of the waxed paper. Place the block on a cutting board. Remove the waxed paper or foil lining and cut into squares. Store in an airtight container in the refrigerator.

Cutting into Perfect Squares and Special Shapes

Cutting candy becomes much easier with the use of parchment paper. Rather than buttering the pan directly, butter a piece of parchment paper larger than the pan and press it into the bottom and up the sides of the pan, tucking and creasing the paper as needed to create corners, and leaving a generous overhang over the sides of the pan. Pour the candy into the parchment-lined pan. Once the candy has cooled, use the parchment to lift the entire block of candy out of the pan. Place the block of candy on a cutting board and use a long, serrated knife to cut straight, uniform rows of the candy, and then cut the rows into squares. For a special presentation, cut the block of candy into diamonds, triangles or other shapes, as desired.

The parchment paper method is optional, but over the years I have found it much easier than cutting candy in the pan, and it saves my pans from deep scratches left by sharp knives. At times I have shipped large blocks of candy to friends and family with the candy still wrapped in the parchment paper and then wrapped again in foil wrap. It simplifies shipping and allows others to cut the candy as they choose.

Luscious Raspberry-Fudge Truffles

2 cups	semisweet chocolate chips	500 mL
1 lb	cream cheese, softened	500 g
1 cup	seedless raspberry preserves	250 mL
2 tbsp	raspberry liqueur, such as Chambord	30 mL
1²⁄₃ cups	very finely crushed vanilla wafer crumbs (see Cook's Notes, right)	400 mL
18 oz	chocolate candy coating	540 g

Decorative White Chocolate Drizzle (optional)

| 3 oz | white chocolate, chopped | 90 g |
| 1 tbsp | solid vegetable shortening | 15 mL |

A longtime personal favorite, these "little bites of heaven" are worth the time it takes to make them.

Cook's Note

For step-by-step photographs, see color page J.

Skill Level: Novice, Easy

Makes about 75 truffles

- 2 large baking sheets, lined with waxed paper
- Double boiler

1. In a small heavy saucepan over low heat, melt the chocolate chips, stirring until smooth. Remove from the heat. Set aside to cool slightly.

2. In a large mixing bowl, beat the cream cheese with an electric mixer until smooth. Add the melted chocolate, raspberry preserves and liqueur, beating until well blended. Blend in the wafer crumbs, mixing well. Cover and freeze 1 hour to make the filling firm enough to handle. If preferred, cover and refrigerate up to 1 week before shaping into truffles.

3. Working with approximately one-third of the cold truffle mixture at a time, shape the mixture into balls ¾ inch (2 cm) in diameter. Place the balls on the prepared baking sheets. Cover and freeze 1 hour or more.

4. Cover a large countertop area or 2 large baking sheets with waxed paper.

5. In the top pan of a double boiler over hot but not boiling water, melt the chocolate coating, stirring until smooth. Using a toothpick, fork or specially designed dipping tool, dip the frozen balls into the melted chocolate until coated. Drop the coated truffles onto the waxed paper. Let stand until the chocolate is firm.

Cook's Notes

The key to making these truffles ultra smooth and delicious is to process the vanilla wafer crumbs in a food processor until they are almost the consistency of a powder.

This recipe appears to be more difficult than it is. It is not necessary to shape or dip all truffles at one time. The filling may be placed in an airtight container and frozen for at least 2 months and then shaped and dipped as needed.

The mixture is much easier to form into balls when very cold. By working with approximately one-third of the mixture at a time, the remaining mixture remains cold until ready to be shaped.

If a toothpick is used to dip the truffles into the melted chocolate, the hole left by the toothpick must be covered with chocolate or the raspberry filling will ooze from the hole. Let the chocolate coating harden and then use a spoon to dab a tiny amount of the melted chocolate over the hole.

For helpful tips, see Dipping Candies in Chocolate (page 22). For alternate chocolate coating recipes, see Chocolate Coatings (page 185).

6. *To prepare the Decorative White Chocolate Drizzle, if desired:* Place the white chocolate and shortening in a small, heavy-duty self-sealing plastic bag. Seal the bag tightly. Submerge the bag in hot water until the chocolate melts. (The hot water left in the bottom of the double boiler pan used to melt the chocolate coating is usually perfect for melting the white chocolate.) Gently knead the bag until the chocolate and shortening are blended. Poke a tiny hole in one corner of the bag. Gently squeeze the white chocolate mixture through the hole in the bag, drizzling it over the tops of the dipped truffles in a decorative pattern. Let the truffles stand until the white chocolate is firm.

7. Store the truffles in an airtight container in the refrigerator for up to 3 weeks or in the freezer for up to 2 months. The truffles may be served at room temperature but taste best when chilled.

Variation

If desired, substitute 3 oz (90 g) white chocolate candy coating for white chocolate and shortening used for the drizzle.

Farmhouse Favorites

Even the most devoted *chocolate lovers need a change of pace now and then, and Farmhouse Favorites are the perfect choice. Packed with the treasures of a bountiful harvest, these candies are a gift from Mother Earth.*

Savor a shiny red apple smothered in velvety smooth caramel or an oven-roasted pecan dressed in a bouquet of winter spices. Sample unusual jelly candies from the Pacific Northwest, where lush fruit orchards burst into bloom each spring to flaunt the beauty of nature's palette. Celebrate Indian summer with the crunchy goodness of popcorn candies flavored with nuts, orange or natural sorghum syrup. Let the poetry of sugarplums hypnotize you with their charm as you prepare for that special Christmas Eve with loved ones.

Snacks made of fruits and honey date back thousands of years and were the first candies to be enjoyed by man. Whether tucked away in a backpack or served on a tray for guests, Farmhouse Favorites will always remind us of sunshine, springtime and all things good.

Packed with the treasures of a bountiful harvest, these candies are a gift from Mother Earth.

Candied and Spiced Nuts

Roasted Cinnamon Pecans

2 cups	pecan halves	500 mL
1 cup	granulated sugar	250 mL
1 to	ground cinnamon,	5 to
3 tsp	to taste	15 mL
1½ to	vanilla extract, to taste	7 to
3 tsp		15 mL
5 tbsp	water	75 mL

> Oh, my! The first time I made this recipe I ate the whole batch before anyone else could taste them. Roasting gives the pecans a deep, rich flavor and a double dose of vanilla just makes them doubly delicious.

Cook's Note

The amount of cinnamon and vanilla extract used is often a matter of personal preference and can easily be adjusted within the ranges listed.

Although the timing method can be used in this recipe, a candy thermometer is preferred to make certain that the syrup has reached the soft ball stage.

Skill Level: Novice, Easy

Makes about 3 cups (750 mL)

- Preheat the oven to 350°F (180°C)
- Large baking sheet, buttered
- 2-quart heavy saucepan
- Candy thermometer

1. Scatter the pecans on an unbuttered baking sheet. Roast the pecans in preheated oven for 8 to 10 minutes, stirring once.

2. In heavy saucepan, combine the sugar and cinnamon, mixing well. Stir in the vanilla and water. Bring to a boil over medium heat, stirring until the sugar dissolves. Cook at a medium boil, without stirring, about 5 minutes or until the mixture reaches the soft ball stage 234°F to 240°F/112°C to 116°C, with 236°F/113°C recommended).

3. Remove from the heat. Stir vigorously about 1 minute. Add the pecans and stir until the syrup thickens and coats the pecans.

4. Pour the mixture onto the prepared baking sheet. Separate the pecans using two forks. Cool. Store in an airtight container.

Important Tip

In many recipes, it is important to be prepared for all the steps because timing can be critical. Have all ingredients available and ready to use, and have the pan, baking sheet, or surface prepared before you begin cooking.

Spiced Pecans

1 cup	granulated sugar	250 mL
1/2 tsp	ground cinnamon	2 mL
1/4 tsp	ground nutmeg	1 mL
1/8 tsp	ground allspice	0.5 mL
1/2 tsp	salt	2 mL
1/2 cup	water	125 mL
1/2 tsp	vanilla extract	2 mL
2 cups	pecan halves	500 mL

Nothing speaks of fall quite like fresh pecans smothered with the spices of your favorite apple pie.

Gourmet Nuts

Candied and spiced nuts are so simple, so easy and oh, so good; these wonderful delicacies are welcome any time of year. Serve them with ice cream or baked apples or just as a snack.

Makes about 3 cups (750 mL)

- Large baking sheet, buttered
- 2-quart heavy saucepan
- Candy thermometer

1. In heavy saucepan, combine the sugar, cinnamon, nutmeg, allspice and salt, mixing well. Stir in the water. Bring to a boil over medium heat, stirring until the sugar dissolves. Cook, without stirring, to the soft ball stage (234°F to 240°F/112°C to 116°C, with 236°F/113°C recommended).

2. Remove from the heat. Add the vanilla and stir vigorously about 1 minute. Add the pecans and stir until the syrup thickens and coats the pecans.

3. Pour onto the prepared baking sheet. Separate the pecans using two forks. Cool. Store in an airtight container.

Cinnamon-Sugar Pecans

1 cup	granulated sugar	250 mL
1/4 tsp	salt	1 mL
1/2 tsp	ground cinnamon	2 mL
6 tbsp	milk	90 mL
1/2 tsp	vanilla extract	2 mL
2 cups	pecan halves	500 mL

From my mother's collection, this recipe for cinnamon-sugar pecans has a creamier texture than similar recipes because of the milk.

Makes about 3 cups (750 mL)

- Large baking sheet, buttered
- 2-quart heavy saucepan
- Candy thermometer

1. In heavy saucepan, combine the sugar, salt and cinnamon, mixing well. Stir in the milk. Bring to a boil over medium heat, stirring until the sugar dissolves. Cook, stirring occasionally to prevent scorching, to the soft ball stage (234°F to 240°F/112°C to 116°C, with 236°F/113°C recommended).

2. Remove from the heat. Add the vanilla and stir vigorously about 1 minute. Add the pecans and stir until the syrup thickens and coats the pecans.

3. Pour onto the prepared baking sheet. Separate the pecans using two forks. Cool. Store in an airtight container.

Crispy Sugared Walnuts

2½ cups	walnut halves	625 mL
1 cup	granulated sugar	250 mL
1 tsp	ground cinnamon	5 mL
½ tsp	salt	2 mL
½ cup	water	125 mL
1 tsp	vanilla extract	5 mL

Sugared walnuts have a milder flavor than similar recipes made with pecans.

Makes about 3 cups (750 mL)

- Preheat the oven to 350°F (180°C)
- Large baking sheet, buttered
- 2-quart heavy saucepan
- Candy thermometer

1. Scatter the walnuts on a baking sheet. Roast the walnuts in preheated oven for 5 minutes, stirring once.

2. In heavy saucepan, combine the sugar, cinnamon and salt, mixing well. Stir in the water. Bring to a boil over medium heat, stirring until the sugar dissolves. Cook, without stirring, to the soft ball stage (234°F to 240°F/112°C to 116°C, with 236°F/113°C recommended).

3. Remove from the heat. Add the vanilla and stir vigorously about 1 minute. Add the walnuts and stir until the syrup thickens and coats the walnuts.

4. Pour onto the prepared baking sheet. Separate the walnuts using two forks. Cool. Store in an airtight container.

County Fair Nuts

1	large egg white	1
1 tbsp	cold water	15 mL
1 cup	granulated sugar	250 mL
1 tsp	salt	5 mL
1 tbsp	ground cinnamon	15 mL
1 lb	whole almonds, pecan halves or walnut halves	500 g

My cousins Peggy and Lynda sent me this recipe after they had tasted the nuts at an arts and crafts fair in Shelby, North Carolina.

Makes 3 to 4 cups (750 mL to 1 L)

- Preheat the oven to 275°F (140°C)
- Rimmed baking sheet, buttered

1. In a small mixing bowl, beat the egg white and water with an electric mixer on high speed until frothy. In a separate small bowl, combine the sugar, salt and cinnamon until well blended.

2. Drop the nuts, a few at a time, into the egg white mixture, turning with a fork until coated. Drop the coated nuts into the sugar mixture, turning with a fork until well coated with the sugar mixture. Place the nuts on the prepared baking sheet. Bake in preheated oven 45 minutes, stirring every 15 minutes or until crispy. Remove from the oven. Cool. Store in an airtight container.

Sugared Peanuts

1 cup	granulated sugar	250 mL
1/2 cup	water	125 mL
2 cups	raw unsalted peanuts	500 mL

With a crunchy sugar coating, these crispy peanuts are best eaten by the handful.

Makes about 2 1/2 cups (625 mL)

- Preheat the oven to 325°F (160°C)
- Rimmed baking sheet, buttered
- 2-quart heavy saucepan

1. In heavy saucepan, combine the sugar, water and peanuts. Cook over medium-high heat, stirring occasionally, until the nuts are well coated in syrup and most of the moisture has evaporated.

2. Remove from the heat. Pour onto the prepared baking pan. Bake in preheated oven for 15 minutes, stirring twice. Remove from the oven. Cool. Store in an airtight container.

Candied Nuts

1 cup	packed light brown sugar	250 mL
1/2 cup	granulated sugar	125 mL
1/2 cup	sour cream	125 mL
1 tsp	vanilla extract	5 mL
2 1/2 cups	pecan halves	625 mL

A thick, light brown coating with a hint of sour cream gives these nuts a special flavor.

Makes about 3 cups (750 mL)

- Large baking sheet, buttered
- 2-quart heavy saucepan
- Candy thermometer

1. In heavy saucepan, combine the brown and granulated sugars and sour cream. Bring to a boil over low heat, stirring until the sugar dissolves. Cover and cook 2 to 3 minutes to dissolve the sugar crystals on the sides of the pan. Remove the lid and cook slowly, stirring occasionally, until the mixture reaches the firm ball stage (244°F to 248°F/118°C to 120°C, with 246°F/119°C recommended).

2. Remove from the heat. Add the vanilla and stir vigorously about 1 minute. Add the pecans and stir until the candy thickens and coats the pecans.

3. Pour onto the prepared baking sheet. Separate the pecans using two forks. Cool. Store in an airtight container.

Glazed Nuts

1 cup	granulated sugar	250 mL
1/3 cup	light (white) corn syrup	75 mL
1/2 cup	water	125 mL
2 cups	pecan halves, walnut halves or whole raw almonds	500 mL

With a hard, clear, glossy coating, glazed nuts and fruits are usually used as a garnish.

Cook's Note

This recipe may also be used to glaze dried, candied or fresh fruits such as cherries, pineapple, grapes, strawberries or raisins, though fresh fruits will not store well and should be used immediately.

Skill Level: Average

Makes about 3 cups (750 mL)

- Large baking sheet, buttered
- Candy thermometer

1. In a very small saucepan, combine the sugar, corn syrup and water. Bring to a boil over medium heat, stirring until the sugar dissolves. Cook, without stirring, to the hard crack stage (300°F/149°C).

2. Remove from the heat. Set the saucepan in a pan of boiling water to prevent the syrup from hardening. Drop the nuts, one at a time, into the syrup, coating the nuts well. Using a fork, remove the nuts and drop onto the prepared baking sheet. Do not stir the syrup while dipping the nuts. If the syrup becomes too thick to use, reheat the syrup over medium heat until it reaches a boil. Cool. Store in an airtight container.

Storing Candy

Most candies should be stored in an airtight container to keep them fresh. Unless specifically instructed in the recipe, refrigeration is often a matter of personal choice, but generally, most fudges and fudge-like candies should keep at least 1 week at room temperature and at least 1 month, sometimes much longer, if refrigerated. Excessive heat, high humidity, or added ingredients such as fruit may shorten the storage time so it is important to use common sense. If the color or texture of the candy has changed, dispose of it and make a fresh batch.

Cowboy Crunch

8 cups	freshly popped popcorn, unsalted	2 L
1 cup	coarsely chopped pecans, toasted	250 mL
1 cup	sliced almonds, toasted	250 mL
1⅓ cups	granulated sugar	325 mL
1 cup	butter or margarine	250 mL
½ cup	light (white) corn syrup	125 mL
1 tsp	vanilla extract	5 mL

This is a personal favorite, and one batch of this buttery gourmet candied popcorn is never enough to satisfy friends and family.

Cook's Note

The cooking temperature for the syrup can vary a few degrees without harming the candy. Do not cook the syrup beyond 270°F (132°C) or the popcorn will be hard and difficult to chew.

Skill Level: Average

Makes about 11 cups (2.75 L)

- 13- by 9-inch (33 by 23 cm) pan or a large roasting pan, sprayed with nonstick spray
- 2-quart heavy saucepan
- Candy thermometer

1. In a very large mixing bowl, combine the popcorn, pecans and almonds, tossing them together until the nuts are evenly distributed. Pour the popcorn mixture into the prepared pan.

2. In heavy saucepan over medium heat, bring the sugar, butter and corn syrup to a boil, stirring until the sugar dissolves and the mixture begins to boil. Cook, stirring constantly to prevent scorching, to a point between the hard ball and soft crack stages (265°F to 268°F/129°C to 131°C), about 15 minutes. The syrup will not darken significantly and will be a very light golden color when cooked.

3. Remove from the heat. Stir in the vanilla. Pour the hot syrup over the popcorn mixture and stir until the popcorn and nuts are well coated. Cool slightly, 5 to 10 minutes. Break the candy apart into small pieces. Cool completely. Store in an airtight container.

Orange-Nut Popcorn

12 cups	freshly popped popcorn, unsalted	3 L
1 cup	coarsely chopped pecans, walnuts or toasted almonds	250 mL
2 cups	granulated sugar	500 mL
1/2 cup	half-and-half (10%) cream	125 mL
	Freshly grated zest of 1 orange	
1/2 cup	orange juice	125 mL
Pinch	salt	Pinch
1 tbsp	butter or margarine	15 mL

Not your usual popcorn candy, this zesty version has a wonderful orange flavor.

Cook's Note

If preferred, the mixture may be shaped into popcorn balls. Wrap each cooled popcorn ball in plastic wrap.

Skill Level: Average

Makes about 14 cups (3.5 L)

- 13- by 9-inch (33 by 23 cm) pan or a large roasting pan, sprayed with nonstick spray
- 2-quart heavy saucepan
- Candy thermometer

1. In a very large mixing bowl, combine the popcorn and nuts, tossing them together until the nuts are evenly distributed. Pour the popcorn mixture into the prepared pan.

2. In heavy saucepan over medium-low heat, bring the sugar, half-and-half, orange zest, orange juice and salt to a boil, stirring until the sugar dissolves and the mixture begins to boil. Cook, stirring only as needed to prevent scorching, to the soft ball stage (234°F to 240°F/112°C to 116°C, with 236°F/113°C recommended).

3. Remove from the heat. Stir in the butter until melted. Slowly pour the hot syrup over the popcorn mixture and stir until the popcorn and nuts are coated. Cool slightly, 5 to 10 minutes. Break the candy apart into small pieces. Cool completely. Store in an airtight container.

Honey-Nut Popcorn

8 cups	freshly popped popcorn, unsalted	2 L
1 cup	blanched slivered almonds	250 mL
1 cup	coarsely chopped pecans	250 mL
1 cup	roasted salted cashews	250 mL
1 cup	packed light brown sugar	250 mL
1/2 cup	butter or margarine	125 mL
1/4 cup	honey	60 mL
1 tsp	vanilla extract	5 mL

Sweet, golden honey slowly baked onto popcorn, almonds, pecans and cashews creates a magnificent combination.

Makes about 12 cups (3 L)

- Preheat the oven to 250°F (120°C)
- Very large roasting pan, buttered
- 2-quart heavy saucepan

1. Pour the popcorn, almonds, pecans and cashews into the prepared pan, tossing them together until the nuts are evenly distributed.

2. In heavy saucepan over medium heat, bring the sugar, butter and honey to a boil, stirring until the sugar dissolves and the mixture begins to boil. Boil 5 minutes without stirring.

3. Remove from the heat. Stir in the vanilla. Pour the hot syrup over the popcorn mixture and stir the popcorn and nuts until well coated. Bake 1 hour, stirring every 15 minutes. Remove from the oven and cool completely. Break into pieces. Store in an airtight container.

Old-Fashioned Caramel Popcorn

12 cups	freshly popped popcorn, unsalted	3 L
1 cup	granulated sugar	250 mL
1/2 cup	dark (cooking) molasses (see Glossary, page 20)	125 mL
1/2 cup	water	125 mL
1 1/2 tsp	cider vinegar	7 mL
2 tbsp	butter	30 mL
1/2 tsp	baking soda	2 mL
1 tsp	vanilla extract	5 mL

With a crunchy texture and rich molasses flavor, it is no wonder that this recipe has been enjoyed by many generations.

Makes about 12 cups (3 L)

- 3-quart heavy saucepan
- Candy thermometer

1. Pour the popcorn into a large mixing bowl.

2. In heavy saucepan over medium heat, bring the sugar, molasses, water, vinegar and butter to a boil, stirring until the sugar dissolves and the mixture begins to boil. Cook, stirring gently a few times, to the soft crack stage (270°F/132°C).

3. Remove from the heat. Stir in the baking soda. Add the vanilla. Pour the hot syrup over the popcorn and stir until the popcorn is well coated. Cool and separate into pieces. Store in an airtight container.

Southern-Style Caramel Popcorn

16 cups	freshly popped popcorn, unsalted	4 L
1 cup	pure sorghum syrup or sorghum with molasses	250 mL
1 cup	packed light brown sugar	250 mL
¼ cup	butter	60 mL
¼ cup	water	60 mL

> Made with Southern-style sorghum syrup, this gooey, flavorful caramel-coated popcorn may taste familiar, especially to seniors who remember the days when sorghum was used as a sugar substitute.

Cook's Note

Sorghum syrup is made from sorghum cane and was once quite common in the southern United States. It is becoming popular as a sweetener again because of its high antioxidant content.

Skill Level: Average

Makes about 16 cups (4 L)

- 3-quart heavy saucepan
- Candy thermometer

1. Pour the popcorn into 2 large or one very large mixing bowl.
2. In heavy saucepan over medium heat, bring the sorghum, sugar, butter and water to a boil, stirring until the sugar dissolves and the mixture begins to boil. Cook, stirring gently a few times, to the soft ball stage (240°F/116°C).
3. Remove from the heat. Cool slightly, 1 to 2 minutes. Pour the hot syrup over the popcorn, stirring the popcorn until well coated. Cool and separate into pieces. Store in an airtight container. If preferred, the coated mixture may be shaped into popcorn balls. Wrap each cooled popcorn ball in plastic wrap.

Sorghum Syrup

During the Depression of the 1930s, sugar was a luxury item that few could afford. Like many Southerners, my grandfather built a mule-operated sorghum mill on his land so that his family could still enjoy sweets. Once a year, the family harvested their sorghum cane by hand, hauled it to my grandfather's mill in a horse-drawn wagon and then cooked the sorghum juice in a flat pan over a large open fire until it thickened into a sweet, brown syrup. With a few days of hard work, the family had enough sorghum syrup to last an entire year, plus a little extra to share with neighbors.

Popcorn-and-a-Prize

20 cups	freshly popped popcorn, unsalted	5 L
1 cup	salted peanuts	250 mL
2 cups	packed light brown sugar	500 mL
½ cup	butter	125 mL
½ cup	light (white or golden) corn syrup	125 mL
⅛ tsp	cream of tartar	0.5 mL
1 tsp	baking soda	5 mL
1	small toy prize (optional)	1

Popcorn, peanuts and a prize, this candy might have a familiar taste.

- Preheat the oven to 200°F (100°C)
- 2 large rimmed baking sheets, buttered
- 3-quart heavy saucepan

1. In 2 large mixing bowls, combine the popcorn and peanuts, tossing them together until the peanuts are evenly distributed.

2. In heavy saucepan over medium heat, bring the sugar, butter, corn syrup and cream of tartar to a boil, stirring until the sugar dissolves and the mixture begins to boil. Boil 5 minutes without stirring.

3. Remove from the heat. Stir in the baking soda. Pour the hot syrup over the popcorn mixture, dividing equally between bowls, stirring the popcorn and peanuts until well coated.

4. Spread out on prepared baking sheets. Bake in preheated oven for 40 minutes, stirring every 10 minutes. Remove from the oven and cool completely. Break into pieces. Hide the toy prize inside the popcorn, if using. Store in an airtight container.

Storing Candy

Most candies should be stored in an airtight container to keep them fresh. Unless specifically instructed in the recipe, refrigeration is often a matter of personal choice, but generally, most fudges and fudge-like candies should keep at least 1 week at room temperature and at least 1 month, sometimes much longer, if refrigerated. Excessive heat, high humidity, or added ingredients such as fruit may shorten the storage time so it is important to use common sense. If the color or texture of the candy has changed, dispose of it and make a fresh batch.

Microwave Caramel Popcorn

16 cups	freshly popped popcorn, unsalted	4 L
1 cup	packed light brown sugar	250 mL
6 tbsp	butter or margarine	90 mL
1/4 cup	light (white or golden) corn syrup	60 mL
1/4 tsp	salt	1 mL
1 tsp	vanilla extract	5 mL
1/2 tsp	baking soda	2 mL

> One bite of this microwave popcorn will leave you "shaking" for more.

Skill Level: Novice, Easy

Makes about 16 cups (4 L)

- Very large roasting pan, sprayed with nonstick spray
- Large brown paper bag

1. Pour the popcorn into a large brown paper bag.

2. In a large microwave-safe bowl, combine the sugar, butter, corn syrup and salt, stirring to blend. Microwave, uncovered, on High for 2 minutes. Stir. Microwave on High 3 minutes, stirring after each minute. Stir in the vanilla and baking soda until well blended.

3. Pour the hot syrup over the popcorn in the paper bag. Seal the top of the bag. Microwave on High 1 minute. Shake the bag. Microwave 1 minute and shake the bag. Microwave 30 seconds and shake the bag. Microwave 30 seconds and shake the bag.

4. Pour the popcorn into the prepared roasting pan. Cool and break into pieces. Store in an airtight container.

Popcorn Snap

1½ cups	granulated sugar	375 mL
½ cup	packed light brown sugar	125 mL
½ cup	light (white or golden) corn syrup	125 mL
	Butter the size of a walnut (2 tbsp/30 mL butter)	
½ cup	water	125 mL
Pinch	salt	Pinch
¼ tsp	baking soda	1 mL
3 cups	ground popped popcorn (see Cook's Note, page 239)	750 mL
½ cup	ground peanuts	125 mL

Almost like peanut brittle but made with ground popcorn, this interesting old recipe may be one of a kind.

Skill Level: Average

Makes about 1½ lbs (750 g)

- 2 large baking sheets, buttered
- 5-quart heavy candy kettle or pot
- Candy thermometer

1. In heavy candy kettle over medium heat, bring the sugars, corn syrup, butter, water and salt to a boil, stirring until the sugars dissolve and the mixture begins to boil. Cook, stirring gently a few times, to the hard crack stage (300°F/149°C).

2. Remove from the heat. Stir in the baking soda until well blended. Add the popcorn and peanuts. Quickly pour the mixture onto the prepared baking sheets, spreading evenly across both pans. Cool slightly and cut into pieces or cool completely and break into pieces. Store in an airtight container.

Old-Fashioned Popcorn Balls

12 cups	freshly popped popcorn, unsalted	3 L
1 tsp	salt	5 mL
1 cup	granulated sugar	250 mL
1 cup	light (white) corn syrup	250 mL
1 tbsp	cider vinegar	15 mL
1 tbsp	butter or margarine	15 mL

These classic white popcorn balls are just as tasty as you remember them being.

Cook's Note

If the syrup is too hot to handle, use two large spoons to loosely form the popcorn into balls or large clusters and then drop the clusters onto a prepared baking sheet. Cool slightly and then finish forming the balls by hand.

Skill Level: Average

Makes about 12 balls

- 1-quart saucepan
- Candy thermometer

1. Pour the popcorn into a large mixing bowl. Sprinkle with the salt.

2. In saucepan over medium to medium-high heat, bring the sugar, corn syrup and vinegar to a boil, stirring until the sugar dissolves and the mixture begins to boil. Cook, without stirring, to the hard ball stage (265°F/129°C).

3. Remove from the heat. Stir in the butter. Slowly pour the hot syrup over the popcorn and stir until the popcorn is well coated. Let the popcorn cool slightly.

4. Using lightly buttered hands, quickly form the popcorn mixture into balls 3 inches (7.5 cm) in diameter. (Use caution when forming the balls; the syrup can be dangerously hot. See Cook's Note, left.) Cool completely. Wrap each cooled popcorn ball in plastic wrap.

Painter's Popcorn Balls

20 cups	freshly popped popcorn, unsalted	5 L
2 cups	granulated sugar	500 mL
1 cup	light (white) corn syrup	250 mL
2 tsp	cream of tartar	10 mL
1 tbsp	butter	15 mL
	Few drops food coloring of choice	
1/2 tsp	baking soda	2 mL

Always a favorite, these tinted popcorn balls make a wonderful party favor for a child's birthday.

Makes about 20 balls

- 2-quart saucepan
- Candy thermometer

1. Pour the popcorn into a large mixing bowl.
2. In saucepan over medium heat, bring the sugar, corn syrup, cream of tartar and butter to a boil, stirring until the sugar dissolves and the mixture begins to boil. Cook, without stirring, to the hard ball stage (265°F/129°C).
3. Remove from the heat. Stir in a few drops of food coloring, as desired. Stir in the baking soda. Slowly pour the hot syrup over the popcorn, stirring the popcorn until well coated. Let the popcorn cool slightly. Using lightly buttered hands, quickly form the popcorn mixture into balls 3 inches (7.5 cm) in diameter. (Use caution when forming the balls because the syrup can be dangerously hot; see Cook's Note, page 235.) Cool completely. Wrap each cooled popcorn ball in plastic wrap.

Variation

Up to 1½ cups (375 mL) chopped pecans may be mixed with the popcorn in the bowl. Omit the food coloring, if desired.

Kid Pleasin' Popcorn Cake

16 cups	freshly popped popcorn, unsalted	4 L
8 oz	small gumdrops	250 g
8 oz	salted peanuts	250 g
1 lb	large or miniature marshmallows	500 g
1/2 cup	butter	125 mL
1/2 cup	vegetable oil	125 mL

> Aunt Lucy always knew how to bring out the kid in all of us, especially through food. This was one of her best kid pleasers.

Important Tip

In many recipes, it is important to be prepared for all the steps because timing can be critical. Have all ingredients available and ready to use, and have the pan, baking sheet, or surface prepared before you begin cooking.

Skill Level: Novice, Easy

Makes about 12 servings

- Large roasting pan, buttered
- 10-inch (25 cm) tube pan, buttered or sprayed with nonstick spray
- 3-quart heavy saucepan

1. Combine the popcorn, gumdrops and peanuts in the prepared roasting pan.

2. In heavy saucepan over low heat, melt the marshmallows, butter and oil together, stirring until smooth.

3. Remove from the heat. Pour the marshmallow mixture over the popcorn mixture, stirring until the popcorn is well coated. Press the popcorn mixture into the prepared tube pan. Cool completely. Remove the cake from the pan. Wrap the cake in foil until ready to serve. To serve, slice into pieces.

Variation

Candy Popcorn Cake: Substitute plain M&M's chocolate candies for the gumdrops. Let the marshmallow mixture cool slightly before pouring it over the popcorn mixture so the candies do not melt. Mixed nuts may be substituted for the peanuts, if desired.

Popcorn Party Cake

6 cups	popped popcorn, unsalted	1.5 L
½ cup	salted peanuts	125 mL
1 cup	sweetened flaked coconut	250 mL
1 cup	granulated sugar	250 mL
½ cup	half-and-half (10%) cream	125 mL
1 cup	light (white) corn syrup	250 mL
Pinch	salt	Pinch
1 tbsp	butter	15 mL
1 tsp	vanilla extract	5 mL

Packed with peanuts and sweet, flaky coconut, this version of popcorn cake is held together with an old-fashioned cooked syrup, much like syrups used in popcorn balls.

Important Tip

In many recipes, it is important to be prepared for all the steps because timing can be critical. Have all ingredients available and ready to use, and have the pan, baking sheet, or surface prepared before you begin cooking.

Makes about 8 servings

- 10-inch (25 cm) tube pan, buttered or sprayed with nonstick spray
- 2-quart heavy saucepan
- Candy thermometer

1. In a large mixing bowl, combine the popcorn, peanuts and coconut.

2. In heavy saucepan over medium heat, bring the sugar, half-and-half, corn syrup and salt to a boil, stirring until the sugar dissolves and the mixture begins to boil. Cook, stirring occasionally to prevent scorching, to the soft ball stage (234°F to 240°F/112°C to 116°C with 238°F/114°C recommended).

3. Remove from the heat. Stir in the butter and vanilla until the butter melts. Pour the hot syrup over the popcorn mixture and stir until the popcorn mixture is well coated. Press the popcorn mixture into the prepared tube pan. Cool. Remove the cake from the pan. Wrap the cake in foil until ready to serve. To serve, slice into pieces.

Nutty Popcorn Candy

3 cups	ground popped popcorn (see Cook's Notes, below)	750 mL
1 cup	finely chopped salted peanuts	250 mL
1/2 cup	granulated sugar	125 mL
1/2 cup	light (white or golden) corn syrup	125 mL
1/2 cup	peanut butter	125 mL
1/2 tsp	vanilla extract	2 mL

Chewy and packed with peanut butter, this unusual popcorn candy may be like none you have ever tasted.

Cook's Note

To make this candy like our grandmothers did, grind popcorn in a food grinder, measuring 3 cups (750 mL) when finished. If a food grinder is not available, a food processor may be used, although many food processors only chop the popcorn into slightly smaller pieces.

Makes about 1 1/4 lbs (625 g)

- 8-inch (20 cm) square pan, lined with parchment (see below) or buttered

1. In a large mixing bowl, combine the popcorn and peanuts, stirring until well mixed.
2. In a very small saucepan over medium-high heat, bring the sugar and corn syrup to a boil, stirring until the sugar dissolves and the mixture begins to boil. Boil 1 to 2 minutes without stirring.
3. Remove from the heat. Add the peanut butter and vanilla, stirring until smooth. Pour the syrup over the popcorn and peanuts, mixing well. Pack into the buttered pan. Cool and cut into squares. Store in an airtight container.

Cutting into Perfect Squares and Special Shapes

Cutting candy becomes much easier with the use of parchment paper. Rather than buttering the pan directly, butter a piece of parchment paper larger than the pan and press it into the bottom and up the sides of the pan, tucking and creasing the paper as needed to create corners, and leaving a generous overhang over the sides of the pan. Pour the candy into the parchment-lined pan. Once the candy has cooled, use the parchment to lift the entire block of candy out of the pan. Place the block of candy on a cutting board and use a long, serrated knife to cut straight, uniform rows of the candy, and then cut the rows into squares. For a special presentation, cut the block of candy into diamonds, triangles or other shapes, as desired.

The parchment paper method is optional, but over the years I have found it much easier than cutting candy in the pan, and it saves my pans from deep scratches left by sharp knives. At times I have shipped large blocks of candy to friends and family with the candy still wrapped in the parchment paper and then wrapped again in foil wrap. It simplifies shipping and allows others to cut the candy as they choose.

Washington State Apple Squares

3 cups	applesauce, at room temperature, divided	750 mL
4	envelopes (each ¼ oz/7 g) unflavored gelatin	4
4 cups	granulated sugar	1 L
1 cup	coarsely chopped walnuts	250 mL
1 tsp	vanilla extract	5 mL
Pinch	salt	Pinch
2 to 3 cups	confectioner's (icing) sugar, for rolling	500 to 750 mL

Similar to Washington state's famous Aplets candy, these fruity squares are a popular treat throughout the Pacific Northwest.

Storing Candy

Most candies should be stored in an airtight container to keep them fresh. Unless specifically instructed in the recipe, refrigeration is often a matter of personal choice, but generally, most fudges and fudge-like candies should keep at least 1 week at room temperature and at least 1 month, sometimes much longer, if refrigerated. Excessive heat, high humidity, or added ingredients such as fruit may shorten the storage time so it is important to use common sense. If the color or texture of the candy has changed, dispose of it and make a fresh batch.

Skill Level: Average

Makes about 3 lbs (1.5 kg)

- 11- by 8-inch (28 by 20 cm) pan, lined with parchment (see Cook's Notes, page 239) or buttered
- Large airtight plastic container, bottom lined with waxed paper
- 4- to 5-quart heavy candy kettle or pot

1. In a small bowl, combine 1 cup (250 mL) of the applesauce and the gelatin, stirring until blended.

2. In heavy candy kettle over medium heat, bring the remaining 2 cups (500 mL) applesauce and the sugar to a boil over medium heat, stirring until the sugar dissolves and the mixture begins to boil. Gradually add the gelatin mixture, by spoonfuls, working out the lumps with the back of a spoon as the mixture cooks. Boil rapidly, stirring occasionally, over medium heat 20 minutes.

3. Remove from the heat. Cool slightly, 5 to 10 minutes. Stir in the walnuts, vanilla and salt. Pour into the prepared pan. Cool at room temperature about 30 minutes. Cover and refrigerate until firm.

4. Cut into 1-inch (2.5 cm) squares. Roll each square in the confectioner's sugar once a day for 2 to 3 days or until they have a white coating. After the first coating, place the squares in the prepared plastic container, separating each layer with waxed paper to prevent sticking. Place the squares back in the same container after the second rolling. If needed, roll a third time. Store at room temperature for up to 2 days or in the refrigerator for up to 5 days. Once they begin to lose their eye appeal, they are spoiled and should be discarded.

Apricot Squares

2	cans (each 15.25 oz/430 mL) apricots	2
2 tbsp	unflavored gelatin	30 mL
1/2 cup	cold water	125 mL
2 cups	light (white) corn syrup	500 mL
1 tbsp	lemon juice	15 mL
1 cup	chopped walnuts	250 mL
2 cups	confectioner's (icing) sugar, for rolling (approx.)	500 mL

> This version of Washington state's famous candy offers a slightly different cooking method to Washington State Apple Squares (page 240).

Cook's Note

The easiest way to make this candy is to use canned apricots. If preferred, 2 cups (500 mL) cooked fresh apricot purée may be substituted for the canned apricots. If using fresh apricots, peel, core and slice the fruit into thin slices. Cook over low heat in a small saucepan until tender, using as little water as possible. Sieve and place in the heavy 3-quart saucepan.

Skill Level: Average

Makes about 2 lbs (1 kg)

- 8-inch (20 cm) square pan, lined with parchment (see Cook's Notes, page 239) or buttered
- Food processor
- 3-quart heavy saucepan

1. Drain the apricots in a colander, removing as much excess juice as possible. Chop the apricots in a food processor until reduced to a purée. Measure 2 cups (500 mL). In a small bowl, dissolve the gelatin in the cold water, stirring to mix.

2. In heavy saucepan over medium heat, bring the apricot purée and the corn syrup to a boil, stirring constantly. Cook at a medium boil, stirring constantly, about 20 minutes or until the excess moisture has evaporated and the mixture is very thick.

3. Remove from the heat. Add the gelatin mixture and stir until the lumps dissolve. Cool slightly, about 3 minutes. Stir in the lemon juice and walnuts. Pour into the prepared pan. Cool completely. When firm, cut into squares and roll in the confectioner's sugar. Store in an airtight container, separating each layer with waxed paper to prevent sticking. After 24 hours, roll the squares in confectioner's sugar again. The squares should maintain a white, powdery coating. If not, wait a few hours and roll in confectioner's sugar a third time. Store in an airtight container at room temperature for up to 2 days or in the refrigerator for up to 5 days. Once they begin to lose their eye appeal, they are spoiled and should be discarded.

Variation

Apple Squares: Replace the 2 cans of apricots with 2 cups (500 mL) applesauce.

Apple-Cinnamon Walnut Squares

1 cup	applesauce	250 mL
1 tbsp	small hot cinnamon candies	15 mL
1	package (3 oz/86 g) strawberry-flavored gelatin	1
1 cup	granulated sugar	250 mL
¾ cup	chopped walnuts	175 mL
1 cup	granulated or confectioner's (icing) sugar, for rolling (approx.)	250 mL

The combination of apples, cinnamon and strawberry just makes these gelatin candies more flavorful.

Important Tip

In many recipes, it is important to be prepared for all the steps because timing can be critical. Have all ingredients available and ready to use, and have the pan, baking sheet, or surface prepared before you begin cooking.

Skill Level: Average

Makes about 1 lb (500 g)

- 9- by 5-inch (23 by 12.5 cm) loaf pan, lined with parchment (see Cook's Notes, page 239) or buttered
- 2-quart heavy saucepan

1. In heavy saucepan over low heat, bring the applesauce and candies to a boil. Stir in the gelatin and sugar. Bring to a second boil, stirring constantly. Boil 2 minutes, stirring constantly.

2. Remove from the heat. Add the walnuts and mix well. Pour into the prepared pan. Cover and refrigerate until firm, about 3 hours. Cut into squares and roll the squares in the sugar. Place in an airtight container, separating each layer with waxed paper to prevent sticking. After 24 hours, roll the squares in sugar again. Store in an airtight container at room temperature for up to 2 days or in the refrigerator for up to 5 days. Once they begin to lose their eye appeal, they are spoiled and should be discarded.

A Candy Memory

Many of the people I met while writing this book shared their memories of homemade candy with me, often reminiscing about their childhoods with stories such as this one.

"I remember making apricot candy when I was a child," one man told me. "We were very poor and could not afford gifts, so every year my family made little balls of apricot candy and gave them to family and friends for Christmas. I am not sure what recipe we used, but it sure was good!"

All of those who heard this story agreed that a gift of homemade candy is always special.

Apricot Bars

4	envelopes (each ¼ oz/7 g) unflavored gelatin	4
1½ cups	apricot juice, divided	375 mL
2 cups	granulated sugar	500 mL
2 tsp	freshly grated orange zest	10 mL
¼ cup	orange juice	60 mL
1 cup	dried apricots, finely chopped	250 mL
1 cup	confectioner's (icing) or granulated sugar for rolling (approx.)	250 mL

The addition of orange gives a slightly different spin to Washington's famous Cotlets candy.

Cook's Note

These candies will spoil within about 1 week of being cooked, perhaps sooner. Once they begin to lose their eye appeal it is time to dispose of them.

Skill Level: Average

Makes about 2 lbs (1 kg)

- 8-inch (20 cm) square pan
- 3-quart heavy saucepan

1. Line pan with waxed paper, leaving a 1-inch (2.5 cm) overhang on the sides of the pan. Lightly spray the waxed paper in the pan with nonstick spray.

2. Soften the gelatin in 1 cup (250 mL) of the apricot juice.

3. In heavy saucepan over medium heat, bring the sugar, remaining apricot juice, orange zest, orange juice and gelatin mixture to a boil, stirring until the sugar dissolves and the mixture begins to boil. Cook at a medium boil 20 minutes, stirring constantly. Add the chopped apricots. If the apricots stick together use the back of a spoon to separate any large lumps. Return to a boil and cook 2 minutes longer.

4. Remove from the heat. Cool 10 minutes. Pour into the prepared pan. Cool completely, refrigerating, if desired. When the candy is firm, use the waxed paper overhand and remove it from the pan. Cut into squares.

5. Cover a medium-size area of the countertop with waxed paper. Wet the tips of your fingers and lightly dip in the sugar to prevent the candy from sticking to your fingers. Pick up each piece and roll in the sugar. Place on the waxed paper to dry. If needed, roll in sugar again until the candy can be handled and no longer has a sticky coating. Store in an airtight container at room temperature, placing waxed paper between layers to prevent sticking, for up to 2 days or in the refrigerator for up to 5 days.

Aunt Shirley's Apricot Sugarplums

11 oz	dried apricots	330 g
3 cups	water, divided	750 mL
2 cups	granulated sugar	500 mL
2 tbsp	light (white) corn syrup	30 mL
1 tbsp	orange or almond liqueur or pinch ground ginger (optional)	15 mL
3 cups	walnut halves (approx.)	750 mL
1 cup	granulated sugar, for rolling	250 mL

Each holiday season, Aunt Shirley enchants her family and friends with these elegant apricot sugarplums. To spice up your holidays, try adding a dash of ginger.

Skill Level: Average

Makes 30 to 36

- 3-quart saucepan
- 10-inch (25 cm) skillet

1. In heavy saucepan over medium heat, combine the apricots and 2 cups (500 mL) of the water. Cover and bring to a boil. Remove from the heat. Cool 10 minutes. Drain the apricots, discarding the water.

2. In skillet over medium heat, bring the 2 cups (500 mL) sugar, remaining 1 cup (250 mL) water and corn syrup to a boil, stirring until the sugar dissolves. Cook, without stirring, 15 minutes. Add the apricots, stirring gently to separate them. Gently stir in the liqueur, if using. Simmer, uncovered, until the apricots are translucent, about 20 minutes.

3. Remove from the heat. Cool to room temperature, about $1\frac{1}{2}$ hours.

4. Remove each apricot half from the skillet and place on a wire rack. Let stand, uncovered, at room temperature until dry. Fill the cavity of each apricot with a walnut half. Roll the stuffed apricots in the sugar. Store in an airtight container at room temperature for up to 3 days or freeze for up to 1 month.

Apple Crystals

6	firm apples	6
2 cups	granulated sugar	500 mL
2 tbsp	small hot cinnamon candies	30 mL
2	drops red food coloring	2
2¼ cups	water (approx.), divided	550 mL
2 cups	granulated sugar, for rolling	500 mL

> When cut into fancy shapes, these dried apple crystals make an elegant garnish for a favorite cake or dessert.

• 1- to 2-quart saucepan

1. Peel the apples and cut into halves or quarters. Remove the cores using a half teaspoon (2 mL) measuring spoon or a French ball cutter (melon baller). Cut the apples into fancy shapes or rings or slice the apple halves crosswise using a fluted edge cutter. Cut each apple half into about 6 slices.

2. Cover a large countertop area or 2 large baking sheets with waxed paper.

3. In saucepan over medium heat, bring 2 cups (500 mL) sugar, candies, food coloring and 1 cup (250 mL) water to a boil, stirring until the sugar dissolves and the mixture begins to boil. Drop up to 12 pieces of apple (no more than one apple at a time) into the syrup and cook on medium heat until the apple pieces are tender when pierced with a toothpick. Remove the apple pieces from the syrup, drain and place on the waxed paper to cool. Repeat until all of the apple pieces are cooked, adding ¼ cup (60 mL) more water to cook each apple (or 12 pieces), until all the apples are cooked or the syrup gets too low to use (the syrup will be absorbed by the apples).

4. Let the apple pieces stand, uncovered, for 24 hours. Roll the pieces in the sugar. Roll twice again at 24-hour intervals, turning the apples and keeping them in as dry a location as possible, especially if weather is damp. Dry the apples at room temperature until they have no moisture. Pack in an airtight container and store in a cool, dry location for up to 3 days. Use as a candy or as a garnish.

Fresh Coconut Chips

1	fresh coconut	1	
	Salt, to taste		

For a simple, elegant dessert, fill stemmed glasses with scoops of vanilla ice cream, add a spoonful of Kahlúa and top with oven-toasted coconut chips.

Skill Level: Novice, Easy

Makes about 2 cups (500 mL)

- Preheat the oven to 350°F (180°C)
- Large pick or nail

1. Using an ice pick or a large nail, punch holes into the coconut eyes. Drain the coconut water, discarding the water or saving it for another recipe. Place the coconut on a baking sheet and bake in preheated oven for 30 to 40 minutes. Remove the coconut from the oven and cool until it is comfortable to the touch.

2. Using a hammer, crack the center of the coconut shell. Run a knife blade between the coconut meat and the shell, loosening the coconut meat from the shell. Remove any shell fragments from the coconut meat by rinsing under cold water.

3. Using a vegetable peeler, cut the coconut into thin ribbons by drawing the peeler toward you. Use a paring knife to cut the ribbons into smaller pieces.

4. Spread the thinly sliced coconut on 2 baking sheets. Place in the oven and reduce the temperature to 200°F (100°C). Dry the coconut in the oven for 2 to 3 hours, stirring occasionally. If desired, increase the oven temperature to 250°F (120°C) the last few minutes to toast the chips. Sprinkle the toasted chips with salt. If the chips lose their crispness, heat in the oven a few minutes. Cool the chips completely. Store in an airtight container.

Candied Citrus Peel

4	medium oranges, 6 lemons or 2 grapefruits (see Cook's Note, below)	4
	Cold water	
1 cup	granulated sugar	250 mL
1/3 cup	water	75 mL
1 cup	granulated sugar, for coating (approx.)	250 mL

Candied citrus peel makes a wonderful garnish for the top of a special cake or a holiday tray filled with other sweets.

Cook's Note

When purchasing the citrus fruit for this recipes, select thick-skinned fruit. Buy a few extra pieces so you can choose the ones with the thickest skin.

Skill Level: Average

Makes about 2 cups (500 mL)

1. Remove the peel and cut into slender strips using a sharp knife or kitchen shears. Place the strips in a small saucepan and cover with cold water. Bring to boil over medium heat. Boil for 10 to 15 minutes and then drain. Add fresh cold water, repeating the process up to three times or until the peel is tender. (Changing water helps remove excess bitterness.) Do not mix different types of fruit peels because cooking times vary with different fruits.

2. In a small saucepan over low heat, bring 1 cup (250 mL) sugar and the 1/3 cup (75 mL) water to a boil, stirring until the sugar dissolves and the mixture begins to boil. Add the peel, boiling until the syrup is almost completely absorbed by the peel, stirring occasionally.

3. Lift the peel from the syrup and place into a strainer to drain. Spread in a single layer on waxed paper to cool. Sprinkle sugar over the peel, mixing with a fork so that each piece is coated with sugar. Let dry 12 to 24 hours. Add more sugar as needed so that the candied peel does not stick together. Store in an airtight container.

Banana Tidbits

2	ripe medium bananas	2
1/2 cup	sweetened condensed milk	125 mL
1/2 cup	finely chopped peanuts	125 mL
1/2 cup	sweetened flaked coconut	125 mL

This recipe was a favorite with an elderly woman I knew as a child. Ruby would be thrilled to have you try her peanut-and-coconut-covered treats.

Skill Level: Novice, Super Simple

Makes about 16 pieces

1. Peel the bananas and cut into 1-inch (2.5 cm) slices. Dip each banana piece into the milk. Roll half of the banana pieces in the peanuts and half in the coconut. Cover and refrigerate until ready to serve. This treat is best served within 1 day.

Cuppa Fruit Candy

1 cup	ground or finely chopped dried peaches or apricots	250 mL
1 cup	ground or finely chopped raisins	250 mL
1 cup	ground or finely chopped figs	250 mL
1 cup	ground or finely chopped dried apples	250 mL
1 cup	ground or finely chopped dates	250 mL
1 cup	toasted almonds, ground or finely chopped	250 mL
1 cup	honey (approx.)	250 mL
1/2 cup	sesame seeds	125 mL
1/2 cup	sunflower seeds	125 mL

Skill Level: Novice, Super Simple

Makes 40 to 45 pieces

1. In a large mixing bowl, combine the fruits and almonds. Blend together, adding just enough honey to hold the fruit together. Shape small bits of the fruit mixture into patties. Roll the patties in the sesame seeds and sunflower seeds. Store in an airtight container at room temperature for up to 2 days or in the refrigerator for up to 5 days.

A cup of this, a cup of that, add a little honey and you have a natural, healthy candy. Using a food processor, grind or finely chop the fruit before measuring. Grind or chop the nuts after measuring.

Cook's Note

If the fruit is particularly dry, cover it in water and soak for 30 minutes. Drain off the liquid before chopping the fruit.

Nature's Candy

½ cup	peanut butter	125 mL
10 tbsp	ground or very finely chopped sunflower seeds	150 mL
½ cup	chopped raisins	125 mL
¼ cup	instant nonfat dry milk	60 mL
½ tsp	salt	2 mL
¼ cup	honey	60 mL
¼ cup	wheat germ (approx.)	60 mL
½ cup	sweetened flaked coconut, for rolling (approx.)	125 mL

Skill Level: Novice, Super Simple

Makes about 12

1. In a medium mixing bowl, combine the peanut butter, sunflower seeds, raisins, dry milk, salt and honey. Shape the mixture into balls 1 inch (2.5 cm) in diameter. Roll the balls in the wheat germ and the coconut. Cover and refrigerate until chilled. Store in an airtight container in the refrigerator for up to 5 days.

> Choosy mothers may want to choose this candy as an after-school treat.

Cook's Note
If desired, 1 tbsp (15 mL) brewer's yeast can be added to the mixture if you like its unusual flavor.

Persian Sweets

4 oz	pitted dates	125 g
4 oz	dried figs	125 g
1 cup	raisins	250 mL
1 cup	pecans or walnuts	250 mL
	Honey or fruit juice, if needed	
¼ cup	confectioner's (icing) or granulated sugar, for rolling (approx.)	60 mL

Skill Level: Novice, Super Simple

Makes about 18 pieces

1. Finely chop the dates, figs, raisins and nuts and place in a bowl. Blend or knead the mixture by hand until thoroughly mixed. If the mixture is too dry to hold together, stir in honey, by teaspoonfuls (5 mL), to moisten.

2. The mixture may be pressed into a small pan and cut into squares, shaped into logs and sliced or shaped into small balls. Roll each piece of candy in confectioner's or granulated sugar. Store in an airtight container in the refrigerator for up to 5 days.

> This is the perfect snack for skiers and hikers to stash away in their pockets.

Figgie Nuggets

1 lb	dried figs	500 g
8 oz	pitted dates	250 g
1/2 cup	raisins	125 mL
1 lb	dried apricots	500 g
2 cups	walnuts or pecans	500 mL
1 tsp	grated orange zest	5 mL
	Honey or orange juice, if needed	
1 1/2 to 2 cups	sweetened flaked coconut, for rolling	375 to 500 mL

Loaded with figs and apricots, this tasty treat is packed with sunshine.

Cook's Note

If a food grinder is not available, very finely chop the fruits and nuts in a food processor or by hand.

Skill Level: Novice, Super Simple

Makes 45 to 50 pieces

- Food grinder (see Cook's Note, left)
- 8-inch (20 cm) square pan

1. Grind the figs, dates, raisins, apricots and nuts in a food grinder until finely ground. Transfer to a medium bowl. Stir in the orange zest. Mix the ingredients by hand until well blended. If the mixture is too dry to hold its shape, stir in a few teaspoons (10 mL) of honey to moisten.

2. Press into pan. Cut into squares and roll each square in the coconut. Store in an airtight container in the refrigerator for up to 5 days.

Storing Candy

Most candies should be stored in an airtight container to keep them fresh. Unless specifically instructed in the recipe, refrigeration is often a matter of personal choice, but generally, most fudges and fudge-like candies should keep at least 1 week at room temperature and at least 1 month, sometimes much longer, if refrigerated. Excessive heat, high humidity, or added ingredients such as fruit may shorten the storage time so it is important to use common sense. If the color or texture of the candy has changed, dispose of it and make a fresh batch.

Carnival Candied Apples

8	medium red apples	8
3 cups	granulated sugar	750 mL
½ cup	water	125 mL
½ cup	light (white) corn syrup	125 mL
1	drop cinnamon oil or to taste	1
1 tsp	red food coloring	5 mL

Remember those delicious, sticky, bright cinnamon red apples you loved as a kid? Once a common carnival treat, they can easily be made at home.

Cook's Note

These apples are lightly flavored with cinnamon. The amount of cinnamon oil may be increased, if desired.

Skill Level: Average

Makes 8

- Large baking sheet, lined with aluminum foil, sprayed with nonstick spray
- 8 Popsicle sticks
- Candy thermometer

1. Wash, dry and polish the apples. Remove the stems. Insert a stick into the stem end of each apple, using a twisting motion so that the apple will not split.

2. In a large, heavy, deep saucepan over medium heat, bring the sugar, water and corn syrup to a boil, stirring until the sugar dissolves and the mixture begins to boil. Cook, without stirring, to the soft crack stage (285°F/141°C).

3. Remove from the heat. Stir in the cinnamon oil and food coloring just until mixed.

4. Working very quickly, hold an apple by the wooden skewer and quickly twirl it into the syrup, tilting the pan to cover the apple. Remove the apple from the syrup, allow the excess syrup to drip into the pan and then twirl the apple again to spread the syrup smoothly over the apple. Place on the prepared baking sheet. Repeat with remaining apples and syrup. Let stand until firm. Store in a cool, dry place.

Mrs. McDonald's Red Candied Apples

20	small apples	20
2 cups	granulated sugar	500 mL
1¾ cups	milk	425 mL
1½ cups	light (white) corn syrup	375 mL
¼ cup	margarine	60 mL
1/16 tsp	baking soda	0.25 mL
1 tbsp	red food coloring	15 mL

Once upon a time, a kind lady named Mrs. McDonald gave each child in a small town a red candied apple for Halloween. With a soft, creamy coating, these apples are just as special today as they were in the 1950s.

Cook's Note

If preferred, this recipe may be doubled and cooked in a heavy 8-quart kettle.

Skill Level: Average

Makes 20

- 2 large baking sheets, buttered
- 20 Popsicle sticks
- 5-quart heavy candy kettle or pot
- Candy thermometer

1. Wash, dry and polish the apples. Remove the stems. Insert sticks into the stem end of each apple, using a twist-like motion so that the apple will not split.

2. In heavy candy kettle over medium-low to medium heat, bring the sugar, milk, corn syrup, margarine and baking soda to a boil, stirring until the sugar dissolves and the mixture begins to boil. Cook, stirring occasionally to prevent scorching, to between 240°F and 242°F (116°C to 117°C), about 40 minutes. Add the food coloring, stirring until well blended.

3. Remove from the heat. Working very quickly, hold an apple by the stick and quickly twirl it into the syrup, tilting the pan to cover the apple. Remove the apple from the syrup, allow the excess syrup to drip into the pan and then twirl the apple again to spread the syrup smoothly over the apple. Place on the prepared baking sheet. Repeat with remaining apples and syrup. Let stand until firm. Wrap each apple in plastic wrap.

Old-Fashioned Caramel Apples

12	medium apples	12
2 cups	granulated sugar	500 mL
1 cup	packed light brown sugar	250 mL
2/3 cup	light (white or golden) corn syrup	150 mL
1/2 cup	butter or margarine	125 mL
1 cup	half-and-half (10%) cream or evaporated milk	250 mL
1 tsp	salt	5 mL
2 tsp	vanilla extract	10 mL
2 cups	chopped pecans, 1 1/2 cups (375 mL) sweetened flaked coconut or 2 cups (500 mL) crisp rice cereal (optional)	500 mL

What could be better than a crisp fall apple smothered in rich, creamy homemade caramel? Here is the real McCoy.

Skill Level: Average

Makes 12

- 12 Popsicle sticks
- Large heavy kettle or pot
- Candy thermometer

1. Wash and dry the apples. Remove the stems. Insert a stick into the stem end of each apple, using a twist-like motion so that the apple will not split.

2. Cover a large countertop area or a large baking sheet with waxed paper.

3. In a large heavy kettle over medium-low heat, bring the granulated and brown sugars, corn syrup, butter, half-and-half and salt to a boil, stirring until the sugars dissolve and the mixture begins to boil. Cook, gently stirring to prevent scorching, to the firm ball stage (246°F/119°C). Stir in the vanilla.

4. Remove from the heat. Cool until the mixture thickens slightly. Hold each apple by the wooden skewer and quickly twirl into the caramel, tilting the pan to cover the apple with caramel. Remove the apple from the caramel, allow the excess caramel to drip into the pan and then twirl the apple again to spread the caramel smoothly over the apple. Use a spoon to coat any part of the apple not covered with caramel. If desired, roll the coated apples in the pecans before the caramel sets. Place on the waxed paper until the coating is firm. Store in a cool, dry place.

Variation

Red Caramel Apples: Use 2/3 cup (150 mL) butter or margarine. Stir in about 1 tbsp (15 mL) red food coloring with the vanilla.

Short and Sweet

Sometimes just the simplest combination of ingredients is enough to satisfy a screaming sweet tooth or feed a starving crowd. When those busy days arrive, nothing pleases us more than to have a ready supply of easy recipes that we can make in a matter of minutes.

Perfect for everyday entertaining or filling a holiday gift tin, the cool, refreshing taste of peppermint bark is always a favorite, no matter which recipe is used. Chocolate, butterscotch and peanut butter lovers will delight in the many simple clusters and confections they can make using ingredients already on hand. And what grandparent can resist introducing the grandkids to fun and creative recipes such as Caramel-Nut Marshmallows, Chocolate Birds' Nests or Chipper Nutty Fudge?

With a little something for everybody, the only difficult part about these recipes is choosing just one favorite.

> When those busy days arrive, nothing pleases us more than to have a ready supply of easy recipes that we can make in a matter of minutes.

Cherry-Almond Bark

12 oz	white chocolate, chopped	375 g
1/2 cup	chopped almonds, toasted	125 mL
1/2 cup	chopped candied red cherries	125 mL

> Aunt Lucy's simple, colorful candy will brighten up any holiday gift tin.

Skill Level: Novice, Easy

Makes about 1 lb (500 g)

- Large baking sheet, lined with waxed paper
- Double boiler

1. In the top pan of a double boiler over hot but not boiling water, melt the white chocolate, stirring until smooth. Stir in the almonds and cherries.
2. Spread the mixture onto the prepared baking sheet in an even layer. Refrigerate 1 hour or until firm. Break into pieces. Store in an airtight container.

Variations

This candy may also be made using 8 oz (250 g) white chocolate and 4 oz (125 g) white chocolate candy coating or 12 oz (375 g) white chocolate candy coating in place of the white chocolate.

Pistachio nuts may be substituted for the toasted almonds and dried cranberries may be substituted for the candied red cherries.

Chocolate-Nut Bark

1 cup	pecans, in large pieces, toasted	250 mL
10 1/2 oz	sweet chocolate, such as German's by Bakers, chopped	315 g
1 tbsp	butter or margarine	15 mL
1 1/2 lbs	large marshmallows, halved	750 g
1 tsp	vanilla extract	5 mL

> This old favorite can be made in a matter of minutes.

Skill Level: Novice, Easy

Makes about 2 lbs (1 kg)

- Large baking sheet, buttered

1. Sprinkle prepared baking sheet with the pecans.
2. In the top of a double boiler pan over hot but not boiling water, melt the chocolate and butter together. Blend well.
3. Remove from the heat. Stir in the marshmallows. The marshmallows will only partially melt. Stir in the vanilla. Quickly pour the chocolate mixture over the nuts on the baking sheet. Cool until the chocolate is firm, about 1 hour. Break into pieces. Store in an airtight container.

White Chocolate Peppermint Bark

12 oz	white chocolate candy coating	375 g
¼ cup	crushed peppermint candies or candy canes or to taste, divided	60 mL
½ tsp	peppermint extract	2 mL

> A bag of this cool, mint-flavored bark is the perfect gift for those you want to remember during the holiday season. For stronger flavor, add more crushed peppermint.

Variation

This candy can be made using 12 oz (375 g) chopped white chocolate in place of the white chocolate candy coating.

- Baking sheet, lined with waxed paper
- Double Boiler

1. In the top pan of a double boiler over hot but not boiling water, melt the white chocolate, stirring until smooth. Stir in half of the peppermint candy and the peppermint extract, blending well.

2. Spoon the mixture onto the prepared baking sheet. Using a flat metal spatula or knife, spread the mixture evenly to about a ¼-inch (0.5 cm) thickness. Sprinkle the remaining crushed peppermint candy on top. Refrigerate 1 hour or until firm. Break into small pieces. Store in an airtight container.

Storing Candy

Most candies should be stored in an airtight container to keep them fresh. Unless specifically instructed in the recipe, refrigeration is often a matter of personal choice, but generally, most fudges and fudge-like candies should keep at least 1 week at room temperature and at least 1 month, sometimes much longer, if refrigerated. Excessive heat, high humidity, or added ingredients such as fruit may shorten the storage time so it is important to use common sense. If the color or texture of the candy has changed, dispose of it and make a fresh batch.

Gourmet Layered Peppermint Bark

8 oz	dark chocolate candy coating	250 g
2/3 cup	semisweet chocolate chips or chopped semisweet chocolate (4 oz/125 g)	150 mL
2 tsp	peppermint extract, divided	10 mL
12 oz	white chocolate candy coating	375 g
3/4 cup	crushed peppermint candies or candy canes	175 mL

This double-layered peppermint bark is as beautiful as it is delicious. A stunning gift, this is a personal favorite.

Skill Level: Novice, Easy

Makes about 1½ lbs (750 g)

- Baking sheet, lined with waxed paper
- Double Boiler

1. In the top pan of a double boiler over hot but not boiling water, melt the dark chocolate candy coating and chocolate chips, stirring until smooth. Remove from the heat. Stir in 1 tsp (5 mL) of the peppermint extract until well blended. Pour the chocolate mixture onto the prepared baking sheet, spreading into a thin, even layer. Cool about 30 minutes or until the chocolate is firm.

2. In the top pan of a clean double boiler over hot but not boiling water, melt the white chocolate candy coating, stirring until smooth. Remove from the heat. Stir in the remaining peppermint extract until well blended. Pour the white chocolate on top of the dark chocolate layer, spreading evenly. Sprinkle with the crushed peppermint. Cool and break into pieces. Store in an airtight container.

Cherry-Topped Fruit Roll

¼ cup	whole red candied cherries, divided	60 mL
¼ cup	whole green candied cherries, divided	60 mL
½ cup	coarsely chopped candied pineapple	125 mL
1 cup	golden raisins	250 mL
1 cup	coarsely chopped pecans	250 mL
2 cups	miniature marshmallows	500 mL
½ cup	dry bread crumbs, divided	125 mL
½ tsp	ground cinnamon	2 mL
½ tsp	ground nutmeg	2 mL

Bright red and green cherries adorn this fluffy white marshmallow, raisin and pecan roll, but the best part may be the spiced outer coating.

Skill Level: Novice, Easy

Makes about 1½ lbs (750 g)

1. Reserve half of the red candied cherries and half of the green candied cherries. Coarsely chop the remaining cherries.

2. In a medium microwave-safe bowl, combine the remaining red and green cherries with the pineapple, raisins, pecans and marshmallows, mixing well. Microwave the mixture on High, uncovered, 1½ to 2 minutes or until the marshmallows have melted. Stir the ingredients together until well blended.

3. Cover the countertop with a large sheet of waxed paper. Lightly sprinkle the waxed paper with about half of the bread crumbs and then sprinkle the bread crumbs with the cinnamon and nutmeg. Using alternating colors of the reserved whole red and green cherries, place the cherries down the center of the bread crumbs in a straight line, spacing them about ½ inch (1 cm) apart. Spoon the marshmallow mixture into a row next to the row of cherries. Shape the marshmallow mixture into a roll and sprinkle with the remaining bread crumbs. Roll in the waxed paper, pressing the red and green cherries into the marshmallow mixture while rolling, creating a decorative cherry-topped design. Wrap tightly in the waxed paper and then wrap in aluminum foil and freeze.

4. To serve, remove the foil and cut into thin slices, leaving the waxed paper in place while slicing. Let stand at room temperature 10 to 15 minutes, removing the waxed paper before serving. Store tightly wrapped in the refrigerator or freezer.

Marshmallow Date Roll

1 cup	chopped pitted dates	250 mL
1 cup	miniature marshmallows	250 mL
1 cup	golden raisins	250 mL
½ cup	finely chopped pecans or walnuts	125 mL
1 cup	finely crushed graham cracker crumbs	250 mL
⅓ cup	evaporated milk or half-and-half (10%) cream (approx.)	75 mL

For a simple dessert, top a few slices of this old favorite with dollops of freshly whipped cream or your favorite ice cream.

Skill Level: Novice, Super Simple

Makes about 1½ lbs (750 g)

1. In a medium mixing bowl, combine the dates, marshmallows, raisins, nuts and graham cracker crumbs, mixing well. Stir in just enough milk to moisten the ingredients so they can be shaped into a roll.

2. Tear 2 large sheets of waxed paper. Divide the mixture evenly, spooning half the mixture onto each piece of waxed paper. Shape each portion into a roll about 2 inches (5 cm) in diameter. Wrap tightly in the waxed paper and seal in foil. Refrigerate until firm, about 2 hours. Slice as needed. Store wrapped in the refrigerator.

Pineapple Date Roll

1½ cups	chopped pitted dates	375 mL
2 cups	miniature marshmallows	500 mL
1 cup	chopped pecans	250 mL
½ cup	drained canned crushed pineapple	125 mL
3 cups	graham cracker crumbs	750 mL
½ cup	evaporated milk or half-and-half (10%) cream (approx.)	125 mL

Pineapple Date Roll is another old-time treat that tastes particularly good when smothered in whipped cream.

Cook's Note

If preferred, ½ to 1 cup (125 to 250 mL) graham cracker crumbs may be reserved and patted onto the outside of the roll before sealing it in waxed paper.

Skill Level: Novice, Super Simple

Makes about 3 lbs (1.5 kg)

1. In a medium mixing bowl, combine the dates, marshmallows, pecans, pineapple and graham cracker crumbs, mixing well. Stir in just enough milk to moisten the ingredients so they can be shaped into a roll.

2. Cover the countertop with 2 to 3 large sheets of waxed paper. Divide the mixture evenly, spooning equal portions onto each piece of waxed paper. Shape each portion into a roll about 2 inches (5 cm) in diameter. Wrap tightly in the waxed paper and then wrap again in aluminum foil. Refrigerate until firm, about 2 hours. Slice as needed. Store in the refrigerator.

Chocolate Raisin Roll

1 cup	semisweet chocolate chips	250 mL
20	large marshmallows, halved or quartered	20
1 tbsp	milk	15 mL
1 cup	finely chopped pecans	250 mL
1 cup	raisins	250 mL
1 to 1½ cups	sweetened flaked coconut, toasted (see page 246)	250 to 375 mL

Cook's Note

Snip the marshmallows in halves or quarters using a pair of kitchen shears.

Skill Level: Novice, Easy

Makes about 1½ lbs (750 g)

• Double boiler

1. In the top pan of a double boiler over hot but not boiling water, melt the chocolate chips, marshmallows and milk together, stirring until smooth.

2. Remove from the heat. Stir in the pecans and raisins. Let the mixture cool slightly, about 5 minutes or until it begins to thicken and can be shaped into a roll.

3. Cover the countertop with a large sheet of waxed paper. Sprinkle the coconut on the waxed paper. Spoon the cooled mixture on top the coconut. Shape the chocolate mixture into a long roll about 2 inches (5 cm) in diameter, sprinkling with the coconut while rolling. Wrap tightly in the waxed paper and then wrap again in foil. Refrigerate until firm, about 2 hours. Slice as needed. Store in an airtight container in the refrigerator.

Simple Peanut Butter Roll

1 cup	light (white or golden) corn syrup	250 mL
1 cup	smooth peanut butter	250 mL
1 cup	confectioner's (icing) sugar	250 mL
1½ cups	instant nonfat dry milk	375 mL
1 cup	crushed vanilla wafer cookies or cornflakes cereal	250 mL

So simple that a child can make it, this candy is ready to enjoy in a matter of minutes.

Skill Level: Novice, Super Simple

Makes about ½ lb (250 g)

1. In a medium mixing bowl, combine the corn syrup and peanut butter, blending until smooth. Gradually stir in the confectioner's sugar and dry milk until well blended.

2. Shape the candy into small logs and roll in the crushed cookies. Slice into pieces to serve. Store wrapped in plastic wrap.

Variation

If preferred, omit the crushed cookies or cereal and roll the candies into balls. The ball can be rolled in crushed cookies or cereal.

Chocolate Fudge Turtles

3 cups	semisweet chocolate chips (18 oz/540 g)	750 mL
1	can (14 oz or 300 mL) sweetened condensed milk	1
1	jar (7 oz/198 g) marshmallow creme	1
2 tsp	vanilla extract	10 mL
4 cups	pecans, in large pieces	1 L

This 1960s recipe is so popular that candy makers put a new spin on it every few years. See the 1980s version, Chocolate Marshmallow Turtles, below.

Skill Level: Novice, Super Simple

Makes 40 to 50

• Double boiler

1. Cover a large countertop area or 2 large baking sheets with waxed paper.

2. In the top pan of a double boiler over hot but not boiling water, melt the chocolate chips, stirring until smooth. Remove from the heat. Stir in the milk, marshmallow creme, vanilla and pecans.

3. Drop by spoonfuls onto the waxed paper. Cool. Store in an airtight container in the refrigerator.

Chocolate-Marshmallow Turtles

3 cups	semisweet chocolate chips (18 oz/540 g)	750 mL
1	can (14 oz or 300 mL) sweetened condensed milk	1
1	jar (7 oz/198 g) marshmallow creme	1
Pinch	salt	Pinch
1 tsp	vanilla extract	5 mL
1 cup	walnuts, in large pieces	250 mL
1 cup	pecans, in large pieces	250 mL
5 1/2 cups	miniature marshmallows	1.375 L

This recipe will feed an army of kids, and if the kids do not like nuts, omit and add a few more marshmallows.

Skill Level: Novice, Easy

Makes 50 to 60

• Double boiler

1. In the top pan of a double boiler over hot but not boiling water, melt the chocolate chips, stirring until smooth. Remove from the heat. Cool slightly, about 10 minutes.

2. Cover a large countertop area or 2 large baking sheets with waxed paper.

3. In a large mixing bowl, mix together the sweetened condensed milk and marshmallow creme, blending well. Stir in the salt, vanilla and melted chocolate until smooth. Stir in the walnuts, pecans and marshmallows until coated. Drop by spoonfuls onto the waxed paper. Let stand until firm. Store in an airtight container in the refrigerator.

Chocolate Coconut Drops

2 oz	unsweetened chocolate, coarsely chopped	60 g
1	can (14 oz or 300 mL) sweetened condensed milk	1
2²⁄₃ cups	sweetened flaked coconut	650 mL
½ cup	pecans or walnuts, in large pieces	125 mL

Moist and chewy, these addictive little chocolate drops are halfway between a candy and a cookie.

Makes about 36

- Preheat oven to 350°F (180°C)
- Baking sheet, lined with aluminum foil, sprayed with nonstick spray

1. In a small heavy saucepan over low heat, melt the chocolate, stirring until smooth. Remove from the heat. Stir in the milk, coconut and nuts. Drop by spoonfuls onto the prepared baking sheet.

2. Place the baking sheet into the preheated oven. Turn off the heat. Leave in the oven until the candy has a glazed appearance, about 20 minutes. Remove from the oven and cool completely before removing the candy from the baking sheet. Store in an airtight container in the refrigerator.

Ultra-Smooth Chocolate Clusters

1 cup	semisweet chocolate chips	250 mL
3 tbsp	light (white or golden) corn syrup	45 mL
1 tbsp	water	15 mL
1 cup	sweetened flaked coconut or pecans, in large pieces	250 mL

When I can no longer fight that urge for chocolate, I whip up a batch of these smooth clusters.

Skill Level: Novice, Easy

Makes 12 to 18

- 1-quart heavy saucepan

1. Cover a countertop area or medium baking sheet with waxed paper.

2. In heavy saucepan over low heat, heat the chocolate chips, corn syrup and water together, stirring until smooth. Remove from the heat. Add the coconut. Drop by spoonfuls onto the waxed paper. Let stand until the chocolate is firm. Store in an airtight container.

Chocolate Peanut Clusters

1½ cups	semisweet chocolate chips	375 mL
1 cup	roasted peanuts	250 mL

These simple little candies will always be a favorite.

Skill Level: Novice, Easy

Makes about 2½ dozen

- Double boiler

1. Cover a large countertop area or 2 large baking sheets with waxed paper.
2. In the top pan of a double boiler over hot but not boiling water, melt the chocolate chips, stirring until smooth. Stir in the peanuts.
3. Drop by spoonfuls onto the waxed paper. Let stand until firm. Store in an airtight container.

Sweet Chocolate Clusters

4 oz	sweet chocolate (preferably German's by Baker's), chopped	125 g
⅔ cup	sweetened condensed milk	150 mL
1 cup	peanuts or raisins	250 mL

This chocolate is as smooth as velvet.

Skill Level: Novice, Easy

Makes about 25

- Large baking sheet, lined with waxed paper, sprayed with nonstick spray
- Double boiler

1. In the top pan of a double boiler over hot but not boiling water, melt the chocolate, stirring until smooth. Remove from the heat. Stir in the milk and peanuts, mixing well.
2. Drop by spoonfuls onto the prepared baking sheet. Refrigerate until the chocolate is firm. Store in an airtight container in the refrigerator.

Twice-as-Nice Peanut Clusters

1 cup	semisweet chocolate chips	250 mL
1 cup	butterscotch chips	250 mL
1 tbsp	solid vegetable shortening	15 mL
1 to 2 cups	roasted peanuts	250 to 500 mL

These clusters have a double dose of flavor.

Skill Level: Novice, Easy

Makes about 24

- Double boiler

1. Cover a large countertop area or 2 large baking sheets with waxed paper.
2. In the top pan of a double boiler over hot but not boiling water, melt the chocolate chips, butterscotch chips and shortening together, stirring until smooth. Stir in the peanuts.
3. Drop by spoonfuls onto the waxed paper. Let stand until firm. Store in an airtight container.

Triple Delight Pecan Patties

4 oz	sweet chocolate (preferably German's by Baker's)	125 g
1 cup	peanut butter chips	250 mL
1 cup	butterscotch chips	250 mL
1 tbsp	solid vegetable shortening	15 mL
2 to 3 cups	pecans, in large pieces	500 to 750 mL

> Good things come in threes, such as these three-flavor pecan patties.

Skill Level: Novice, Easy

Makes about 36

- Double boiler

1. Cover a large countertop area or 2 large baking sheets with waxed paper.
2. In the top pan of a double boiler over hot but not boiling water, melt the chocolate, peanut butter chips, butterscotch chips and shortening together, stirring until smooth. Stir in the pecans.
3. Drop by spoonfuls onto the waxed paper. Let stand until firm. Store in an airtight container.

Triple Delight Marshmallow Squares

2 cups	butterscotch chips	500 mL
2 cups	semisweet chocolate chips	500 mL
1 cup	smooth peanut butter	250 mL
5½ cups	miniature marshmallows	1.375 L

> Three great flavors blended with marshmallows make this candy every kid's dream.

Skill Level: Novice, Easy

Makes about 30 squares

- 13- by 9-inch (33 by 23 cm) pan, sprayed with nonstick spray
- 2-quart heavy saucepan

1. In heavy saucepan over low heat, melt the butterscotch chips, chocolate chips and peanut butter together, stirring until smooth. Remove from the heat. Stir in the marshmallows until coated.
2. Pour the mixture into the prepared pan. Chill in the refrigerator until firm. Cut into squares. Store in an airtight container.

Rocky Road

3 cups	semisweet or milk chocolate chips (18 oz/540 g)	750 mL
3 cups	miniature marshmallows	750 mL
3/4 cup	pecans or walnuts, in large pieces	175 mL

> The rocky road of life is always easier to travel when first paved with chocolate.

Makes about 2 lbs (1 kg)

- 8-inch (20 cm) square pan, buttered
- Double boiler

1. In the top pan of a double boiler over hot but not boiling water, melt the chocolate, stirring until smooth. Remove from the heat. Cool slightly, 3 to 5 minutes. Stir in the marshmallows and nuts.
2. Spread into the prepared pan. Cover and chill until firm. Cut into squares. Store refrigerated in an airtight container.

Heavenly Hash

2 cups	semisweet chocolate chips	500 mL
1	can (14 oz or 300 mL) sweetened condensed milk	1
5 1/2 cups	miniature marshmallows	1.375 L
2 cups	pecans, in large pieces	500 mL

> An old favorite deserving of its name, this recipe offers two versions.

Cook's Note

If preferred, the candy may be dropped by spoonfuls onto waxed paper.

Makes about 2 1/2 lbs (1.25 kg)

- 13- by 9-inch (33 by 23 cm) pan, buttered
- 2-quart heavy saucepan

1. In heavy saucepan over low heat, melt the chocolate chips with the milk, stirring until smooth. Remove from the heat. Stir in the marshmallows and pecans.
2. Spread in the prepared pan. Cover and chill until firm. To serve, cut into squares. Store in an airtight container in the refrigerator.

Variation

Coconut Heavenly Hash: Reduce the amount of miniature marshmallows to 1 cup (250 mL). Reduce the pecans to 1 1/2 cups (375 mL) and add 1 to 2 cups (250 to 500 mL) sweetened flaked coconut and 1 tsp (5 mL) vanilla.

Chocolate Rum Squares

2½ cups	semisweet chocolate chips	625 mL
1 cup	sweetened condensed milk	250 mL
Pinch	salt	Pinch
2 tsp	rum extract or almond extract	10 mL
1½ cups	chopped pecans or walnuts	375 mL

Rum extract adds a rich flavor to these tasty candies.

Skill Level: Novice, Easy

Makes about 2 lbs (1 kg)

- 8-inch (20 cm) square pan
- Double boiler

1. Line square pan with aluminum foil, leaving a 1-inch (2.5 cm) overhang on the sides of the pan. Spray the foil lightly with nonstick spray.

2. In the top pan of a double boiler over hot but not boiling water, melt the chocolate chips with the milk, stirring until smooth. Remove from the heat. Stir in the salt, rum extract and nuts.

3. Pour into the prepared pan. Cover and refrigerate 24 hours. Lift the candy from the pan and remove the foil lining. Cut into squares. Store in an airtight container in the refrigerator.

Caramel-Nut Marshmallows

1 lb	soft caramels, unwrapped	500 g
3 tbsp	evaporated milk	45 mL
30	large marshmallows	30
1½ cups	pecans, in large pieces	375 mL

Kids enjoy making these caramel-coated marshmallows almost as much as they enjoy eating them.

Skill Level: Novice, Easy

Makes about 30

- 1-quart heavy saucepan

1. Cover a countertop area or a small baking sheet with waxed paper.

2. In heavy saucepan over low heat, melt the caramels and milk together, stirring until smooth. Using a fork, toothpick or specially designed dipping tool, dip the marshmallows into the hot caramel until coated. Immediately roll the dipped marshmallows in the pecans. Place on the waxed paper. Let stand until firm. Store in an airtight container in the refrigerator.

Chipper Nutty Fudge

1½ cups	packed light brown sugar	375 mL
1	can (14 oz or 300 mL) sweetened condensed milk	1
1½ tsp	vanilla extract	7 mL
1 cup	crunchy peanut butter	250 mL
1 cup	semisweet chocolate chips or miniature semisweet chocolate chips	250 mL
½ to 1 cup	salted roasted peanuts, finely chopped	125 to 250 mL

This yummy peanut butter candy comes with an endorsement from my cousin Travis, who hails from a long line of expert candy tasters. It will be an instant favorite with your family, too.

Skill Level: Novice, Super Simple

Makes about 2½ lbs (1.25 kg)

- 13- by 9-inch (33 by 23 cm) pan, lined with parchment (see Cook's Note, below) or buttered

1. In a medium bowl, combine the brown sugar, milk and vanilla, stirring until the sugar dissolves. Stir in the peanut butter until well blended and smooth. Add the chocolate chips and peanuts, mixing well.

2. Spread into the prepared pan. Refrigerate until firm. Cut into squares. Store in an airtight container in the refrigerator.

Cook's Note

Cutting candy becomes much easier with the use of parchment paper. Rather than buttering the pan directly, butter a piece of parchment paper larger than the pan and press it into the bottom and up the sides of the pan, tucking and creasing the paper as needed to create corners, and leaving a generous overhang over the sides of the pan.

Peanut Butter Graham Squares

1½ cups	smooth peanut butter	375 mL
1½ cups	graham cracker crumbs	375 mL
1 cup	butter or margarine, softened	250 mL
1 lb	confectioner's (icing) sugar	500 g
2 cups	semisweet chocolate chips, melted	500 mL

This candy may remind you of a favorite candy bar.

Skill Level: Novice, Super Simple

Makes about 24

- 13- by 9-inch (33 by 23 cm) pan, sprayed with nonstick spray

1. In a medium mixing bowl, combine the peanut butter, crumbs, butter and confectioner's sugar, mixing well.

2. Press into the prepared pan. Spread the chocolate on top of the peanut butter layer. Chill until firm. Cut into squares. Store in an airtight container.

Mom's Peanut Butter Candy

3 to 4 tbsp	smooth or crunchy peanut butter	45 to 60 mL
2 cups	confectioner's (icing) sugar	500 mL
2 tbsp	half-and-half (10%) cream or milk (approx.)	30 mL
1/4 tsp	vanilla extract (optional)	1 mL

Skill Level: Novice, Super Simple

Makes 8 to 10 pieces

1. In a small bowl, mix the peanut butter and confectioner's sugar together. Stir in just enough half-and-half to bind the ingredients and make the candy smooth. Add the vanilla, if desired.

2. Shape the candy into balls 3/4 to 1 inch (2 to 2.5 cm) in diameter. Store in an airtight container in the refrigerator.

> I might not have made it through grade school without this candy. Whether I had a scraped knee or just needed an after-school treat, this yummy-for-the-tummy candy was my solution to all of life's problems. My youngest cousin Anne was so enamored with Mom's special candy that she requested the recipe when she was only six years old. Here are Anne's instructions: "Peanut butter. White Shugger. and Creame. Miks them all tell the shugger goes Away and the creame goes Away then roll them in balls and eat."

Pine Cones

1 cup	smooth peanut butter	250 mL
1/2 cup	sweetened condensed milk	125 mL
1/3 cup	confectioner's (icing) sugar	75 mL
1/2 cup	chopped roasted peanuts	125 mL

> Who can resist smooth peanut butter candy rolled in crispy peanuts.

Skill Level: Novice, Super Simple

Makes 12 to 16 pieces

1. In a small bowl, mix the peanut butter, milk and confectioner's sugar together, blending until well mixed. Knead the candy by hand until smooth.

2. Shape the candy into small logs 3/4 to 1 inch (2 to 2.5 cm) long. Roll in the chopped peanuts to resemble pine cones. Store in an airtight container in the refrigerator.

Peanut Butter Log

¼ cup	smooth peanut butter	60 mL
¼ cup	light (white or golden) corn syrup	60 mL
2 tsp	water	10 mL
3 tbsp	instant nonfat dry milk	45 mL
1⅔ cups	confectioner's (icing) sugar	400 mL
¼ tsp	salt	1 mL
½ cup	sweetened flaked coconut	125 mL

This creamy peanut butter roll coated with coconut is a fun candy to make and eat, with your kids.

Skill Level: Novice, Super Simple

Makes about 12 pieces

1. In a small mixing bowl, combine the peanut butter and corn syrup until well mixed. Stir in the water, dry milk, confectioner's sugar and salt, blending well.

2. Shape the candy into a log 2 inches (5 cm) in diameter. Roll the log in the coconut. To serve, slice into pieces. Store in an airtight container.

Honey Do Candy

1 cup	instant nonfat dry milk	250 mL
1 cup	creamy peanut butter	250 mL
1 cup	honey	250 mL
½ tsp	vanilla extract	2 mL
½ cup	chopped peanuts	125 mL

This classic combination of peanut butter and honey may help you get those household chores done more quickly.

Skill Level: Novice, Super Simple

Makes about ½ lb (250 g)

1. In a medium mixing bowl, combine the dry milk, peanut butter, honey and vanilla, blending until smooth.

2. Shape into balls ¾ inch (2 cm) in diameter. Roll in the peanuts. Store in an airtight container in the refrigerator.

Rhonda Walters' Chocolate-Topped Cereal Bars

6 cups	flake cereal, such as Special K cereal	1.5 L
1 cup	light (white or golden) corn syrup	250 mL
1 cup	granulated sugar	250 mL
1½ cups	creamy peanut butter	375 mL
1¼ cups	semisweet chocolate chips	300 mL
1¼ cups	butterscotch chips	300 mL

Oklahoma's former First Lady Rhonda Walters shares her recipe for a favorite Walters family treat, Special K bars.

Cook's Note

The chocolate chips and butterscotch chips may be melted together in the microwave, if preferred.

Skill Level: Novice, Easy

Makes about 24 bars

- 13- by 9-inch (33 by 23 cm) pan, sprayed with nonstick spray
- 1-quart saucepan

1. Pour the cereal into a large mixing bowl.

2. In saucepan over medium heat, bring the corn syrup and sugar to a boil, stirring until the sugar dissolves and the mixture begins to boil. Boil 1 minute.

3. Remove from the heat. Stir in the peanut butter, blending well. Pour the hot syrup over the cereal, stirring the cereal until well coated. Spread evenly in the buttered pan. Cool.

4. In a saucepan over low heat, melt the chocolate chips and butterscotch chips together, stirring until smooth. Spread the melted chocolate-butterscotch mixture over the cereal mixture. Cool and cut into squares. Store in an airtight container.

Chocolate-Caramel Quickies

8 oz	soft caramels, unwrapped	250 g
8 oz	soft chocolate caramels, unwrapped	250 g
2 cups	chow mein noodles	500 mL

This 1962 recipe came with a note saying, "It costs 64 cents to make these." Imagine what our thrifty candy maker would think now.

Skill Level: Novice, Easy

Makes about 1¼ lbs (625 g)

- 1-quart heavy saucepan

1. Cover a large countertop area or a large baking sheet with waxed paper.

2. In heavy saucepan over low heat, melt the caramels together, stirring until smooth. Remove from the heat. Stir in the noodles.

3. Pour onto the waxed paper. Let stand until firm. Cut into squares. Store in an airtight container.

Chocolate Birds' Nests

2 cups	semisweet chocolate chips	500 mL
1¼ cups	smooth or crunchy peanut butter	300 mL
¼ tsp	vanilla extract	1 mL
10	large shredded wheat cereal biscuits, crushed	10
	Colored jellybeans or miniature candy eggs	

Perfect for an Easter celebration, these egg-filled birds' nests will put a twinkle into any child's eye.

Cook's Note

If desired, slightly less peanut butter may be used.

Skill Level: Novice, Easy

Makes about 40

• Double boiler

1. Cover a large countertop area or 2 large baking sheets with waxed paper.

2. In the top pan of a double boiler over hot but not boiling water, melt the chocolate chips, stirring until smooth. Add the peanut butter, vanilla and cereal, stirring until the peanut butter has melted and the mixture is well blended.

3. Remove from the heat. Quickly drop by spoonfuls onto the waxed paper. Using a thumb or the back of a spoon, make an indention in the center of each candy. Lightly press 2 to 5 brightly colored jellybeans or miniature candy eggs into each indentation before the chocolate cools completely. Cool. Store in an airtight container.

Chocolate-Covered Turtles

2 cups	semisweet chocolate chips	500 mL
2 cups	butterscotch chips	500 mL
1 cup	roasted salted cashews	250 mL
1	can (3 to 5 oz/90 to 150 g) crisp fried chow mein noodles (about 1½ cups/375 mL to 2½ cups/625 mL)	1

Crunchy noodles and roasted cashews make these extra good.

Skill Level: Novice, Easy

Makes about 50

• Double boiler

1. Cover a large countertop area or 2 large baking sheets with waxed paper.

2. In the top pan of a double boiler over hot but not boiling water, melt the chocolate chips and butterscotch chips together, stirring until smooth.

3. Remove from the heat. Stir in the cashews and noodles. Quickly drop by spoonfuls onto the waxed paper. Cool. Store in an airtight container.

Butterscotch Bonbons

1 cup	butterscotch chips	250 mL
1/2 cup	smooth peanut butter	125 mL
1 1/2 cups	corn flakes cereal	375 mL
1 cup	miniature marshmallows	250 mL
1/2 cup	chopped candied cherries, raisins or unsalted peanuts	125 mL

Butterscotch and peanut butter are always a favorite combination, regardless of what else is added.

Makes about 30

• Double boiler

1. Cover a large countertop area or a large baking sheet with waxed paper.

2. In the top pan of a double boiler over hot but not boiling water, melt the butterscotch chips and peanut butter together, stirring until smooth.

3. Remove from the heat. Stir in the cereal, marshmallows and cherries. Refrigerate until lightly set, 10 to 15 minutes. Drop by spoonfuls onto the waxed paper. Cool. Store in an airtight container.

Variations

Double Butter Clusters: Omit the marshmallows and the fruit or nuts. Substitute crunchy peanut butter for the smooth peanut butter. Use 2 cups (500 mL) slightly crushed corn flakes cereal. Stir in 1/2 tsp (2 mL) vanilla extract with the cereal.

Crazy Candy: Omit the corn flakes, marshmallows and the fruit or nuts. Reduce the peanut butter to 4 tsp (20 mL). Stir in 1 can (1.5 oz/45 g) shoestring potatoes.

Hopscotch Candy

1 cup	butterscotch chips	250 mL
1/2 cup	peanut butter	125 mL
2 cups	crispy fried chow mein noodles	500 mL
2 cups	miniature marshmallows	500 mL

An oldie but a goody, this recipe combines soft, fluffy marshmallows with crisp chow mein noodles to create the ultimate quick-style treat.

Makes about 30

• Double boiler

1. Cover a large baking sheet with waxed paper.

2. In the top pan of a double boiler over hot but not boiling water, melt the butterscotch chips and peanut butter together, stirring until smooth.

3. Remove from the heat. Stir in the noodles and marshmallows. Quickly drop by spoonfuls onto the waxed paper. Chill until firm. Store in an airtight container.

Butterscotch Crispies

2 cups	butterscotch chips	500 mL
2½ cups	chow mein noodles	625 mL
2 cups	Spanish peanuts	500 mL

Peanuts give this quick candy
an extra punch.

Makes about 30

- Double boiler

1. Cover a large countertop area or a large baking sheet with waxed paper.
2. In the top pan of a double boiler over hot but not boiling water, melt the butterscotch chips, stirring until smooth.
3. Remove from the heat. Stir in the noodles and peanuts. Quickly drop by spoonfuls onto the waxed paper. Cool. Store in an airtight container.

Variation

Butterscotch Crunch: Use 1 can (3 oz/90 g) or 1½ cups (375 mL) crispy fried chow mein noodles and 1 cup (250 mL) salted peanuts.

Easy Peanut Butter Candy

4 cups	crushed corn flakes cereal	1 L
¾ cup	granulated sugar	175 mL
¾ cup	light (white or golden) corn syrup	175 mL
1 cup plus 1 tsp	peanut butter	255 mL

This peanut butter and cereal candy
is sure to find some new fans among
peanut butter lovers.

Makes about 30

- 1-quart saucepan

1. Cover a large countertop area or a large baking sheet with waxed paper.
2. Pour the corn flakes into a medium mixing bowl.
3. In saucepan, bring the sugar and corn syrup to a boil. Remove from the heat. Add the peanut butter, stirring until smooth. Pour the hot syrup over the corn flakes, stirring until the corn flakes are well coated. Quickly drop by spoonfuls onto the waxed paper. Cool. Store in an airtight container.

Crispy Peanut Butter Treats

2½ cups	crispy rice cereal	625 mL
16	large marshmallows	16
3 tbsp	butter or margarine	45 mL
¼ cup	peanut butter	60 mL
½ tsp	vanilla extract	2 mL

> Surprise your kids with ice cream served in these crispy candy cups.

Cook's Note

If preferred, the mixture can be pressed into the bottom and sides of 6 buttered custard cups to make candy cups used for serving ice cream.

Makes about 16 squares

- Large mixing bowl, sprayed with nonstick spray
- 8-inch (20 cm) square pan, spread with nonstick spray
- Double boiler

1. Pour the cereal into the prepared mixing bowl.
2. In the top pan of a double boiler over hot but not boiling water, melt the marshmallows, butter and peanut butter together, stirring until smooth.
3. Remove from the heat. Stir in the vanilla. Pour the marshmallow mixture over the cereal, stirring until the cereal is well coated. Press the mixture into the prepared pan. Cool and cut into squares. Store in an airtight container.

Peanut Butter Crumb Bars

1	jar (7 oz/198 g) marshmallow creme	1
3 tbsp	butter or margarine	45 mL
⅓ cup	crunchy peanut butter	75 mL
2 cups	crushed toasted rice cereal squares, such as Chex (about 4 cups/1 L whole)	500 mL

> Peanut butter and marshmallows with a slightly different twist.

Makes about 16

- 8-inch (20 cm) square pan, sprayed with nonstick spray
- Double boiler

1. In the top pan of a double boiler over hot but not boiling water, melt the marshmallow creme, butter and peanut butter together, stirring until smooth.
2. Remove from the heat. Stir in the cereal. Press the mixture into the prepared pan. Cool and cut into squares. Store in an airtight container.

S'Mores

⅓ cup	light (white or golden) corn syrup	75 mL
1 cup	semisweet chocolate chips	250 mL
½ tsp	vanilla extract	2 mL
4 cups	graham cracker cereal	1 L
1½ cups	miniature marshmallows	375 mL

What a marvelous invention!

Cook's Note

Cutting candy becomes much easier with the use of parchment paper. Rather than buttering the pan directly, butter a piece of parchment paper larger than the pan and press it into the bottom and up the sides of the pan, tucking and creasing the paper as needed to create corners, and leaving a generous overhang over the sides of the pan.

Skill Level: Novice, Easy

Makes about 16

- 9-inch (23 cm) square pan, lined with parchment (see Cook's Note, left) or buttered
- 2-quart saucepan

1. In heavy saucepan, bring the corn syrup to a boil. Remove from the heat. Stir in the chocolate chips until melted. Stir in the vanilla, cereal and marshmallows until well coated.

2. Turn into the prepared pan. Cool and cut into squares. Store in an airtight container.

Storing Candy

Most candies should be stored in an airtight container to keep them fresh. Unless specifically instructed in the recipe, refrigeration is often a matter of personal choice, but generally, most fudges and fudge-like candies should keep at least 1 week at room temperature and at least 1 month, sometimes much longer, if refrigerated. Excessive heat, high humidity, or added ingredients such as fruit may shorten the storage time so it is important to use common sense. If the color or texture of the candy has changed, dispose of it and make a fresh batch.

Recipes by Skill Level

(For further info see Skill Levels: What Do They Mean?, page 12)

NOVICE, Super Simple

Apricot Nuggets (p. 173)
Apricot Tea Balls (p. 174)
Banana Tidbits (p. 248)
Bourbon Balls (p. 180)
Buttercream Fondant (p. 206)
Chipper Nutty Fudge (p. 268)
Chocolate Cocktails (p. 181)
Chocolate-Dipped Strawberries
 (p. 197)
Chocolate Fudge Turtles (p. 262)
Cinnamon Walnut Balls (p. 178)
County Fair Nuts (p. 226)
Cream Cheese Bonbons (p. 177)
Creamy Apricot Balls (p. 172)
Cuppa Fruit Candy (p. 248)
Dipsy Doodles (p. 181)

Festive Chocolate Nut Balls
 (p. 172)
Figgie Nuggets (p. 250)
French Fudge (p. 134)
Honey Do Candy (p. 270)
Luscious Cream Cheese Mints
 (p. 209)
Marshmallow Date Roll (p. 260)
Marvelous Marbled Mints (p. 208)
Marzipan Potatoes (p. 176)
Microwave Rocky Road Fudge
 (p. 131)
Microwave Toffee (p. 53)
Mom's Peanut Butter Candy
 (p. 269)
Nature's Candy (p. 249)

Orange-Nut Tea Balls (p. 174)
Peanut Butter Graham Squares
 (p. 268)
Peanut Butter Log (p. 270)
Persian Sweets (p. 249)
Pineapple Date Roll (p. 260)
Pine Cones (p. 269)
Potato Fondant (p. 102)
Potato Kisses (p. 103)
Potato Pinwheels (p. 104)
Risky Whiskey Rumba Balls
 (p. 180)
Simple Peanut Butter Roll
 (p. 261)
Ultra-Creamy Fondant (p. 204)
Zesty Apricot Nut Balls (p. 173)

NOVICE, Easy

Almond Coffee Walnuts (p. 196)
Aunt Mary's Turtles (p. 199)
Bittersweet Chocolate Truffles
 (p. 214)
Blue Ribbon Turtles (p. 200)
Buckeyes (p. 190)
Butterscotch Bonbons (p. 273)
Butterscotch Crispies (p. 274)
Caramel-Nut Marshmallows
 (p. 267)
Caramel-Raisin Balls (p. 177)
Cheery Cherry Date Balls (p. 187)
Cherry-Almond Bark (p. 256)
Cherry-Topped Fruit Roll (p. 259)
Chocolate Angel Sweets (p. 171)
Chocolate Birds' Nests (p. 272)
Chocolate-Caramel Quickies
 (p. 271)
Chocolate-Cherry Creams (p. 170)
Chocolate Coconut Drops (p. 263)
Chocolate-Covered Cherries
 (p. 198)
Chocolate-Covered Mint Patties
 (p. 210)
Chocolate-Covered Turtles
 (p. 272)
Chocolate Cream Cheese Fudge
 (p. 133)
Chocolate Fudge Drops (p. 188)
Chocolate-Marshmallow Turtles
 (p. 262)
Chocolate-Nut Bark (p. 256)
Chocolate Peanut Clusters (p. 264)
Chocolate Raisin Roll (p. 261)
Chocolate Rum Squares (p. 267)

Chocolate Velvet Fudge (p. 134)
Cinnamon-Sugar Pecans (p. 225)
Coconut Bonbons (p. 182)
Crispy Peanut Butter Balls (p. 189)
Crispy Peanut Butter Treats
 (p. 275)
Crispy Sugared Walnuts (p. 226)
Date-Nut Balls (p. 178)
Easy Peanut Butter Candy (p. 274)
Elegant Sparkling Strawberries
 (p. 175)
Emergency Chocolate Fudge
 (p. 136)
Fresh Coconut Chips (p. 246)
Golf Balls (p. 191)
Gordon's Christmas Caramels
 (p. 201)
Gourmet Layered Peppermint
 Bark (p. 258)
Heavenly Hash (p. 266)
Honey-Nut Popcorn (p. 231)
Hopscotch Candy (p. 273)
Humdinger Date Balls (p. 179)
Kentucky Bourbon Balls (p. 195)
Kid Pleasin' Popcorn Cake
 (p. 237)
Lemon Curd Truffles (p. 215)
Luscious Raspberry-Fudge
 Truffles (p. 220)
Lynda's Gourmet Chocolate
 Truffles (p. 213)
Magic Truffles (p. 219)
Martha Washingtons (p. 183)
Microwave Caramel Popcorn
 (p. 234)

Microwave Fudge (p. 131)
Nutty Popcorn Candy (p. 239)
Peanut Butter Crumb Bars
 (p. 275)
Peanut Butter–Date Balls
 (p. 192)
Plain Jane Truffles (p. 212)
Quick Walnut Penuche (p. 150)
Reece's Microwave Peanut
 Brittle (p. 45)
Rhonda Walters' Chocolate-
 Topped Cereal Bars (p. 271)
Roasted Cinnamon Pecans
 (p. 224)
Rocky Road (p. 266)
Sensational Orange Mint Patties
 (p. 211)
S'Mores (p. 276)
Spiced Pecans (p. 225)
Sugared Peanuts (p. 227)
Sweet Chocolate Clusters
 (p. 264)
Toasted Coconut Chocolate
 Drops (p. 193)
Triple Delight Marshmallow
 Squares (p. 265)
Triple Delight Pecan Patties
 (p. 265)
Twice-as-Nice Peanut Clusters
 (p. 264)
Ultra-Smooth Chocolate
 Clusters (p. 263)
Wacky Potato Fudge (p. 135)
White Chocolate Peppermint
 Bark (p. 257)

AVERAGE

Almond Brittle (p. 46)
Almond Butter Toffee (p. 50)
Apple-Cinnamon Walnut Squares (p. 242)
Apple Crystals (p. 245)
Apricot Bars (p. 243)
Apricot Squares (p. 241)
Aunt Lucy's Extra-Buttery Brittle (p. 43)
Aunt Mary's Favorite Fudge (p. 124)
Aunt Shirley's Apricot Sugarplums (p. 244)
Blissful Butterscotch-Chocolate Fudge (p. 145)
Brown Sugar Taffy (p. 108)
Buttercrunch Candy (p. 52)
Butternut Toffee (p. 51)
Butter Pecan Toffee (p. 51)
Butterscotch Nut Marshmallows (p. 32)
Candied Citrus Peel (p. 247)
Candied Nuts (p. 227)
Carnival Candied Apples (p. 251)
Charlotte's Extra-Good, Extra-Wicked Fudge (p. 123)
Chewy, Gooey Caramel Pecan Squares (p. 59)
Chocolate Caramels (p. 61)
Chocolate-Cherry Coconut Drops (p. 184)
Chocolate-Covered Haystacks (p. 194)
Christmas Fudge (p. 128)
Classic Combo Fudge (p. 142)
Coconut Haystacks (p. 77)

Cowboy Crunch (p. 229)
Creamy Two-Chocolate Fudge (p. 133)
Dorothy's Never-Fail Caramels (p. 58)
Double-Duty Fudge (p. 146)
Dreamy Date Roll (p. 94)
Dreamy White Christmas Fudge (p. 167)
Easy-Do Divinity (p. 79)
English Toffee (p. 48)
Extra-Firm Fudge (p. 128)
Famous Fudge (p. 127)
Farmers' Market Peanut Brittle (p. 45)
Five-Minute Fudge (p. 127)
Glass Candy (p. 54)
Glazed Nuts (p. 228)
Hall of Fame Chocolate Fudge (p. 126)
Hardtack Candy (p. 55)
Holiday Pineapple Candy (p. 39)
Honey Walnut Caramels (p. 61)
Horehound Candy (p. 56)
Jo-Joe's Million-Dollar Fudge (p. 122)
Katie's Perfect Fudge (p. 132)
Lemon–White Chocolate Fudge (p. 166)
Licorice (p. 55)
Lindsay's Luscious Peanut Butter Fudge (p. 140)
Lynda's Luscious Lemon Truffles (p. 216)
Margaret's Double Fantasy Fudge (p. 125)
Marry Me Toffee (p. 47)

Marzipan Truffles (p. 218)
Microwave Peanut Patties (p. 62)
Mocha Fudge (p. 154)
Molasses Foam Taffy (p. 107)
Molasses Taffy (p. 107)
Mrs. McDonald's Red Candied Apples (p. 252)
Munchabuncha Peanut Brittle (p. 44)
Old-Fashioned Caramel Apples (p. 253)
Old-Fashioned Caramel Popcorn (p. 231)
Old-Fashioned Popcorn Balls (p. 235)
Old-Fashioned Taffy (p. 109)
One-in-a-Million Toffee (p. 49)
Orange-Nut Popcorn (p. 230)
Painter's Popcorn Balls (p. 236)
Peanut Cremes (p. 141)
Peppermint Taffy (p. 106)
Pistol Pete Peanut Brittle (p. 42)
Popcorn-and-a-Prize (p. 233)
Popcorn Party Cake (p. 238)
Popcorn Snap (p. 235)
Pumpkin Fudge (p. 162)
Rocky Road Fudge (p. 130)
Royal Eggnog Fudge (p. 165)
Southern-Style Caramel Popcorn (p. 232)
Super Peanut Butter Fudge (p. 138)
Twice-as-Tempting Two-Tone Fudge (p. 144)
Washington State Apple Squares (p. 240)
White Taffy (p. 105)

ADVANCED

Aunt Erma's Legendary 'Til It's Done Fudge (p. 114)
Banana Fudge (p. 159)
Black Walnut Caramels (p. 60)
Brown Sugar Candy (p. 27)
Brown Sugar Panocha (p. 148)
Bullet Fudge (p. 119)
Butterscotch-Pecan Pralines (p. 71)
Caramel-Coated Date Roll (p. 96)
Cherry-Nut Nougat (p. 89)
Classic Divinity (p. 82)
Classic Pecan Roll (p. 99)
Coconut Fudge (p. 160)
Coconut Pralines (p. 73)
Coffee Fudge (p. 153)
Cowboy Date Roll (p. 90)
Creamy Blonde Fudge (p. 163)
Creamy Bonbon Fondant (p. 205)

Creamy Orange Fudge (p. 158)
Creamy Pecan Pralines (p. 68)
Creamy White Fudge (p. 163)
Dad's Date Loaf (p. 92)
Dainty Mint Puffs (p. 87)
Delta Date Loaf (p. 94)
Delicate Apricot Roll (p. 91)
Down-Home Divinity (p. 80)
Evelyn's Maple Pralines (p. 72)
Extra-Buttery Buttermilk Fudge (p. 151)
Extra-Chocolaty Brown Sugar Fudge (p. 121)
Fancy Chocolate Fudge (p. 143)
Fresh Buttermilk Candy (p. 30)
Fruit Fancies (p. 34)
Golden Butter Nut Candy (p. 29)
Grace's Walnut Butter Fudge (p. 115)

Granny's Best Fudge (p. 116)
Granny's Extra-Sweet Date Roll (p. 95)
Hawaiian Fudge (p. 159)
Holiday Divinity (p. 84)
Jolly Good Fudge (p. 117)
Lollipops (p. 57)
Louisiana Double Divinity Delight (p. 83)
Love Me Pralines (p. 70)
Maple-Pecan Pralines (p. 71)
Maple Sugar Fudge (p. 156)
Marshmallow Cocoa Fudge (p. 129)
Marshmallows (p. 88)
Mexican Pecan Candy (p. 76)
Molasses Pralines (p. 73)
Mom's Divinity (p. 78)

ADVANCED *(continued)*

New Orleans Roasted Pecan Pralines (p. 66)
Norway Black Walnut Fudge (p. 157)
Nut Cream Drops (p. 76)
Nut Cream Loaf (p. 35)
Old-Fashioned Cooked Fondant (p. 202)
Old-Fashioned Pastel Butter Mints (p. 207)
Old-Time Cocoa Fudge (p. 118)
One Sharp Peanut Butter Fudge (p. 138)
Orange Creams (p. 33)
Out-of-This-World Maple Fudge (p. 155)
Panache Penuche (p. 149)
Peanut Butter–Apricot Roll (p. 101)

Peanut Butter–Cinnamon Roll (p. 100)
Peanut Butter Cracker Candy (p. 31)
Peanut Patties (p. 62)
Peanut Smoothies (p. 139)
Penuche Nut Roll (p. 97)
Perfect Pralines (p. 63)
Pineapple Cremes (p. 40)
Pineapple Sherbet Fudge (p. 160)
Pioneer Date Loaf (p. 93)
Pralines-in-a-Pan (p. 37)
Private Collection Fudge (p. 113)
Prizewinning Pralines (p. 64)
Rainbow Divinity (p. 85)
Ruth's Angel Pralines (p. 67)
St. Patty's Pineapple Candy (p. 40)

Sea Foam Candy (p. 86)
Sinfully Rich Buttermilk Fudge (p. 152)
Soft Pecan Pralines (p. 68)
Sour Cream Candy (p. 41)
Sweet Buttermilk Candy (p. 31)
Sweetheart Divinity (p. 81)
Sweet Milk Fudge (p. 120)
Texas Pralines (p. 64)
The Preacher's Pineapple Fudge (p. 161)
Three-Nut Candy (p. 36)
Traditional Peanut Butter Fudge (p. 137)
Tuxedo Fudge (p. 147)
Ultra-Creamy Buttermilk Pralines (p. 65)
White Cherry Fudge (p. 164)

EXPERT

Aunt Bill's Brown Candy (p. 28)
Caramel-Pecan Pralines (p. 69)

Caramel Pecan Roll (p. 98)
Mexican Candy (p. 75)

Mexican Orange Drops (p. 74)
Patience Candy (p. 38)

Library and Archives Canada Cataloguing in Publication

Sharrock, Jane
[Who wants candy?]
   300 best homemade candy recipes : brittles, caramels, chocolates, fudge, truffles & so much more / Jane Sharrock.

Includes index.
Originally published: New York : HP Books, 2004, under title: Who wants candy?
ISBN 978-0-7788-0475-8 (pbk.)

   1. Candy. 2. Cookbooks. I. Title. II. Title: Three hundred best homemade candy recipes. III. Title: Who wants candy?

TX791.S53 2014   641.8′53   C2013-908436-3

Index